WHY THE ARTS MATTER

The arts are many things: a source of entertainment, an industry, and even, in some cases, a luxury item or status symbol. In this book, a philosopher and a cognitive scientist argue that, most foundationally, the arts are fundamental to who we are, a source of transformation and transcendence. Drawing on real-world examples – from visual art and poetry to music and performance – they offer a powerful framework for understanding how art engagement fosters intellectual growth and emotional insight. Each chapter features thought-provoking artworks that invite readers to reflect on their own experiences and grapple with essential questions about empathy, creativity, and what it means to live well. Rich in scholarship yet grounded in everyday relevance, this work offers fresh ways to think about the role of the arts in both individual and collective life. It offers the perfect jumping-off point for anyone curious about how the arts shape our minds.

ALEKSANDRA SHERMAN is Professor of Cognitive Science and Director of the Center for Research and Scholarship at Occidental College. She is an award-winning research mentor and has published across the sciences, humanities, and arts. Sherman's research program exploring the intersection of empirical aesthetics, the arts, and multisensory perception has been supported by the National Endowment for the Arts and the National Science Foundation.

CLAIR MORRISSEY is Professor of Philosophy and Director for Partnerships with Los Angeles at Occidental College. She is an award-winning teacher whose interdisciplinary and cross-divisional work has been supported by the Mellon Foundation, Bringing Theory to Practice, and the National Institutes of Health. Morrissey specializes in moral philosophy, including the relationship between ethics and aesthetics. She is the author of *The Virtue of Wit: Humor, Social Connection, and Flourishing* (2025).

CREATIVITY AND THE ARTS IN CONTEXT

Series Editor
James C. Kaufman, University of Connecticut

Creativity and the Arts in Context presents books in the broad area of creativity studies. Titles in the series offer detailed explorations of timely concepts, theories, or lines of research, written in accessible language. They offer enough background to serve as introductions for their topic, yet deep and nuanced enough coverage to advance the field. Although the arts are highlighted in particular, the series includes volumes by scholars across a wide variety of academic disciplines such as psychology, education, business, engineering, and neuroscience. Examples of topics within the series' scope include dark creativity, artistic prodigies, creative mindsets, the creative process, creativity and gender, evolution of culture and innovation, and how to (not) kill creativity.

A full list of titles in the series can be found at: www.cambridge.org/crac

WHY THE ARTS MATTER

How Art Shapes Our Thinking, Identity, and Wellbeing

ALEKSANDRA SHERMAN
Occidental College, Los Angeles
CLAIR MORRISSEY
Occidental College, Los Angeles

Shaftesbury Road, Cambridge CB2 8EA, United Kingdom

One Liberty Plaza, 20th Floor, New York, NY 10006, USA

477 Williamstown Road, Port Melbourne, VIC 3207, Australia

314–321, 3rd Floor, Plot 3, Splendor Forum, Jasola District Centre, New Delhi – 110025, India

Cambridge University Press is part of Cambridge University Press & Assessment, a department of the University of Cambridge.

We share the University's mission to contribute to society through the pursuit of education, learning and research at the highest international levels of excellence.

www.cambridge.org
Information on this title: www.cambridge.org/9781009344289

DOI: 10.1017/9781009344302

When citing this work, please include a reference to the DOI 10.1017/9781009344302

First published 2026

A catalogue record for this publication is available from the British Library

A Cataloging-in-Publication data record for this book is available from the Library of Congress

ISBN 978-1-009-34428-9 Hardback
ISBN 978-1-009-34431-9 Paperback

For my parents, who nurtured my passion for the arts, and for my husband Sasha, who supports every crazy idea I have.
—A. S.

For the Michigan Morrisseys, who are always up for going to a museum.
—C. M.

Contents

Figures

Foreword

I am delighted to introduce the first book in the new Cambridge book series Creativity and the Arts in Context, *Why the Arts Matter: How Art Shapes Our Thinking, Identity, and Wellbeing,* by Aleksandra Sherman and Clair Morrissey. Sherman and Morrissey focus on the positive effects and outcomes that come from the arts, a topic near and dear to my heart. We're living in a world where funding for creating or studying the arts is regularly being cut or under attack. We're living at a time when general artificial intelligence is alternately portrayed as a great democratizer that allows anyone to be an artist . . . or as an enormous existential and practical threat to actual artists. In this context, it is invaluable to have a book that offers a careful and detailed explanation of the specific mental, physical, and social skills and benefits that come from art creation and art appreciation.

James C. Kaufman
Series Editor, Creativity and the Arts in Context

Acknowledgments

This book has been many years in the making. We are privileged to have had the support of many generous people throughout the process of writing it. Our families have been our greatest champions, supporting us during stressful moments, encouraging us to take writing retreats, and reading through many iterations of our writing. Our dear friends – most especially Q. Ostendorf and Kristi Upson-Saia – have been critical thought partners, always game to brainstorm ideas, read drafts, and provide intellectual and moral support. Our colleagues at Occidental College, especially those in the Cognitive Science and Philosophy Departments, have been not only encouraging but inspiring. We have also had the pleasure of working with undergraduate students who directly contributed to this project and to studies featured in it. We owe special thanks to Jean Meyer for diving headfirst into the world of copyright permissions and collaborating on this process with us. We are also indebted to our editor, Stephen Acerra, for his support and encouragement throughout the life of the project, and to the many audiences and reviewers who provided meaningful feedback throughout the development of these ideas. Lastly, our successful collaboration was facilitated by support from a number of sources at Occidental College, including the Humanities for Just Communities Program funded by the Mellon Foundation, the New Harmonies Program, the Brown Humanities Fund, and the Faculty Enrichment Grant Program.

Introduction

This book began as a conversation between friends and colleagues who love the arts. In our conversations about the latest exhibition we had seen across town, the museum we had visited on our last trip, or the books we were reading, we discussed not only beautiful artworks but also their power to afford us moments of joy and awe. We gravitated most toward discussing the times when art challenged, confused, and provoked us. Art's significance was not confined to what we admired with our eyes but also encompassed the role it played in our lives and how it resonated with us on a deep, personal level.

Sasha's fascination with the arts has been woven into the fabric of her life for as long as she can remember. One of Sasha's earliest memories is of her mother guiding her through the Metropolitan Museum of Art in New York City, teaching her how to discern the brushstrokes and light that distinguished the works of Renoir, Monet, and Degas. Sasha can still vividly picture the joy that lit up her mother's face – the crinkle in her eye, the knowing smirk, and the way she seemed to slip into another world – as she spoke about the soft, glowing cheeks in Renoir's *Girl with a Watering Can*. It was more than "just art" for her mother; it was a language of its own, a source of delight and wonder, a reveling in the expertise it took for an artist to communicate a story using subtle visual cues, as well as in her mother's own expertise in recovering and understanding that story. As Sasha delved into the study of Impressionism and Post-impressionism during an art history course in early high school, the relationship she had formed with these artists that her mother loved took on a new layer of complexity, deepening her childhood awe and personal connection with a richer historical understanding.

Clair's love for the arts also comes from her family. One of Clair's formative memories is staying up late poring over a cherished copy of Edith Hamilton's *Mythology* that her dad had kept from his school days. The stories were bizarre, but familiar; they were jam-packed with symbols she recognized but did not fully understand, and the characters' actions and motivations were often even more mysterious. She spent many nights trying to understand tales like that of Prometheus on the side of a mountain with his guts exposed, liver being picked at by an eagle, and would toss out takes in the cafeteria or at the dinner table when things got boring. The stories felt like a gift from, and a special connection with, both her dad and everyone else who had read and cared about them.

We are certainly not alone in feeling this connection with the arts. From ancient rituals to contemporary galleries, the arts are a fundamental part of human life that foster connection, understanding, and community across time and space (Dissanayake, 1990). Art is what we seek out when we want to experience intense emotions and connect to our inner selves; when we want to feel connected to each other and to our shared cultural histories; when we want to learn something new and interesting; and when we want to challenge ourselves and our views. As Jeannette Winterson (1997) writes:

> Even those from whom art has been stolen away by tyranny, by poverty, begin to make it again. If the arts did not exist, at every moment, someone would begin to create them, in song, out of dust and mud, and although the artifacts might be destroyed, the energy that creates them is not destroyed. (p. 20)

Despite the physical and social isolation during the COVID-19 pandemic, people could not help but create and share art. It was a social lifeline, a friend to many of us, and a means of connecting across and beyond our confined spaces. Neighbors hosted concerts for one another from their front doors, visual art installations appeared on people's windows, and museums exploded with arts challenges like inviting people to recreate their favorite art pieces. It is very telling that creating and appreciating the arts was so central to people's lives at a time of global crisis. The pandemic exposed how indelibly linked the arts are to *who we are* and to our shared humanity (Chan et al., 2022). That moment showed us how much art feels – and is – indispensable.

Kinds of Mattering

The title of our book states our central thesis: The arts matter. They are not a mere luxury for our leisure time, nor are they mere decoration or ornamentation on the things that really count in life. Instead, they are an important part of what makes us human, and they enrich our individual lives and our society in profound ways. Our question, then, is not whether the arts matter, but *how* the arts matter to human life. To take up this question, we find it useful to begin by clarifying what it means to say that something matters in the first place.

In Book II of the *Republic,* Plato makes a distinction between *intrinsic* value and *instrumental* value (Cooper, 1997). Things with intrinsic value are good for their own sakes, or good in themselves. They are worth choosing or pursuing just for what they are. A classic example of something with intrinsic value is joy. Joy is just good. You do not need a further reason to want joy beyond "it's joy." Things with instrumental value, in contrast, are good for or because of their consequences. They are valuable because of what we can use them to do. The standard example of something that is instrumentally valuable is money. We want money because of what we can do with it; wanting money for itself only makes sense for coin collectors. Using this distinction, Plato argues that valuable things fall into one of three kinds. They can be *only* intrinsically valuable, *only* instrumentally valuable, or *both* intrinsically and instrumentally valuable. Some things are valuable in both ways, and a central aim of the *Republic* is to argue that justice is among those things that are both. In this book, we will show that art is another of those things that are both intrinsically and instrumentally valuable.

That these categories are not mutually exclusive may strike some as counterintuitive. We often associate something being "useful" with being merely utilitarian and therefore *not* valuable in its own right. But something can be both good for its own sake *and* be good because of what we can do with it. For example, many people believe physical exercise is only instrumentally valuable; they exercise because it helps them stay fit and healthy. However, other people find exercise to be intrinsically valuable. Whatever exercise you engage in – walking, running, wheelchair basketball, stretching, dancing – can be worth engaging in for no other reason than that it is fun, or that it challenges your body to do something different than it usually does, or that it involves moving in particular ways. Exercise can be valuable both in itself and for its consequences.

We can see the "mutually exclusive" way of thinking in how the "fine arts" came to be defined as separate from craft and other skilled labor. Neither Ancient Greek culture nor Ancient Roman culture had a concept of fine arts in our current sense. The Greek word *techne*, and Latin *ars*, were used far more generally to mean any human skill of making or performing for a purpose. This encompassed painting, pottery, and sculpture, but also cobbling, shipbuilding, medicine, and "horse breaking" among many other pursuits, including theater, poetry, and music (Shiner, 2003, p. 19). The opposite of "art" in this sense was not "science" or "craft," but "nature." The concept of fine arts as we currently understand it was not formed until the seventeenth and eighteenth centuries. Moreover, during the same period, the arts became formally institutionalized in things like museums, secular concerts, and literary criticism (Shiner, 2003, p. 88). These institutions entrenched a growing distinction between the fine arts and "craft," in which the fine arts were experienced, discussed, and physically and temporally located apart from their traditional functions, and craft was thus associated with utility and social use. One can still see remnants of this in museum spaces, concert halls, and libraries, where quiet, internal contemplation is thought to be the "right way" to engage with artworks "for their own sake," and "useful" objects like quilts, ceramics, or furniture are either not included or set apart as their own exhibitions.

Despite this history, we believe that the arts are both instrumentally and intrinsically valuable. There is no shortage of studies and arguments that aim to show that the arts can be instrumentally valuable. Research on the relationship between math competence and music training, for example, suggests that children with more music training excel at math relative to their nonmusically trained peers. These kinds of arguments are often presented in the media as concluding that children should "learn music *so that* they will get a good SAT score." Even while asserting that the arts are instrumentally valuable, we are sympathetic with artists and art lovers who are suspicious of this kind of argument. Reporting on results in this way positions the arts as *only* instrumentally valuable, and it conflates instrumental value with economic value. Economic value is just one way for things to be instrumentally valuable. That music is also good for one's health or wellbeing is also a way for it to be instrumentally valuable, and in our mind, more importantly so. Moreover, being useful, or good for the sake of one's consequences, does not diminish something's intrinsic value. Whether musical training is good for math competence says nothing about whether musical training is good for its own sake.

Instrumental value is complex. It does not just refer to something being useful for economic reasons, but also to something being useful and good for *yourself*: for developing key capacities, ways of thinking, and ways of being that are important to living a good life. In this book, we do exactly that. We argue that the arts are instrumentally valuable for living well, that is, that the arts are *good for us*. They contribute to our health and wellbeing, including our sense of self and sense of others, and they help us to develop cognitive skills like observation, attention, emotional intelligence, and open-mindedness.

Defining "the Arts"

In a series of sculptures from the early twentieth century, Constantin Brâncuși explored the essential qualities of birds. In one version of *Bird in Space*, a slender, elongated piece of polished bronze tapers upward in a smooth, streamlined curve. The sculpture's center of gravity is quite high, with a narrow bottom tapering into a bulbous "body" and tapering again into a thinner "head." The piece is intentionally abstracted rather than a literal bird; it is a study in capturing the essence of "birdness." What Brâncuși arrives at is a work that, he argues, captures the essence of flight and upward movement (Figure I.1).

In 1926, Brâncuși was set to show *Bird in Space* at a gallery in New York. When the sculpture arrived in New York from Paris, US Customs officials refused to recognize it as art, arguing that it did not conform to the traditional definition of sculpture as a realistic imitation of nature. Instead, they classified it as a utilitarian object (a piece of manufactured metal that was essentially a kitchen item) and imposed a tariff on it. Brâncuși challenged the classification in court, and in the 1928 case *Brâncuși v. United States*, the judge ruled in his favor, suggesting that modern art could communicate ideas and aesthetic value without mimetic representation. The case marked a turning point in cultural history and underscored that the nature of "art" is not static, but shaped by evolving social, legal, and aesthetic values and artistic practices (Fincham, 2014; Heinich, 1996).

Throughout the history of philosophy, there have been many and varied attempts to define "art" which aim to identify the necessary and sufficient conditions for being an artwork. In doing so, philosophers argue that a specific property or set of properties is essential to something being an artwork. These attempts are motivated by a concern to unify varied arts practices, and to identify them all as of a single, coherent kind. For example, Charles Batteux argued that art aims to represent and imitate the beauty of nature, whereas Leo Tolstoy suggested that art communicates (and literally transmits) the artist's emotion to the beholder. Others suggest that art can be identified and

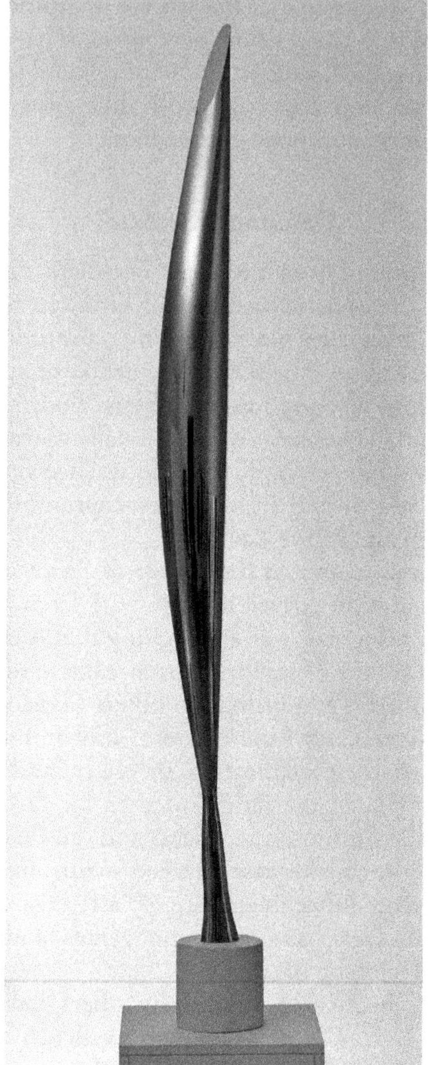

Figure I.1 Constantin Brâncuşi, *Bird in Space* (1931). Norton Simon Museum of Art, Pasadena, CA, USA.
Courtesy of the Norton Simon Museum of Art.

understood based on the specific way we engage with it – and the aesthetic experiences that we have with it, usually feelings of awe or responses to beauty. A different set of approaches defines art institutionally and historically. Some philosophers contend that institutions and practices that make up the "art world" get to say what art is and is not, or they suggest that artworks are things that have a special set of historical and causal relationships to other artworks.[1]

One common problem with these kinds of definitions is that they tend to conflate something's being an artwork with it being a *good* artwork. After all, someone could aim to express and evoke a specific emotion in a painting but fail to actually do so for all kinds of reasons (e.g., they lack relevant skill, or it was just an unsuccessful attempt). Definitions of the kinds above may not allow art like this – "bad art," so to speak – to be categorized as art at all. Additionally, these kinds of definitions are often overly inclusive or overly exclusive, or sometimes both, at the same time. Take, for example, the "aesthetic experience" definition, in which artworks are defined by a characteristic feeling or response to them. These kinds of definitions often do not deal well with negative responses to artworks such as disgust, dislike, or aversion, nor with cases in which someone is confused by a piece, or otherwise does not recognize it as art. The *Bird in Space* example illustrates this: If artworks are defined as things that give rise to aesthetic experiences, then the initial response by customs officers to Brâncuși's piece would call into question its status as an artwork. However, what their response really did was call into question the inadequacy of fixed definitions of art. The fact that *Bird in Space* is widely heralded as an influential masterpiece of modern art confirms its status as an artwork and exposes the flaws of these kinds of definitions. Moreover, this same kind of problem can be found across nearly all attempts to give a definition; for each, we can find ready counterexamples that undermine their claim to universality.

Galileo Galilei, who is sometimes referred to as the "father of the scientific method," was trained in artistic techniques, including linear perspective. Galileo lived during the Renaissance, a period when art and science were not seen as separate domains but were intertwined as part of a broader humanistic worldview. We can see the intermixing of these two domains in the depictions of the moon that he created as part of his scientific investigation of the heavens. In 1609, he produced a series of six watercolors representing the moon in its different phases, based on his observations through a telescope. They are described as the first realistic depictions of the moon in history (Figure I.2; Edgerton, 2009; Roche et al., 2018).

Does it matter whether these watercolors are characterized as artworks? If we set out to observe and appreciate them, would such a characterization

[1] See Thomas Adajian (2024) and Paisley Livingston (2024) for systematic reviews and extensive bibliographies on these issues.

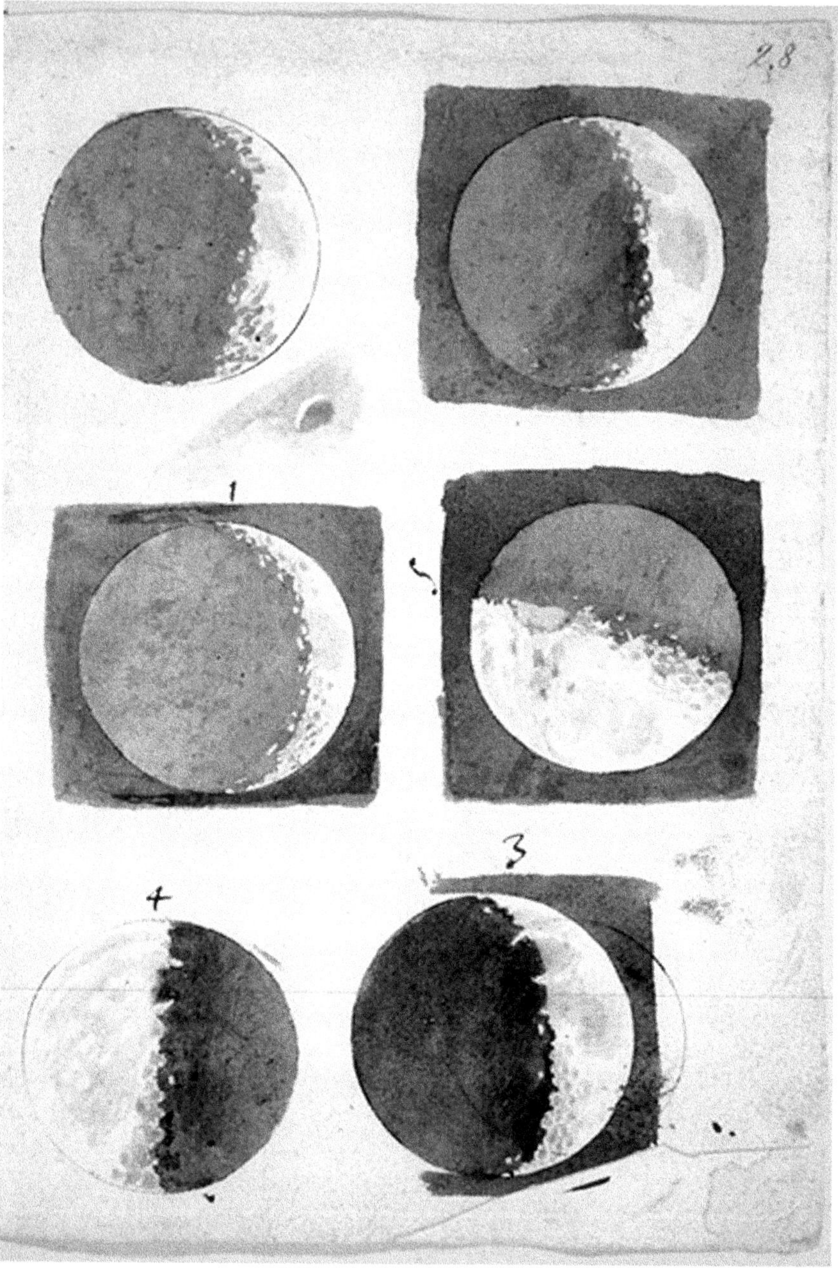

Figure I.2 Galileo Galilei (1609). Watercolors of the moon in different phases. Biblioteca Nazionale Centrale, Florence, Italy.

help us better to understand them, their importance, their role in our understanding of the world, or our responses to them? It is not clear that it would. Moreover, approaching them in this way runs the risk of erasing their connection to Galileo's scientific work. Of course, the paintings can be appreciated aesthetically and independently of any contextual information. However, what is particularly interesting about them – we suggest – is that they are part and parcel of Galileo's scientific investigations, understanding, and communication of ideas and insights to others. The artistic practice Galileo engaged in to create these paintings helped him to make sense of his observations of the moon's surface; more specifically, his artistic training helped him accurately record his scientific discoveries in a visual medium and communicate them to others.

Classifying Galileo's watercolors as either "art" or as "not art" misses the point. If we instead shift our attention to considering the *role that the arts played* in Galileo's life, and more generally, in human life, a whole host of interesting questions arise. Understanding the role of the arts helps us to focus on their social and cultural significance, including how participation in art creation and appreciation helps us to develop important skills and competencies for understanding ourselves, others, and the world. While we recognize the appeal of having a definition of art (in no small part because that would be very useful for our investigation!), we are not going to provide or subscribe to a particular definition here, and we remain agnostic about whether an adequate one exists. Even if there is a correct definition of "art," we believe that the best way to understand the value of the arts is not to focus on giving necessary and sufficient conditions for something being an artwork, but instead to understand how the practices that people care about and recognize as "the arts" are embedded in our lives (Lopes, 2008).

This perspective rests on an important premise that the arts are social practices.[2] They are activities we engage in as communities. They are:

> coherent and complex form[s] of socially established cooperative human activity through which goods internal to that form of activity are realized in the course of trying to achieve those standards of excellence which are appropriate to, and partially definitive of, that form of activity, with the result that human powers to achieve excellence, and human conceptions of the ends and goods involved, are systematically extended (MacIntyre, 1984, p. 187).

[2] We explain and defend this approach to the arts as social practices in more depth in our previous work (Sherman & Morrissey, 2017).

In this view, the arts are not a collection of objects or pieces we create and admire; they are ongoing, collaborative activities through which people come together, share methods, materials, and meanings, and continually shape both their individual skills and the collective understanding of what the practices, themselves, can be. Similarly, Winterson writes that the artifact, or the art object, is not the most important thing for appreciation or art-making; more important is what she calls the "energy," or the creative process and practice itself (Winterson, 1997). Tolstoy also argued for such a view: "In order to correctly define art, it is necessary, first of all, to cease to consider it as a means to pleasure, and to consider it as one of the conditions of human life" (Tolstoy, 2021).

We will understand the arts as active pursuits, as things that we do. We use "arts engagement" throughout the book as an umbrella term for a host of different "doings" encompassing both arts appreciation – experiencing visual artworks, songs, and the like – and arts creation – making artworks for yourself and others to appreciate. Arts engagement is not just a one-off experience or moment; appreciation and creation are things that we *learn how to do* and that we *continue to develop our ability to do well* over time. Importantly, they are shared with others. They are done in the context of other people who are also engaging in them, and with whom we can both learn and mutually engage (Dissanayake, 1990).

Although we emphasize the social nature and importance of arts practices, we would be remiss not to point out that our society often sidelines the arts as mere curiosities, as expendable leisure activities, as secondary or tertiary areas of study to more important disciplines like math or science, or as a mere collection of objects of beauty to be contemplated and judged as such, but ignored when there are more important things to do. Arts programs, including those from the visual arts, music, and performing arts, are often the first to get cut during economic hardships and budget cuts. Dominic McIver Lopes points out that a common scholarly response to this sidelining is to insist on "the great cultural significance of the fine arts" (Lopes, 2018, p. 216). The danger of this response, according to Lopes, is that over-attending to the importance of the *fine arts* risks belittling or ignoring the importance of other kinds of arts practices and aesthetic experiences in our lives, many of which are often the most important to who we are. For instance, "crafting" practices like knitting or quilting are passed down through families and often cultivated in the context of local communities. We follow Lopes in thinking that a better reaction is to "embrace all aesthetic activity" as important. To this end, throughout the book, we take a broad stance, focusing on a host of different kinds of arts practices, all of which we mark as equally relevant.

The Argument and Structure of the Book

The overarching framework of this book is rooted in the idea that the arts are a vital set of social practices that are tied deeply to who we are, to what we know and how we know, and to how we interact with the world around us. The arts offer us unique opportunities for personal identity, growth, and development. Here, we argue that the arts cultivate a specific set of skills that enable us to better connect with the world. The arts help us to sharpen our capacity for observation, to foster our emotional intelligence, and to encourage and enable our open-mindedness and flexible thinking. Moreover, they provide an avenue for self-reflection, expression, and belief revision. Ultimately, we suggest, the cognitive and affective processes that are engaged through art not only enhance our relationship with art itself but also contribute to a richer life, helping us to navigate challenges and to find greater meaning in our everyday experiences.

Chapter 1 discusses the question of what it could mean for the arts to be a source of knowledge. We survey how philosophers have argued for and against the claim that we can gain knowledge through engaging with the arts. We suggest that the arts can make us epistemically better off, not by teaching us new facts per se, but by helping us to grasp the underlying meanings and relationships amongst aspects of our world. Moreover, we argue that "know-how," or skill-based knowledge, can be gained from arts engagement, which serves as a jumping-off point for Chapters 2–4.

Chapters 2–4 each highlight a socio-cognitive skill developed through arts engagement: attention and observation (Chapter 2), emotional intelligence (Chapter 3), and open-minded, flexible thinking (Chapter 4). We describe and define these as cognitive skills that are teachable and malleable even in adulthood, we provide theoretical and empirical evidence for the arts as a venue for cultivating these skills, and we speculate about how the arts may contribute to making people more open and more creative observers of the world, even outside of arts contexts. Although we distinguish and discuss these skills in separate chapters, we also recognize that they build on one another, inform one another, and may not be fully distinct from one another. These discussions draw deeply from existing empirical research and endeavor to provide a fair and comprehensive representation of the relevant literature, although our goal is not to conduct a systematic review or meta-analysis of any particular body of data.

In Chapter 5, we turn our attention to identity and connection. The skills discussed in the earlier chapters are relevant to our sense of self and our connection to other people. By exposing us to a diverse array of perspectives, helping us see things and people anew, and fostering social connection and meaning generation, the arts become indelibly linked to our senses of self, to our identities, to who we think we are, and to how we identify in relation to others and the world. In giving this argument, we pay special attention to personal accounts and both philosophical and empirical investigations into the role the arts can play in the transformation of ourselves and our communities.

In Chapter 6, we take up the connection between the arts and wellbeing. We discuss the relationship between arts engagement and subjective wellbeing (SWB), as well as the relationship between arts and health. We pay special attention to the ways that the arts have been used in therapeutic settings to help patients manage and treat a host of mental and physical disorders, including Parkinson's disease, acute and chronic pain, and anxiety and depression. We conclude by discussing how to understand the argument of our book as an argument for how the arts contribute to our objective wellbeing.

In the Conclusion, we bring our argument together by taking a more practical approach. We suggest several broad habits of mind that can be found throughout the book that we can embrace more fully as appreciators and makers of the arts: slowing down, embracing uncertainty, and making meaning individually and collectively.

Throughout, we approach our investigation in an intentionally interdisciplinary way by using the tools of philosophy, cognitive science, and empirical psychology. Rather than treat disciplinary tools as discrete and separate, we use them *together* to advance arguments and to understand the questions we are trying to answer. Our goal is to contribute a model for how different ways of thinking about central research questions can mutually inform and support one another, and to contribute to building the common language that is emerging across our fields. The empirical voice is not meant to be the authoritative voice, nor the voice needed to show that art matters; instead, it is one among many that can enrich and complicate our understanding of the value of the arts. The conceptual or theoretical considerations are also not taken to be the final word, nor are they simply a hypothesis to empirically verify (or not). Theory is a method for thinking that is in conversation with the empirical, so that each can inform and be informed by the other.

Like the figures in M. C. Escher's *The Bonds of Union* found on the cover, the separate disciplinary positions from which we began our conversation have become enmeshed and deeply intertwined; yet the distinct influences and positions remain. It may not be clear where the psychology begins and the philosophy ends, where the philosophy begins and the psychology ends, but the presence of both ways of thinking is manifest throughout. In this way, the work is not transdisciplinary (merely covering multiple disciplines), but *inter*disciplinary, integrating different literatures and ways of thinking and arguing into a single contribution.

CHAPTER 1

Art as a Source of Knowledge

Starting Point

Can works of art teach us something, perhaps about ourselves, about the world, or about what matters? Many believe the answer is yes. As Iris Murdoch writes, "[t]he good artist is a vehicle of truth, [they formulate] ideas which would otherwise remain vague and [focus] attention upon facts which can then no longer be ignored" (Murdoch, 1999, p. 235). Even so, because a great deal of art is imaginative and fictional, it may seem that art could not even be in the business of communicating *truths* or being a source of *knowledge*. What Gregory Currie writes of fiction is true for the arts more generally: "the idea of learning from fiction is immensely important to us but the nature and extent of that learning is obscure" (Currie, 2020, p. 2). This is reflected in the cultural distinction often drawn between the arts and the sciences: the belief that the sciences give us objective facts, whereas the arts only offer us a way to engage our emotions and imagination.

To frame this discussion, we begin with two very different artworks. In the 1860s, French painter Édouard Manet created a series of works depicting characters from the streets around his studio in Paris. The series, referred to as the "philosophers," includes a ragpicker and two beggars. To Manet's contemporaries, the men's clothing would have been easily recognized as indicating a lower status in society. Such individuals were prominent on the streets during the renovation of Paris, under the direction of Emperor Napoleon III, when medieval neighborhoods were demolished in favor of broad boulevards, parks, and squares. Each of the three paintings in the series features an individual person, centered in the frame, depicted precisely and with care. The background for each philosopher is relatively flat and undifferentiated, which focuses the viewer's attention on the subject himself. The works are very large, about three-and-a-half feet by six feet, so the figures appear nearly life size (Figure 1.1).

Figure 1.1 Édouard Manet. *The Ragpicker* (c.1865–1870). Norton Simon Museum, Pasadena, CA, USA.
Courtesy of the Norton Simon Museum of Art.

Manet's paintings may be said to be about any number of different things. They seem to confer a worth or dignity on the subjects and perhaps draw attention to the cruelty of poverty. The paintings require the viewer to recognize the humanity of the subjects, despite their being physically displaced and socially marginalized. Moreover, the subjects and the paintings take up space. Their size requires that they be considered, be attended to, and that their existence be reckoned with. Manet uplifts people who would have otherwise been ignored as worthy of respect and consideration.

Consider now a different kind of artwork created in a different kind of place: Richard Serra's sculpture *Tilted Arc* (Figure 1.2). Serra's sculptures are characterized by their size and their seeming simplicity. The works are imposing and heavy, both physically (people have died installing them) and metaphysically (their massiveness requires navigation that inevitably forces engagement). The sculptures must be gone through or gone around. They cannot be ignored. Moreover, standing next to them, the viewer feels small, perhaps insignificant.

Figure 1.2 *Tilted Arc* (1981), by Richard Serra. David Aschkenas (1985). © Courtesy of David Aschkenas.

Tilted Arc was a public installation displayed in Foley Federal Plaza in Manhattan from 1981 to 1989, outside the Jacob K. Javits Building, home to many federal offices in New York City. The Javits Building was widely thought to be a dreary and poorly designed office building in which to work. The sculpture was 120 feet long, 12 feet high, and two-and-a-half inches thick; composed of a solid piece of unfinished, rusted steel. The installation of it was met with passionate reactions from both critics and defenders. Many critics argued that the piece was not only ugly but that it dominated the entire plaza. It was a nuisance to walk around and made the plaza unusable. Defenders argued that the aim of the artwork was to make the space of the public square counterintuitive, and thus to cause those who came across the sculpture to engage differently within the larger space. In this way, the piece required a kind of attention to the viewer's location and to the viewer's own body that many may take for granted during their daily work routines. After a series of public hearings and a trial, the sculpture was removed.

Stepping back from the details of the physical description and historical context of the creation of *Ragpicker* or *Tilted Arc*, let us return to the central question of this chapter: What, if anything, do viewers who encounter these artworks learn? What does it mean to "learn" from art, or to say that one has "gained knowledge" through art engagement? Does encountering a work of art lead us to form a new belief, know something that we did not before, or reconsider something we did know in a new light?

To meaningfully address whether and how the arts contribute to learning, we need to first clarify the question itself and the different kinds of knowledge at stake. In the sections that follow, we draw on insights from epistemology – the branch of philosophy concerned with the nature of knowledge – to explore the various ways of knowing that philosophers distinguish: propositional knowledge (also called "know-that"), experiential knowledge, understanding, and skill-based knowledge (also called "know-how"). "Learning" is "epistemic improvement" (Currie, 2020, p. 81). In other words, to learn something is to become better off than you were before with respect to what you know, regardless of what kind of "knowledge" that is. Here, we consider how the arts contribute to each of these types of knowledge, and how they make us epistemically better off by helping us gain or refine our knowledge. Ultimately, we suggest that "know-how" – or skill-based knowledge – is an especially fruitful concept for understanding how we become epistemically better off through engagement with the arts. In this sense, becoming epistemically better off through engagement with the arts is not about acquiring knowledge of facts, but rather about developing ways of seeing, perceiving, interpreting, and responding to the world more skillfully. Chapters 2–4 elaborate on these claims by examining three key sets of cognitive skills that are cultivated through sustained arts engagement: observation, emotional intelligence, and open-minded engagement.

Propositional Knowledge

Philosophers and psychologists tend to think of knowledge as something an individual person has, or fails to have, in virtue of the beliefs they hold and how those beliefs align with the world we live in.[1] In other words, knowledge is always *someone's* knowledge, and it exists in relation to the external world. Imagine that someone points to a tree and says: "That is an oak tree." Whether or not their claim is true depends on the features of the

[1] Note that whether knowledge is itself a mental state is a matter of disagreement within philosophy (e.g., see Nagel, 2013). In contrast, most psychologists do list knowledge among mental states (such as desire, belief, intention, feeling, and perception).

tree. It depends on whether the tree they pointed at is actually an oak tree. Moreover, the person pointing to the tree only counts as *knowing* that it is an oak tree if that person believes that it is one. They cannot just be pointing and declaring it an oak as a joke or game or as part of a performance of a play.

This kind of knowledge is what philosophers call propositional knowledge. It is about "knowing that" some claim or belief is true. Propositional knowledge, although it belongs to an individual, can be common across individuals. Multiple people could come to have the same true belief – that what they are observing is an oak tree – because these claims are themselves accessible across people. The processes by which we come to believe things are also reproducible and communal. The process by which you came to know that something is an oak tree can work for someone else too. Sometimes, these processes of knowledge acquisition require networks of people and collaboration. The scientific method is often cited as a gold standard here. The process of experimentation is well equipped to determine the truth of some propositions through a strategy that employs public and communal methods of observation, data collection, and replication.

For propositional knowledge, learning or epistemic improvement can occur in a number of ways. First, you might replace a false belief with a true belief, or you may gain a true belief that you did not have before. In both cases, you are straightforwardly better off with respect to what you know, and better in touch with the world as it is. Moreover, epistemic improvement with respect to propositional knowledge could include developing skills related to gaining beliefs, or to replacing weaker beliefs with stronger ones. For example, we may learn how to make distinctions between ambiguous concepts, learn how to observe leaf shapes to determine membership in tree species, or learn about fallacious reasoning and how to identify it. In these cases, you are epistemically better off because you have gained or improved an ability to identify true beliefs.

The value of having propositional knowledge is relatively straightforward. Knowledge is a good thing because it is accurate to the way the world is, which is both intrinsically and instrumentally valuable. If a tree is an oak tree and you claim it is an elm tree, you do not have accurate propositional knowledge, no matter the reasons you cite in favor of your position. Instead, we would say that you *believe* it is an elm (and, in this case, you believe falsely). It is better to know that something is true than to believe falsely that it is. In addition, such knowledge can be instrumentally valuable. If there were an invasive species of beetle that harmed the environment by inhabiting only oak trees, knowing which trees are oaks (and not elms) would make us better able to target our interventions.

When we think of learning in this way – as expanding our store of true beliefs – arts engagement may not seem to be a promising avenue for learning. First, we might be suspicious of the arts helping us arrive at *true* beliefs, at least in part because of the long history of propaganda. Second, and more deeply, we may be concerned that the arts are simply not the kinds of things that can make us epistemically better off with respect to our specific beliefs. Returning to Manet's *Ragpicker*, we may reasonably ask: What beliefs do we learn from encountering the painting? Someone may suggest that we gain the true belief, "everyone has dignity." In response, a skeptic may ask: Is this a *new* belief that someone would have only after viewing the painting? How would someone who didn't have this belief learn it *from* this painting? The painting represents a specific individual, so the path to "everyone" is unclear; and how would one understand what is being represented as "dignity (in spite of poverty)" unless they already believed that dignity does not depend on wealth or other circumstances? Instead, it seems more plausible that someone *already* needs to have the belief "everyone has dignity" to make sense of this meaning of Manet's painting in the first place. If so, then in what sense would "everyone has dignity" be a belief that we learned through an interaction with this specific painting? Similar questions can be raised for Serra's installation. Even if by encountering *Tilted Arc* you came to be aware of your bodiliness, or became attentive to the way in which your daily life has become rote and routine, surely the beliefs "I have a body" and "labor can make life dull and predictable" were not *newly learned* through or from your encounter, for the same reasons as above. Unless you already had those beliefs, it is unclear how the encounter with the artwork could give them to you.

The genre in which Manet painted the *Ragpicker* indicates that it is meant as a realistic depiction of the subject. Thus, someone defending the arts as a source of propositional knowledge may suggest that we can learn facts directly from viewing the painting, such as how ragpickers would have been dressed in late nineteenth-century Paris. One can then apply and generalize this new knowledge, so that were they to come across another depiction of a similarly dressed individual in nineteenth-century Paris, they would be able to identify them as a ragpicker. Those skeptical of the arts as sources of propositional knowledge may challenge this move. Even granting that we could learn what ragpickers look like in nineteenth-century Paris from engaging with Manet's painting, this kind of learning would only apply to artworks in certain genres – namely, those novels, paintings, and sculptures that present realistic depictions. That is a fairly narrow set of works in the history of the arts as social practices. Moreover (and again granting that someone could learn some facts from the artwork in the first place), beliefs like "ragpickers wore dirty clothes" are not what the painting is *about* anyway. Acquiring beliefs about what people wore in a particular social station in a particular cultural context is not what people are generally referring to when they say they have "taken something away" from the artwork.

Another skeptical worry concerns the generality of what is learned. One person may encounter *Tilted Arc* and be overwhelmed by its size and weight, feel it to be hard and cold, and in contrast, feel their body to be small and soft. This vulnerability might cause them to contemplate what it means to be alive, to be human, and to be mortal. Another person, encountering the same sculpture and also overwhelmed by its size and un-movingness, might consider, instead, the weight of their daily routine and nine-to-five job, and feel stuck and overwhelmed by that. When the two people talk about it later, the first may say "that sculpture is about mortality" and the second may say "that sculpture is about capitalism," and, in this way, they appear to be disagreeing with one another about the meaning of the artwork. Yet, in both cases, it is natural to say that the person learned from their respective engagement with the artwork. In contrast to the scientific method that privileges reproducibility across individuals, it seems that the arts invite us to interpret for ourselves.

At the same time, there are some experiences with *Tilted Arc* that we would not think of as "learning" from engaging with it. Imagine that our dreary worker, instead, leaves the Javits building and, upon encountering the large sculpture, has the thought: "I left important contracts I have to work on tonight upstairs in my office." Perhaps it is true that they left the documents, and they have good reason to believe that they did, and the encounter with the sculpture is in some way causally related to their coming to have the belief that the documents are in the office. The massiveness of the sculpture and its being such a pain in the neck to walk around caused them, perhaps, to reflect on the work they need to do tonight after dinner, which led them to remember that the documents they need are still inside. Although coming into contact with the sculpture was causally related to the dreary worker having a true belief, we think this is *not* a case of learning *from* the artwork. *Tilted Arc* is not about the location of documents. Simply encountering a work of art and coming to have a true belief as a result is not sufficient to say that someone has learned something from their engagement with the artwork.

The practical value of propositional knowledge, its utility, explains why there seem to be such high stakes to whether a particular practice – in this case, the arts – contributes to knowledge. If the person's job really is a drain, they may be in an epistemically better position after encountering *Tilted Arc*, because they are getting the world right in a way they were not before. (Of course, they may not be all-things-considered better off, especially if they have limited options with respect to earning money in another way.) If knowledge is good because it is useful, the line of thought seems to go, a practice that does *not* contribute to knowledge is not useful, or at least not useful for pursuing our important interests and goals. But this reasoning is clearly faulty. Propositional knowledge is not the only thing that helps us to live successful, healthful, and happy lives. As Aristotle famously points out in the *Nicomachean Ethics*, luck and access to sufficient material goods and opportunities are also important to things turning out well for us (Aristotle, 1999). Nevertheless, this way of thinking seems to permeate many of our cultural assumptions about the value of the arts in comparison to the importance of the sciences, at least in the United States. Propositional knowledge has long been the primary focus not just of academic philosophers but seemingly also of American education systems and of our social understandings of what it means to learn, or to be "smart." Many of us can probably recall that the standard way that learning was assessed in school was through tests in which we repeated or applied information by rote. The importance we place on "knowing that" also coheres with the cultural pride of place reserved for the sciences as sources of knowledge, and the utility of studying science, rather than other things.

Beyond Propositional Knowledge

Given the skeptical worries described above, propositional knowledge is probably not the right concept to explain what or how we learn from engaging with artworks. In some philosophical traditions, propositional knowledge is not even the central or privileged conception of knowledge. As Brian Burkhart (2019) characterizes it, Indigenous American philosophizing is more rooted in the use of play and narrative to learn and know, rather than in the use of generalizable empirical inquiry. Many of the Indigenous American cultural traditions are rich with stories as the primary objects of philosophical reflection and concern, and several of the characters identified as doing philosophy (e.g., coyote and spider) are "trickster" characters. The meaning of the stories, and the meaning of what these philosophizing characters do and say, must be interpreted and understood by the hearer. The stories are not meant to directly convey true propositions or supply deductive arguments. Alexandra Mouriki-Zervou similarly contends that the traditional model that privileges fact-based knowledge is narrow and inadequate, discounting the importance of knowing how to perceive, imagine, experience, or feel (Mouriki-Zervou, 2011).

These insights suggest the need to expand our conception of knowledge beyond propositional knowledge. Learning, or epistemically improving, could be a process of acquiring other *kinds* of knowledge that do not neatly fit into the account of propositional knowledge above, rather than just gaining justified true beliefs or replacing false beliefs with true ones. In this section, we consider three alternative ways of thinking about knowledge to explore their usefulness for understanding the role the arts play in our epistemic lives. We suggest that both "understanding" and "know-how" are potentially useful frameworks to adopt; we take these up in more detail in Chapter 5 and Chapters 2–4, respectively.

Experiential Knowledge and Knowledge by Acquaintance

In addition to learning that something is true, we also sometimes talk about learning from or about what it is like to experience something in particular. Bertrand Russell (2013) characterizes this as knowledge by acquaintance in contrast to knowledge by description, and Frank Jackson (1986) characterizes it as experiential knowledge. Russell's distinction is between knowing by being acquainted with something and knowing a fact. The things you are acquainted with are experiences, what philosophers call "sense data." These things are more immediate than propositions or beliefs. This kind of knowing is more akin to being familiar with something than it is to acquiring information about it. As Russell describes it, knowledge by acquaintance applies to anything we are directly aware of and does not need intermediaries such as processes of inference or any other knowledge of "truths." Acquaintance, in this sense, is a more intimate and direct relation than knowing that a proposition is true.

In a well-known philosophical thought experiment, Jackson captures a related conception of knowledge. He argues that perceptual experiences teach us things we could not possibly learn any other way. Jackson describes a thought experiment where a person named Mary is raised from birth in a completely achromatic environment. Mary learns everything there is to know – all of the propositional knowledge – about color perception and the neuroscience of vision, but she has never experienced color herself. When one day Mary leaves her achromatic environment and sees red for the first time, Jackson asks whether Mary learns something new from her experience of red that she didn't already know from her neuroscientific investigations of color in her black-and-white room. Jackson argues that Mary's propositional knowledge about how vision works is not sufficient to know everything there is to know about "seeing red." Her experience, he says, teaches her something *new* about color vision; namely, *what it is like* to see red.

Art experiences can seem similarly intimate and direct. A fitting example of an artist whose work both grips us emotionally and helps us to experience our world in a new way is James Turrell. Turrell creates immersive spaces that explicitly explore how we perceive light. In commenting on what his art is about, he states that his "work has no object, no image and no focus. With no object, no image and no focus, what are you looking at? You are looking at you looking" (*James Turrell | Artist | Royal Academy of Arts*, n.d.). When entering *Breathing Light*, an installation that was housed in its own building at the Los Angeles County Museum of Art for many years, you are immediately engulfed in thick, imposing, bright light. It feels as if you are wading through hazy fog, struggling to locate yourself in depth. "What it's like" to experience *Breathing Light* seems to be importantly different from any proposition you could learn about depth perception and is plausibly something that can only be learned by encountering the work for yourself.

In their 2007 paper, David Freedberg and Vittorio Gallese provide additional compelling examples of artworks to which viewers have strong physical responses that suggest a kind of learning or knowing through acquaintance (Freedberg & Gallese, 2007). In Michelangelo's *Prisoners*, the bodies of prisoners appear to be trapped in blocks of stone. When scientists bring people into the lab to investigate bodily responses to these sculptures, they show that there is a physical response such that the muscles that appear to be activated in the viewer are similar to those being "activated" within the sculpture itself, "as if in perfect consonance with Michelangelo's intention of showing his figures struggle to free themselves from their material matrix" (p. 197). Such physical responses also often happen when we see or even imagine someone else experiencing physical or emotional pain. If you imagine watching a needle piercing someone's skin, or a finger touching someone's open wound, you are likely to have a visceral physiological response. One potential explanation for these physical responses is that they reflect our knowledge about what it is like to be physically trapped or to feel metaphorically trapped. Such a response could facilitate a more profound understanding of a particular physical or mental state that might otherwise be difficult to communicate without direct experiences (Sherman & Anderson, 2025).

Of course, we can also experientially learn about depth, the perceptual confusion that arises from being engulfed in diffuse light, or the feeling of being trapped, without these artworks, or any artworks, for that matter. Consider driving through a very heavy rainstorm at dusk. Presumably, that real-life scenario can similarly teach you about the limits of your depth perception and the importance of context and reference points for your eyes. Crucially, however, in the real world, driving in such extreme circumstances is scary and disconcerting. Similarly, we can learn about the feeling of being trapped by actually experiencing a small space that we cannot seem to get out of, but just about the last thing you would be doing in such a situation is reflecting on, contemplating, and intellectualizing the nature of being trapped. What the artworks allow us to do, according to defenders of this experiential knowledge approach to arts' epistemic contribution, is to have these experiences "safely," but in a way that does not seem to qualitatively change the affective response. After all, being immersed in Turrell's work can also be scary and disconcerting. In this way, engaging with artworks may be seen to be similar to riding a roller coaster. The roller coaster can "safely" give you experiences of falling great distances, of being very high off the ground. This can acquaint you with the relevant "what it is like," in a more controlled and intentional way. But, they can still raise fear, exhilaration, and confusion.

Thus, whereas its status as "fictional" was one reason for worrying about an artwork's ability to contribute to propositional knowledge, some hold that a reason for thinking art may be an especially good way to gain this kind of experiential knowledge is precisely because it is *not* "the real world." In everyday life, experiencing situations that cause sadness and fear is not desirable, enjoyable, or epistemically rewarding. In contrast, many people often *seek out* negative emotions in art (and roller coasters). Some people enjoy listening to intensely sad music, watching horror films, or looking at disturbing and even disgusting visual art. In these cases, research shows that people experience negative emotions at the very same time as they experience positive emotions like pleasure and joy (Hanich et al., 2014; Oliver et al., 2012). We discuss complex emotional responses in more depth in Chapter 3.

A potential difficulty for assessing the claim that engagement with artwork can acquaint us with experiences in a way that could count as learning or gaining knowledge, is determining what it would mean to have empirical evidence that this learning has occurred. Self-reports from the people engaging with artworks would not be useful for determining whether or not they have learned something in this way. Imagine that after watching the film *127 Hours* (2010), which depicts a climber's five-day struggle to free himself – alone – after a boulder falls and pins his arm against a canyon wall, someone claims to have learned what it is like to be trapped. How could the truth of this claim be empirically tested? If the person has not experienced being physically trapped, they cannot determine whether what they glean from the film is accurate about what it is like to be stuck in this way. Moreover, if "what it is like" knowledge is truly different from propositional knowledge, *in principle*, it cannot be communicated to others in a way that would allow researchers to test it for accuracy independently of someone's self-report. Consider what it would be like to describe your experience of seeing red. Could it be done in a way that would allow a researcher to determine that you are correct, that you know what it is like to see red? The closer one gets to being able to articulate the precise content of what one has learned through acquaintance – "being trapped is psychologically brutal" or "It feels like *that* to be dumped," or "red looks like *that*," – the more plausible it is that we are talking about propositional knowledge, not experiential knowledge, and then we are back to the considerations and limitations raised above for the position that we can learn from art.

Furthermore, even if you can gain experiential knowledge from arts engagement, it does not exhaust the set of things that people have wanted to claim that you can and do learn. Experiential knowledge does not seem to capture learning about dignity from Manet's painting, or drudgery from Serra's sculpture. So, regardless of whether it is possible to learn what it is like to have a certain experience from an artwork, it does not offer us a conception of learning from art that is a genuine alternative to propositional knowledge or fully satisfying as an answer to the question with which we began.

Understanding

Linda Zagzebski characterizes the history of Western epistemology as giving pride of place to two different concepts: "understanding" on the one hand, and "certainty" on the other. But rarely, as she points out, are they given priority at the same time (Zagzebski, 2001). She characterizes the first as primarily concerned with explanation, while the second is primarily concerned with justification. The first concept has to do with explaining how things work, how ideas fit together, how something came to be, or what something means and why it matters. The second has to do with proving that some belief is true, or that we have good reason to believe it. These ideas, of course, are not mutually exclusive (e.g., you may think that giving a justification requires being able to explain it), but they are also not the same. Returning quickly to the oak tree example above, it may be enough that a tree expert told you it is an oak tree for you to be justified in thinking that something is an oak tree. Their expertise may be enough to offer you certainty. But, it would not mean that *you* understand much at all about oak trees, trees, biology, or ecology.

Certainty concerns the status of a discrete object: whether a specific belief is true or false, justified or unjustified. Understanding, though, "is not directed toward a discrete object, but involves seeing the relation of parts to other parts and perhaps even the relation of parts to a whole" (Zagzebski, 2001, p. 241). This is because, as Catherine Elgin argues, "cognitive progress often consists in reconfiguration – in reorganizing a domain so that hitherto overlooked or underemphasized features, patterns, opportunities, and resources come to light" (Elgin, 2002, p. 1). Elgin contends that this kind of reconfiguration is found in many different forms across the arts. For example, encountering surprising new information that violates your expectations or challenges common assumptions can trigger you to question your own beliefs and then revise them in light of the new information. Or, rather than adding a new belief or revising a belief, progress can look like organizing and connecting things that we already know or believe. The arts are frequently a context for calling into question default assumptions about what things are and how they are related. Reconfiguration can also occur when we draw new lines or connections between things, or when we erase "or relocate previously accepted boundaries" (Elgin, 2002, p. 3).

In *The Imaginary Museum,* Ben Eastham describes having exactly this kind of experience with Andreas Lolis's extraordinarily realistic imitation trash bags made of marble installed at the 2019 Venice Biennale (Eastham, 2020). Eastham writes that when he first encountered people viewing Lolis's trash bags at the Biennale, he was annoyed, thinking it a rather dull attempt at getting people to reflect on the "what is art?" question. Been there, done that, he thought. Instead, he discovered that after he saw Lolis's work, he "started noticing real [bin bags] on the streets of Venice, meaning that much of the day on which I was supposed to be writing a review [was instead spent] contemplating the vast amount of waste produced in making a major exhibition" (p. 26). Lolis's work highlighted a feature of the world that Eastham had not previously attended to. We take our trash and store it in places that we cannot see; it is unsightly. The experience of having this feature of contemporary human life highlighted led Eastham to reflect on this daily inattention and, as a result, to see the trash everywhere around him. It led to a revision of his understanding of the event he was participating in, a recontextualization of its meaning, and a sense of place that he did not have before.

An emphasis on learning or epistemic improvement as developing understanding, rather than developing knowledge (of either the propositional or the experiential kind), might focus not on the experiences or pieces of information we come to have, but on how we develop connections between beliefs or information, or how we enrich or deepen our conceptual resources. When people report an experience with an artwork as shedding a new light, or as causing an "aha moment," or, as Iris Murdoch characterizes it above, as "focus[ing] attention on facts that can no longer be ignored," it may indicate that an artwork's contribution to our epistemic improvement is found in our developing a depth or connection or focus on a belief that matters through our engagement with it. Thus, understanding may better capture the idea that you are "taking something away" from the arts encounter, that is not reducible to specific claims about the artwork, but is instead about one's larger web of beliefs or how to navigate it.

There are at least two ways this kind of epistemic improvement may take place: "change by accretion" or "change by reconfiguration" (Walden, 2015). Starting with the first, change by accretion refers to a kind of conceptual sharpening or enriching. We could come to have greater credence in a particular belief, or make a concept more precise in our minds, and thus shift our application of it or our extension of it. Reading Mark Twain's *Huckleberry Finn* may lead us to have greater faith in, or support for, our prior beliefs about the moral wrongness of racism. Or it may lead us to have a more precise, or perhaps more careful, conception of friendship, and a better, sharper appreciation for the kinds of relationships the concept describes.

Along these lines, Noël Carroll introduces a kind of accretion view, clarificationism, about moral understanding developed through arts engagement (Carroll, 2002, 2012). For Carroll, understanding is an ability to recognize, respond to, and perhaps forge connections between our beliefs. Because this involves being able to see connections, the process is one of focusing our attention and our practiced judgment on what we already know (or believe). Such a view may provide a compelling explanation of the epistemic growth that goes on in the case of the people who navigate *Tilted Arc*. In encountering the piece, we may have thoughts or experiences that were wholly unexpected or unique, and thus cause us to reflect on things that we ordinarily do not (e.g., having a body, having to navigate the world physically). This may foster insights into the relative importance of what we are doing or cause us to consider how often we do not recognize how the world has or has not been built for our convenience. Similarly, the encounter may bring to the surface important fears, hopes, dreams, harms, or other aspects of our psyches that are often quite peripheral.

Thus, one way to characterize what art engagement does might be to say that it does not (just) transmit new propositions or experiential knowledge, but instead that it can make a particular belief salient or vivid in a way that is phenomenologically meaningful, or in a way that leads one to make it more central to how one understands oneself or the world. In these terms, we learn from engaging with an artwork because doing so helps us to attend to a belief, value, or other commitment, by bringing it front of mind or otherwise into focus. We not only "see" it clearly but are also able to recognize ourselves more fully as the person who has this belief. While you quite certainly know-that poverty does not make someone less than human when you encounter *Ragpicker*, the attention that the works bring to this fact is notable. Thus, this shift may constitute epistemic improvement by spotlighting a belief you already have and drawing your attention to it as important, more precise, and more clear. We will examine the relationship between this kind of epistemic change and self-identity in greater depth in Chapter 5.

A second way our understanding may be enriched through arts engagement is through "change by reconfiguration." Unlike change by accretion, reconfiguration depends on the specific content of the beliefs, values, and commitments at issue. Engagement with art may foster deeper, more radical conceptual change, so much so that we change "the background framework that conditions our thinking about that subject" (Walden, 2015, p. 285). This kind of growth is more profound in that it involves the nature of the conceptual scheme itself including changes to the "rules" or heuristics we use for drawing inferences or determining whether something is a good or bad belief, or changes with respect to the unity or coherence of our conceptual schemas. With change by accretion, we may grow at the level of individual concepts or beliefs. With change by reconfiguration, in contrast, growth is about introducing a whole class of concepts or bringing our conceptual scheme under a (new) principle.

An archetype of this kind of change is what Thomas Kuhn characterized as a scientific revolution, through which individuals and the community more broadly undergo a paradigm shift with respect to the foundational or background scientific framework (Kuhn, 2009). It is an open question whether arts engagement can effect this kind of whole-scale reconstruction. Many believe that it has this power. Wilhelm Richard Wagner, a nineteenth-century German composer, was explicit in his belief that art (and particularly music) could play an important role in moral revolution because it is potentially "revelatory." That is, he believed music can be a context for contact with ideals, values, or beliefs that are otherwise obscured. This is what he took to be art's disruptive power, and Wagner was intentional in writing his operas in a way that aimed to achieve this kind of revelation in the audience. (See Walden, 2015, pp. 290–292 for a detailed explanation of this as applied to Wagner's *Tristan and Isolde.*)

The line between these two kinds of epistemic change is not a bright one. More important than our ability to rigidly classify experiences into one of them is the question of whether either is what people mean when they say that they have learned something through engagement with the arts. Perhaps it is easy to see how the accretion case is plausibly what many mean when they report this kind of learning. The arts are experientially engrossing, and they have the capacity to draw attention to a belief, a value, or a commitment in a nuanced, organic, and novel way. If this is right, then perhaps it is also plausible that arts engagement could give rise to something that we would call a conceptual or paradigm shift for an individual, if the relevant belief, value, or commitment were deep and foundational enough to their understanding of the world. We return to these ideas more fully in Chapter 5 in our discussion of transformative experience (TE).

Know-How

What we find especially interesting and fruitful from this investigation is the emphasis that the concept of understanding gives to the value and importance of cognitive *skills* with respect to our own beliefs and learning. In focusing not on the content of specific ideas we come to have, but on how ideas hang together, and how we come to revise and develop them, the concept of understanding points to the abilities we have to navigate our own cognitive lives. In this way, it invites us to think about the third kind of epistemic status beyond propositional knowledge, and the one we will be focusing more fully on in Chapters 2–4: know-how. Acquiring this type of knowledge concerns learning how to do things, rather than acquiring discrete pieces of information.[2] Consider learning how to drive a car. Although there is a great deal of propositional knowledge required in the learning process (e.g., knowing which pedal applies the brakes, that you must stop when you come to a red light), learning the facts relevant to driving is not the same as learning *how* to drive. Learning how to drive also means that you have to gain the requisite perceptual-motor abilities, such as knowing how to apply the right amount of pressure on the clutch of a manual car, or knowing how far you must turn the steering wheel without overturning it and hitting a curb.

The concept of skill is foundational in both Eastern and Western philosophy: Both Plato and Aristotle took *techne* (translated as art, craft, technique, or skill) to be a kind of knowledge, and the conception of skill plays various and important roles in Mahayana Buddhism, Daoism, and Chan/Zen thought (Garfield & Priest, 2020). Although philosophers disagree about the precise relationship between skills and know-how, we will assume that the two are tied closely together (noting that many use the terms interchangeably). Standardly, skills have two general attributes (Pavese, 2022). First, they are manifested in purposeful, goal-directed activities. That is, they are displayed in actions or other "doing" that is aimed at some end or outcome. The nature of "action" and "outcome" ranges widely, from something like kicking a ball for the purpose of scoring a goal, to reasoning through the formula to determine the volume of the ball. Second, they are learnable and improvable through practice. This is evident in both examples here: Kicking and mathematical reasoning can both be taught and improved.

Importantly, knowing how to do things in many cases also involves honing skills important to *knowing or learning* itself. For instance, becoming a more careful observer helps us to make better inferences about our surroundings. Becoming better at perspective-taking (i.e., understanding the mental states of others) may help us to be more creative (i.e., considering alternative possibilities) in how we respond to a situation. This can be seen through comparison to the motor skills of driving. You may know all the relevant facts about driving, and how to properly turn the wheel, apply pressure, and get the car moving. But, once you take that car out of an empty parking lot and onto a busy road with other cars, those discrete or task-specific skills alone are not sufficient. You must also carefully observe what other cars around you are doing prior to making moves, keep a safe

[2] For discussion of whether know-how and know-that are really that distinct, see Currie (2020), p. 83.

driving distance, use your reasoning and perspective-taking skills to determine what another driver might be thinking based on the relatively minimal information you have about their previous movements, and so on. These kinds of cognitive knowing-how-to-know skills can also be seen in our description of understanding above, particularly in Carroll's clarificationism (e.g., "the capacity to see and be responsive to connections between our beliefs," "recognizing connections between parts of our knowledge stock" and "bringing what we already know to clarity through a process of practice and judgment.")

With respect to whether and how the arts are a venue for epistemic improvement of skills and know-how, let's return to Manet's *Ragpicker*. Rather than focusing on pieces of information that we might learn from viewing the painting, let's consider what you need to know how to do to engage with it, or what skills would allow you to learn from it in the ways discussed above. First, there are cognitive skills related to what we refer to as observation: the ability to perceive and attend closely to what you are viewing. But there is also an ability to practice what we refer to as open-minded engagement: to be open to the painting, to take it on its own terms, to think with it and through it, while looking at it. Additionally, the painting's depiction of the person encourages the viewer to understand the emotions shown by and implied by the subject and gives rise to emotions in the viewer that need to be understood, interpreted, and regulated.

Know-how is also not subject to some of the most important objections raised about know-that and experiential knowledge as gained through arts engagement. Unlike experiential knowledge, it is subject to experimental investigation, and empirical evidence can bear on whether or not it has been gained. Moreover, it is not subject to the same kind of circularity worries as propositional knowledge, because we do not need to claim that arts engagement imparts a skill or is the only way to gain a skill, in order for it to be true that arts engagement can be a context through which we develop a skill. For know-how, being epistemically better off only requires the development or improvement of a skill, not learning a skill that you did not have before. Finally, know-how embraces the complexity and individuality at the heart of arts engagement (e.g., interpretation, meaning-making, discussion, disagreement) as part of what makes the arts especially well suited for epistemic growth, rather than seeing these features of it as problematic or otherwise bad for the arts' role in knowledge production.

We thus suggest that examining know-how is a promising, interesting, and rich ground for thinking about what we learn from arts engagement.

In focusing on knowing-related skills, we take up the idea that the arts are a venue for making us better knowers. The evidence is too complicated and too specific to particular skills to do justice in this section alone, and thus, we expand on this argument in three discrete chapters. The chapters themselves build on one another and contain common threads that suggest rich interrelationships. Nevertheless, for clarity and focus, we organize them into three discrete sets of cognitive skills.

Summary

It is natural to think that we learn something from the arts, and it is natural to think that learning involves acquiring knowledge. Precisely what knowledge is, and how the arts can lead to epistemic improvement, are complex and difficult questions that we do not believe have singular or straightforward answers. We have surveyed four different kinds of knowledge: propositional knowledge, experiential knowledge, understanding, and know-how. With respect to each, there are promising ways of working out how they may contribute to our epistemic growth. At the same time, each candidate type of knowledge faces challenges and complications that limit its ability to be the singular answer regarding learning from and through the arts. Given this, we primarily focus, in what follows, on "know-how," and more specifically on cognitive skills that are foundational for how we learn and know in the first place. Each of the next three chapters takes up a set of cognitive skills – observation, emotional intelligence, and open-minded engagement – in service of elaborating on how engaging with the arts can help us develop ways of seeing, perceiving, interpreting and responding to the world more skillfully.

CHAPTER 2

The Arts and Becoming a Better Observer

Starting Point

Mexican folklórico dance, or *ballet folklórico*, has its roots in the ceremonial and social dances of Indigenous people of Mexico, in the amalgamation of influences from Spain during the sixteenth- to early nineteenth-century colonial period, and in nineteenth-century post-independence immigration, primarily from Germany, France, and parts of Asia and Africa. The blending of cultural influences in different regions of Mexico gave rise to regionally distinct dances that represent different states. Folklórico performance invites us to *see* and *notice* all there is to observe: the intricate movements and shapes of the dancers; the music; the connections between those movements and the music. But even more than this, keen observation is central to understanding the stories being performed. The rhythms, the footwork, how dancers manipulate their skirts, the specific instruments accompanying the dance, the dancers' costumes (i.e., colors, textures, hats, hairpieces, how ribbons are adorned or not, what shoes are worn, etc.), are all indicative of the regional specificity of the dance, and reflect elements of the unique history, cultures, and peoples of the region from which it comes (Friscia, 2019).

Figure 2.1 shows performers in the traditional attire of folklórico in Veracruz, home to one of the oldest and most important ports in Mexico. The beauty of the attire encourages us to carefully attend to it, bringing to light not only the craftsmanship, but the influences of the communities that interacted through the port, including those of Spain and of the Afro-Caribbean, especially Cuba. The same influences inform the music of the dance, which is uniquely characterized by the sounds of a special 39-string harp (*arpa jarocha*) and a small guitar (*jarana*). The Son Jarocho songs from this region are a mixture of Spanish Seguidillas and Fandangos and Cuban "Zapateados and Guajiras" (*Dance from the State of Veracruz*, n.d.), of which "La Bamba" is perhaps the most well known. The rhythm of

Figure 2.1 "La Bamba."

these songs is distinctively Cuban, but the dance style and structure are derived from a Spanish courtship dance. It involves partners performing intricate foot-stamping dance sequences while jointly tying a red ribbon into a bow with their feet to symbolize everlasting love. The result is a wholly novel, unique, and vibrant expression of a particular place and people.

The first time you see "La Bamba" performed (perhaps, as in Figure 2.1, performed by the Ballet Folklórico de México de Amalia Hernández at the Palacio de Bellas Artes in Mexico City), you will not see and hear everything there is to see and hear. As engrossing as any one performance is, there is just so much to take in and to understand. Quick glances or passive attention can give us the visual and perceptual basics – the colors, the shapes, the sounds – but keen observation and recurring engagement are required to grasp the significance of these sensory properties and their relationships to each other, and to the relevant social and historical contexts. In this chapter, we expand on the idea we introduced in Chapter 1 that the arts are an avenue through which we practice and develop cognitive skills that allow us to apprehend and appreciate these connections.

In his new book on creativity, Keith Sawyer suggests that the most important skill that arts professionals cultivate is *seeing*. Training in the arts is itself a training in *really* and *carefully* seeing the world (Sawyer, 2025).

The mechanisms by which the arts can facilitate the development of our abilities to attend and to notice are complex. One way they do so is through inviting us to look slowly and mindfully at the things we are looking at. When we do so, we notice details we may have missed, we make connections and arrive at a more relational understanding of the object of observation, and we can gain insights into our own attentional capacities and cognitive biases. The main point of this chapter is not only to suggest that the act of careful observation helps deepen one's understanding of art, but to suggest that art engagement hones one's skill of observation in general, thus helping you to become a better observer of the world *more broadly.*

Defining Observation and Attention

Before we turn to the evidence linking arts engagement with improvements in observation, it is important to pause and clarify what we mean by "observation" and the cognitive skills it involves. Observation, as we use the term, refers to our ability to notice, analyze, and interpret information from our environment. It is a complex and trainable set of mental processes that includes carefully allocating our attention, recognizing patterns, spotting subtleties and anomalies, and making meaning, in the sense of identifying, characterizing, naming, organizing, sorting, or connecting information. While observation is often most closely associated with the sense of sight (as is reflected in many idioms such as "open your eyes," "see the point," "seeing eye to eye"), observational skill spans sense modalities. People can be careful listeners, or especially sensitive with respect to touch, smell, or taste. Moreover, it is not uncommon to have differently developed sensitivities across these sense modalities. In this chapter, we use observation as an umbrella term for multisensory noticing, although we default in places to examples of visual observation.

Observation within any sensory modality is not a static or fixed ability. It is something that we can be better or worse at, and it is something that we can improve. Becoming a better observer involves cultivating attentional control, patience, and reflectiveness. However, there are limits to our observational capacities, which are constrained by the features of our sensory systems and by our brain's processing power. A vivid demonstration of these limits is provided by the famous "Monkey Business Illusion" (Chabris & Simons, 2010). In the experiment, participants are directed to watch a video of two teams of players in different colored shirts passing two basketballs back and forth to one another. Their goal while watching is to count the number of times one team passes the ball. While the players are passing the ball, a person in a gorilla costume slowly walks through the frame, thumps on their chest, and walks out of the frame. Strikingly, about 50 percent of people fail to notice the gorilla despite their eyes having clearly passed over it while watching the video. This phenomenon, called inattentional blindness, illustrates the gap between visual availability and conscious awareness: Looking at something does not equate to seeing it.

The illusion underscores a crucial point: Attention is limited and selective, and our expectations shape what we look for and what we eventually notice. Because viewers tend to be focused on the task of accurately counting and do not expect to see a gorilla on a basketball court, their attention tends to filter the gorilla out as task irrelevant, resulting in their failing to see it. This filtering mechanism is not inherently bad. Attending takes a great deal of cognitive effort, and we would not want to waste our limited energy attending to every detail of the world. Imagine how exhausting it would be, and how long it would take, to process every single detail of the shapes, colors, and movements in New York City's Times Square. Not being able to limit, restrict, or direct attention would make getting across town impossible. Attention helps our brains to highlight only the details we actually care about at any given time.

We deploy our attention in two ways: involuntarily, through automatic cognitive processes informed by our prior experiences and expectations, and voluntarily, through effortful, deliberate control. Our involuntary, automatic attention helps us to quickly and efficiently recognize the gist of our environment and detect potential threats in it. Careful voluntary observation, in contrast, is slower and intentional, and demands that we override our usual cognitive shortcuts. Crucially, improving our observational skills is not only about learning how and when to slow down and deploy our selective, deliberate attention; it also involves developing our attentional flexibility. It means learning when and how to deploy attention from moment to moment, including shifting it and sustaining it, and in doing so, potentially overcoming the effects of cognitive shortcuts such as those that lead to inattentional blindness .

One method for developing these skills is to practice mindful attention. Consider the practice of mindfully eating an orange. When done with intention, this apparently simple act can be revealed to be quite complicated. We can actively "tune into" various aspects of the sensory experience by noticing subtle variations in colors, textures, temperature, weight, and smells. Mindful eating demands that we slow down, sustain our attention, filter out irrelevant distractions, flexibly shift attention in a deliberate way from one sensory modality to another, control our desire to move more quickly and simply eat the orange, and listen to our own bodily responses to the sensations. Slowing down any task that we typically engage in rapidly also means actively monitoring our attention, noticing the moments when our attention waxes and wanes, and working to bring ourselves back into the present experience when needed. Each of these actions draws on cognitive capacities central to observation. Practicing mindful attention in this way has been shown to improve a variety of attentional and observational skills. For example, having a long-term mindfulness meditation practice improves practitioners' ability to sustain their attention, to inhibit distractions, and to appropriately switch between tasks (Sumantry & Stewart, 2021).

Mindfulness can be, and often is, practiced both in making art and in appreciating art. Whether painting, sculpting, playing an instrument, or simply viewing a piece of art, creative practices demand focused, moment-to-moment awareness. Engaging with art mindfully can not only enhance the creative experience but can also reinforce habits of close looking and embodied attention. Mindful engagement with art encourages individuals to recognize that such focused and deliberate attention is difficult; to accept frustrations, confusion, or attentional lapses that occur while trying to maintain focus, and to return to their engagement with curiosity rather than criticism. In this way, the arts may help cultivate observational acuity over time by training us to be comfortable with deliberately paying attention and training our metacognitive capacities to notice, reflect, and respond attentively to subtle sensory details over time.

We must address one more conceptual question before turning to the empirical studies that explore the connection between observational skills and art engagement: Are observation skills domain-general or domain-specific? In psychology, this is often discussed as the problem of transfer, or transfer effects. Domain-general skills are those that apply broadly across contexts, while domain-specific skills are confined to the context in which they are developed and do not generalize. Does training observation in one context (i.e., art creation or art appreciation) transfer to another context (e.g., everyday social interaction)?

The robustness of transfer effects is a topic of widespread debate in cognitive science, including what evidence can demonstrate such an effect. Researchers distinguish between *near* transfer, where skills apply to a domain that is closely related to the context in which they were learned, and *far* transfer, where skills apply to more distantly related domains. For example, learning to search for crickets in a forest by carefully observing small movements and sounds might transfer to observing and looking for other types of bugs, like beetles. This would be a near-transfer effect. If someone's expert cricket-finding skills translated into an improved ability to notice variations in their friends' facial or bodily movement patterns, or even further, to notice distinctions between slight variations in color shades, this would constitute a far-transfer effect. Far transfer is exceptionally hard to demonstrate, but even near-transfer effects can be notoriously difficult to establish with sound evidence.

In what follows, we review evidence that suggests arts engagement can contribute to training observational skills that can be broadly applied to observations outside of the trained arts context. At the outset, we acknowledge the limitations of the current evidence; specifically, that many of the studies we discuss are either correlational or cross-sectional, and few can definitively demonstrate causality. We are thus careful not to suggest that arts training will *cause* improvements in specific skills across arts domains. Even with experimental studies, it can still be challenging to distinguish the role of natural ability with respect to learned or developed observational skills. For example, in their systematic review of the music training literature, E. Glenn Schellenberg and César Lima suggest that even for training studies that contain control groups, we cannot disentangle whether listening skills are a *result* of music training, or whether individuals with greater listening skills are drawn to or are more motivated to persist in music (Schellenberg & Lima, 2024). Nevertheless, we believe the hypothesis that arts engagement can help cultivate observational skills is worth taking seriously.

Enhancing Observation through Arts Practices

Art Creation

In *A Treatise on Painting*, Leonardo da Vinci describes drawing not only as the best way to disseminate his discoveries but also as fundamental to keen observation, asserting that lacking the ability to draw was akin to lacking the ability to see (Roche et al., 2018). If you have taken a drawing class, you know that one of the most important things you learn when you learn to draw is how to *see.* To draw or paint with any level of accuracy, depth, or sophistication, you must attend to what in other contexts are seemingly minute details. You attend to color differences based on the way light is hitting the object, the width and depth and shape of folds in drapery, or the exact distance between objects. Perceptual precision through keen observation is key to accurate representation. By drawing a subject's eyes slightly too far apart, or in the shape of an almond rather than slightly rounder, you may immediately compromise their likeness. You must thus train yourself (or be trained by your teacher) to carefully examine your environment and to notice details that typically go unnoticed. Artists are trained to spend extensive time closely observing without even picking up a pencil, studying light, shadow, and texture, examining the shapes, angles, and spatial relationships of things around them. Artists also often revisit the same subject repeatedly to understand how it may change as a function of the context, moods, and time.

This is not to say that improving one's drawing skills only concerns enhancing one's visual attention. In drawing, the hand is not merely translating what the eyes and brain perceive. The movements made while drawing are as important to understanding an object as one's visual perception of it. Museum educators emphasize and encourage drawing in museums for precisely this reason. They see drawing as a means of discovery, rather than simply a means to reproduce or depict. As Elliott Kai-Kee, Lissa Latina, and Lilit Sadoyan (2020) explain:

> The hand helps capture and elucidate fine detail and also tests visual hypotheses. The hand and drawn line answer questions that the eye asks: How smooth or rough is this surface? Where does the surface turn away? Similarly, each drawn line asks to be confirmed or contradicted by the eye. Eye and hand learn from each other to the point that the eye learns to "draw" while the hand begins to "see." (p. 116)

Many studies demonstrate that trained visual artists attend to, observe, and think about objects differently than nonartists. Eye-tracking evidence shows that artists scan scenes more holistically and move their gaze broadly around a scene while drawing, suggesting they are attending to the relationships and organization of the scene, whereas nonartists spend more time examining local details (Park et al., 2022). Artists also have better visual memory for an object's form (Perdreau & Cavanagh, 2015), and they tend to segment an object's form into line groupings that allow them to draw the shape in fewer strokes (Tchalenko & Chris Miall, 2009). Together, these findings suggest that artists develop a specialized way of attending to and representing form that is shaped by their training and experience.

To some extent, these findings about drawing expertise are unsurprising. After all, developing expertise in a particular domain should mean that domain-specific skills are becoming better trained. Skilled poker players have better memory spans than novices (Meinz et al., 2012). Skilled chess players represent the chessboard and the various possible moves in memory differently from novices (Gobet & Simon, 1996). Part of developing expertise is adopting novel, distinct, or more efficient approaches to a task from nonexperts. We should thus expect that training in drawing, as in any domain, will help individuals identify better and more efficient strategies to draw. Moreover, practice and expertise help us to better plan and identify relevant goals, to know which strategies are dead ends on the path to achieving those goals, and to assess which aspects of the task should take more or less time to complete.

More interesting to consider, as we suggested above, is whether drawing expertise affords artists a different way of examining the world more generally, even when they are not engaged in a drawing task. There are a host of questions we may want to ask and investigate to illuminate this relationship: Does a portrait painter examine faces differently than a non-painter during their everyday non-painting life? Does training your artistic eye make you a better observer, full stop, or only while you are engaging in the artistic task you are already an expert in? Or is the relationship more complicated than either of these? Perhaps artists have the biggest observational advantages in situations when they are engaged in tasks that most closely resemble their training, as in the eye-tracking research pointing to differences during drawing. The current empirical evidence does not provide a direct answer to these questions, and substantially more research is needed to understand the details and complexity here. Even so, current research does provide some insight into how arts expertise may train up more generalized cognitive processes relevant to observation.

In the eye-tracking study discussed above, the differences in looking strategies between artists and nonartists emerge *while* drawing. When participants just look at the images with no intention to draw them, similar looking strategies are observed in both artists and nonartists (Park et al., 2022). This mitigates the support this evidence provides for the position that art engagement contributes to domain-general observational skills, as it may suggest that this specialized way of attending to and representing form is employed specifically in the process of artistic creation, rather than being a general feature of the way artists see the world. However, several other studies have shown that artists employ distinct attentional strategies, including exhibiting greater attentional flexibility, even when they are not engaged in the task of drawing. For example, artists and nonartists differ in their performance on generalized tasks measuring perceptual and attentional abilities (Drake et al., 2021). The tasks that have been tested include shifting one's attention from the general gist to the details, identifying discrete objects within blurry images, finding simple figures or shapes within larger, more complex figures, and mentally rotating or visualizing objects in your head. Artists and art students outperform nonartists on many of these general perceptual tasks, and this is especially true for participants who produce the best drawings. Drawing skill also predicts better attentional switching; that is, the capacity to flexibly switch between focusing on local details and focusing on more general features of the world, like shape (Chamberlain & Wagemans, 2015). Better drawing skill seems to predict greater domain-general perceptual performance, and stronger attentional and visuospatial reasoning skills.

However, visual artists are not better at all such tasks. They seem to be better only at those tasks that align with the skills they exercise in their arts practice. For example, research finds no difference in performance between artists and nonartists on tasks assessing digit span memorization (a measure of verbal working memory test that asks participants to repeat a sequence of numbers), or in their susceptibility to visual illusions (Chamberlain et al., 2019). This may indicate that visual artists' visuospatial skills are honed only insofar as they are helpful for drawing. Relatedly, longitudinal evidence with high school students enrolled in intensive arts courses shows improvements in geometric reasoning skills over the course of the year for visual arts students but not for students engaged in a theater-intensive curriculum, presumably because of the relevance of those specific skills to their drawing practice (Goldsmith et al., 2016).

Generally, researchers take these studies to suggest that those attentional and visuospatial skills that are essential for visual artists to physically render objects in two or three dimensions (e.g., geometric reasoning, envisioning and visualization, global and local attentional processing) become honed over time as a function of one's arts practice. However, another plausible explanation of the evidence is that individuals self-select into the arts because of a fit between these practices and how they are already disposed to examine the world. In other words, people who already have increased attentional flexibility may be more likely to become visual artists. To determine whether arts training causes an improvement in visual abilities, we would need to conduct more controlled experiments. A gold standard experiment would randomly assign people to different arts training groups and compare their performance with control groups once the arts training was complete (see Benear et al., 2024 for review). We know of no such experiments currently published. The closest the scientific community seems to have come is longitudinal studies examining changes in visuospatial and geometric reasoning measured after one and two years of visual arts training, as we described above.

Similar complexities arise for studies examining expertise in other arts domains. There is a vast literature showing that music training develops a host of auditory skills. The auditory analog of visual observation is careful listening, and behavioral and physiological evidence suggests that musically trained individuals are better listeners than their musically untrained counterparts. Music training helps people discriminate between complex sounds that differ in pitch and time. Musically trained people perform better than untrained people on pitch discrimination tasks in which they are asked to identify which sound is higher or lower. This difference is evident in the brain responses of trained musicians, which show more distinct neural representations of similar pitches than the brains of individuals who are musically untrained. (See Kraus & Chandrasekaran, 2010, for review.)

Relevant careful listening skills go beyond pitch discrimination. There have also been documented improvements in other auditory tasks as a result of musical training, including better pure-tone frequency discrimination, better ability to detect complex sounds (including speech) that are embedded in white noise, and increased capacity to discriminate between emotion-related sounds in speech (e.g., happy, sad, or neutral tones people take on when talking). (Martins et al., 2021). In fact, some researchers have suggested that music lessons can mitigate the effects of age-related declines in hearing (Alain et al., 2014). The superior cognitive abilities that seem to be linked to music training are stable, widespread, and persist into older age. (See reviews by Hannon & Trainor, 2007; Moreno, 2009; Paquette & Mignault Goulet, 2014; Schellenberg, 2005; Schellenberg & Weiss, 2013.)

More careful listening is also related to attention. Research points to musicians' improved ability to sustain attention over prolonged periods of time during auditory tasks (Wang et al., 2015), as well as their more efficient attentional processing, such that they are less affected by irrelevant information (Medina & Barraza, 2019). Musicians also have higher auditory and visual working memory capacity (George & Coch, 2011), as well as greater brain activation in neuronal networks that govern executive function during demanding working memory tasks compared to nonmusicians (Bergman Nutley et al., 2014). Working memory refers to holding information in memory for brief periods of time, as well as being able to manipulate it in memory, which requires focused attention and the ability to limit the influence of distracting information. Having a lower working memory capacity correlates with increased mind-wandering in challenging and effortful daily tasks (Kane et al., 2007). Longitudinal work suggests that improvements in working memory and attention are directly related to the number of hours that one spends every week practicing (Bergman Nutley et al., 2014).

Despite these promising findings, far transfer effects have been difficult to demonstrate. Whereas musicians' extensive training with rhythm and time keeping strengthens their auditory attention, this may not extrapolate to other types of attention tasks, such as those involving visual attention. This is akin to the visual arts findings, suggesting that while the arts and music hone perceptual and attentional expertise, that development does not improve all cognitive abilities relevant to observation. Still, together, these findings are highly suggestive of the important role that artistic training across arts domains plays in cultivating observational skill, particularly by strengthening specific perceptual skills and our attentional control capacities.

This is not to say that these questions regarding causality and expertise are limited to the field of artistic engagement. There is debate in the broader literature on expertise about the interaction between deliberate practice and perceptual and cognitive capacities. For example, larger working memory capacity predicts how good a poker player you are (Meinz et al., 2012). This suggests that working memory capacity might predispose people to be more interested in, or more successful in, poker and thereby influence their motivation to continue pursuing the game. Domain knowledge (e.g., knowledge of the odds of a specific poker hand winning), however, is also highly predictive of poker skills. Thus, it also seems plausible that practicing poker and increasing domain-specific knowledge of the game may increase working memory capacity in general. However, the evidence is currently mixed with respect to this claim (Melby-Lervåg et al., 2016).

Art Appreciation

Like art creation, art appreciation can hone our observation skills. Some of the strongest evidence that it fosters not only the use of but the development of these skills comes from the medical humanities. This is a relatively new field that emphasizes an interdisciplinary approach to medical education by integrating the arts and humanities into the traditional scientific practice of medicine. Those adopting this approach believe that arts engagement can make medicine and patient care more well-rounded, compassionate, and human-centered, because it provides "the potential for trainees at all levels to step outside their comfort zone, become open to new methods of learning, and access competencies in tangential ways that are not possible through the traditional medical school curricula" (Katz & Khoshbin, 2014, p. 332). Medical humanities programs often incorporate close study of literature, narrative, poetry, theater, and the visual arts into their curricula, and often collaborate with local museums to create art materials, workshops, or courses aimed at cultivating students' observational skills with the aim of teaching them to make more accurate diagnoses.

In the last decade, a number of researchers have attempted to measure the effects of arts programs on medical students' clinical skill sets and their mindsets, as well as on patient outcomes. In many such studies, medical or nursing students are randomly assigned either to a control group or to an art "intervention" group, through which they participate in some type of visual or literary arts workshop, often with an arts educator acting as facilitator. Arts interventions vary in length from short multi-hour formats to multiple-week programs, or even to entire semester courses. Pre–post test designs are often employed to evaluate the success of these interventions; at the start of programs, students' general and medically-relevant observation skills are often tested using a set of patient photographs and then retested using a new set after they have completed their assigned participation. These studies tend to employ one of two approaches to foster visual literacy and refine observational skills: Visual Thinking Strategies (VTS) and Artful Thinking (AT). Both of these approaches ask viewers to answer three questions: What is going on in this picture?, What do you see that makes you say that?, and What more can you find? These strategies invite participants to closely examine an artwork, to make observations based on what they see, and to work with their peers and museum facilitators to interpret their observations. Importantly, participants' interpretations are to be grounded in visual evidence, rather than additional context like the placard next to the artwork or reading a book about the artist. (See Yenawine, 2013, for a fuller explanation of the strategies.) Discussions among participants are also key to the practice. The goal is for participants to refine their observation and description skills, their investigative skills, their reasoning skills, their ability to explore various viewpoints, and their capacities to compare, connect, find complexity, and make meaning out of the visual experience (Tishman & Palmer, 2006).

The findings are notable: Students who complete visual arts appreciation training programs embedded in their medical school curricula show improved clinical observation skills compared with their peer control group. In one study, first-year medical students from the University of Pennsylvania were either randomly assigned to receive a free pass to visit the Philadelphia Museum of Art on their own or to an art-training course consisting of six custom-designed, 90-minute live art observation sessions with an arts educator at the museum. All participants' observation skills were tested both before and after the study: They were asked to describe a set of images, including both artworks and ophthalmological clinical images, such as photographs of the retina or photographs of the face showing the eye in detail. In addition to the measured objective improvements in their observational skills, those assigned the art-training course self-reported "applying the skills they learned in the museum in clinically meaningful ways at medical school" (Gurwin et al., 2018, p. 8).

Researchers have also shown that shorter-term art workshops meaningfully affect students' perceptual skills. For example, engaging in just one 90-minute art education workshop at a university museum, in which participants learned to discriminate, compare, and contrast artistic intentions, as well as how to decode objects' meanings and extract information by direct observation, led participants to make significantly more written observations, more plausible clinical interpretations, and more potential diagnoses than the students in the control condition (Pellico et al., 2009). The art appreciation experience demonstrated to participants that it is easy to categorize ambiguous imagery (and concepts) too quickly, to ignore conflicting cues, and to jump to confirmatory conclusions – lessons they extended to their clinical practice.

Art appreciation outside of a museum context – in this case, looking at art reproductions in the classroom – has also been shown to refine observational skills. Students who engaged in a classroom workshop outperformed a control group in both patient description and analysis (Jasani & Saks, 2013). Although students in the workshop and those in the control group made the same number of observations before and after the exercise, the quality of their responses was notably different. While prior to the art observation activity, students used more subjective language, after the activity, their descriptions were more clearly based on visual evidence. For example, in the pretest, they wrote things like "His arm and leg are positioned normally," whereas in the posttest, they omitted subjective words like "normal" and instead wrote things like "Her right arm and leg are straight and lay flat. Her left arm is flexed at the shoulder and elbow with the hand clenched in a fist with the thumbs extended away from the fingers. The left leg is flexed at the hip and knee" (Jasani & Saks, 2013, p. e1328).

Moreover, after the workshop, students demonstrated more speculative thinking, used more visual analogies in their responses, and made more comprehensive descriptions that contained the patient's surroundings, the patient's perspective, or their emotional state. Finally, students' own self-reflections indicated that they felt their skills had broadened, particularly with respect to mindfulness and attention.

Whether, and in what ways, arts interventions are uniquely valuable for the development of observational skills is still an open question. In one study, researchers tested the comparative value of the arts intervention by comparing a control group, who completed a close-looking workshop engaging with clinical photographs and cases, with groups who engaged with art (Shapiro et al., 2006). They showed that, on the posttest, students who examined clinical photographs were better at recognizing disease symptoms and patient patterns than those who participated in the art workshop. However, the art sessions seemed to encourage consideration of multiple perspectives and more holistic observation skills of "the whole person" depicted in the image. This suggests that the art engagement affected students' socio-emotional skills, consistent with a widespread idea that empathy is intricately linked to the arts (a suggestion we take up at length in Chapter 3).

Overall, these findings point to the visual arts as an effective way to train our visual literacy skills, including visual reasoning and pattern identification. The process of engaging with visual art may help people see better, or perhaps see what others miss. Although this evidence base is exciting and becoming stronger, more large-scale and controlled studies need to be conducted to better understand the precise role visual art engagement plays in developing our more general visual literacy and to extend these investigations to other sense modalities. Outside of the medical context, there is still limited research examining how and whether observation skills are honed through arts appreciation. For instance, comparing the observational skills of arts experts, such as art historians or art critics, to arts novices would offer considerable insights. Moreover, many of the studies utilize very small sample sizes, lack randomization in group assignment, or do not have strong control groups. Conducting multi-institution studies would be particularly valuable in this regard.

Summary

Observation is a dynamic process important to our successful navigation of the world around us. It is not mere passive absorption of sensory input, but the ability to carefully attend to the richness, complexity, and interestingness of our daily experiences. The arts invite us to look more closely and intentionally, to notice patterns, to see nuance, and to seek the meaning of and in our observations of ourselves, others, and the world. We have argued that emerging evidence suggests that observational and attentional skills developed through domain-specific arts training may generalize beyond arts contexts. Both art appreciation and art-making have been associated with improvements in perceptual acuity and attentional control. Trained artists, for example, often demonstrate using distinct attentional strategies, exhibit greater attention flexibility and perceptual accuracy, and tend to process information more holistically than nonartists. Drawing, in particular, appears to sharpen specific observational capacities such as mental rotation, pattern detection, and sustained attention. Likewise, guided close-looking in visual arts contexts – whether in museums or classrooms – has been linked to improvements in clinical observational skills, diagnostic accuracy, and a willingness to engage with ambiguity.

However, the extent of this generalizability remains uncertain. Some evidence suggests that the relevant cognitive benefits are context dependent and most noticeable when individuals are engaged in art-making. But several open questions remain: Does sustained arts practice "switch on" a more attentive cognitive mode that remains active across contexts? Or is this attentive cognitive mode situationally activated by artistic engagement? Similarly, questions of causality remain: Do we develop attentional skills because of our arts practice, or do those with stronger attentional capacity in the first place gravitate toward the arts?

As we continue to explore in the next chapters, the attentional capacities honed through observation also underpin our abilities to experience empathy, to detect, interpret, and regulate our emotions (Chapter 3), and to approach differences with curiosity, openness, and flexible thinking (Chapter 4). The arts, then, do more than enhance how and what we see; they also shape how we relate to others, to the world around us, and to ourselves.

CHAPTER 3

Cultivating Emotional Intelligence through the Arts

Starting Point

The arts can undeniably be emotionally evocative (Chatterjee & Vartanian, 2014; Zentner et al., 2008). Consider Rainer Maria Rilke's poem "The Panther."

The Panther

His vision, from the constantly passing bars,
has grown so weary that it cannot hold
anything else. It seems to him there are
a thousand bars; and behind the bars, no world.

As he paces in cramped circles, over and over,
the movement of his powerful soft strides
is like a ritual dance around a center
in which a mighty will stands paralyzed.

Only at times, the curtain of the pupils
lifts, quietly–. An image enters in,
rushes down through the tensed, arrested muscles,
plunges into the heart and is gone.

—Rainer Maria Rilke (1907/2013)

Through his description of the movements of the creature, Rilke portrays a haunting and emotionally complex depiction of captivity. This is done not by stating the captivity outright, but by letting the reader feel the complex constellation of emotions. The poem never names "him" (outside of the title), nor does it explicitly say that he is captive. Instead, the precision of the description of his movements and his experiences conveys the weight and deep despair of involuntary, solitary confinement. The repetitive movements, the dulled perceptions, and the fleeting moments of engagement reflect both physical and emotional constraint.

Reading this poem, many feel they come away with some recognition of what it feels like to be captive. The emotional insights we gain from this poem are not purely intellectual; they are also embodied. We may *feel* despair in response to the descriptions Rilke provides. We may be moved to sadness for the fate of the creature, and perhaps others – both human and nonhuman – who are similarly captive. We may feel these emotions in specific parts of our bodies. In this way, the poem becomes a vehicle for emotional understanding and empathy, allowing readers to feel their way into another being's world, to recognize the depth of suffering that may lie beyond one's own lived experiences.

That poetry, and the arts more broadly, make us *feel* something may help explain why we are so drawn to them in the first place. Arts' emotionality is often cited as the hallmark of our aesthetic experiences, and as a primary motivation for our engagement with it, and sometimes serves as a marker of artistic quality. People routinely describe feeling a range of emotions in response to art, including happiness, sadness, anger, surprise, and disgust, as well as more complex emotional states like interest, curiosity, nostalgia, pride, tenderness, inspiration, peace, serenity, transcendence, wonder, and awe (e.g., Juslin, 2016; Pelowski, 2015; Silvia, 2005, 2009). Notably, as with "The Panther," people commonly experience negative emotions in response to artworks, including feelings of sadness, sorrow, grief, confusion, or even anger and outrage.

Our emotional responses can be subtle or overwhelming. They can be momentary or linger for longer periods of time. They can arise straightforwardly in response to narrative content or literal depictions, or they can arise indirectly in response to more abstract forms like lines, colors, sounds, or textures. The emotions we feel during art engagement may not be the same as those depicted or expressed in the artwork. In our starting-point poem, you may be able to tell that the panther is suffering and feeling despair, but you yourself may not feel that suffering deeply; you may instead feel something more like sadness for the creature. This distinction helps illustrate that the arts are both a site for emotional communication and for emotional reception. Our responses to art are shaped not only by the formal properties of artworks, but also by the context we are in, our own prior experiences, and a host of other dispositions and factors.

In this chapter, we focus on our complex emotional entanglement with the arts. We argue that because of their ability to express and evoke emotionally complex experiences, the arts are a fertile ground for the development of a critical set of cognitive skills associated with *emotional intelligence*. The core components of emotional intelligence that we elaborate on include perceiving, interpreting, regulating, and acting on emotions experienced by oneself and others (Mayer & Salovey, 1997). In what follows, we focus on three sub-skills: emotional perception and recognition, emotional understanding, and emotional regulation. As we did for observation in Chapter 2, and building on that argument, we marshal evidence that the arts present us with novel opportunities to observe and examine how emotions are expressed in varied, nuanced, or even exaggerated ways, which offers us insight into the emotional experience of others. Additionally, we show that feeling and actively reflecting on a host of emotions evoked during art-making and art appreciation can help us to recognize and appropriately label our emotions, which is a key to healthy self-regulation.

Emotions, Art, and Learning

Even though emotions serve as a central organizing force in our learning and meaning-making, precisely defining "emotion" is surprisingly difficult. Most theories agree that emotions are coordinated responses to meaningful events that involve subjective experience (e.g., feeling excited or content), physiological changes (e.g., heart rate increasing or decreasing, muscles tensing), and behavioral tendencies (e.g., smiling, attending to something in the environment). Emotions typically unfold over the course of seconds or minutes and include perceiving and attending to an external or internal situation, determining how the situation affects our goals, and acting accordingly. Emotions can be used (or can fail to be used) to appropriately guide our sensory, perceptual, and cognitive processing. They can help us make better and quicker decisions, better understand others' intentions, and more successfully navigate our social landscape; or they can act against our ability to do these things well. In addition to their value for successfully navigating the world, emotions also increase our attachment to people, places, and experiences, and they play a powerful role in memory formation (Gross, 2015). Emotionally charged experiences are more likely to be remembered with greater vividness and persistence than neutral experiences (Conway, 1990; Hamann, 2001). Try recalling vivid details from the same day and month you are reading this, but three years ago. We suspect it will be quite challenging unless that day had a high number of emotionally salient experiences.

Although people experience a wide array of emotions through the arts, certain complex, intense emotions stand out as especially important to arts experience and can help us better understand how and why these kinds of experiences may contribute to learning or epistemic improvement. Awe and its cousins – curiosity, wonder, surprise, interest, confusion, and being moved – are especially relevant to consider in the context of knowledge generation, knowledge updating, and critical thinking. Awe is often described as an "epistemic emotion" because of its connection to feelings of expanded understanding, of insight, and of a heightened drive to experience new things (Silvia, 2010; Vogl et al., 2021).

Awe is a multifaceted feeling of amazement, admiration, inspiration, or elevation in response to perceived vastness or the sublime. People experiencing awe describe feeling overwhelmingly small compared to everything else around them, or feeling like they are in the presence of something grander, or feeling a sense of oneness with all things (Shiota et al., 2007). When astronauts see Earth in its entirety from space, and report feelings of self-transcendence, of being overwhelmed, and of connection with all of humankind, they are describing awe. Large vistas like the Grand Canyon, architectural spaces like large churches with vaulted ceilings, and many paintings and musical compositions can all evoke such feelings. Awe is associated with physiological phenomena like goosebumps, chills, gasps, or jaw dropping, and with feeling as if time is slowing down (Hur et al., 2020; Yaden et al., 2019). Although it is most typically experienced as a positive emotion, some awe experiences are tinged with fear, unease, or anxiety. For instance, when people watch videos of the solar system, especially when those videos are accompanied by somewhat ominous music, they report feeling positive awe and fear simultaneously (Lazarus, 1991; Stellar et al., 2024).

In museum environments, experiences of awe are quite common, and those experiencing it often attribute the feeling to a recognition of an artist's exceptional skill (Luke, 2021). One especially awe-inducing space is the Rothko Chapel in Houston, Texas, which features fourteen monumental paintings by abstract expressionist Mark Rothko. Rothko himself intended the space to evoke awe, spirituality, feelings of smallness, wonder, and connection to oneself, and visitors tend to agree, so much so that people report crying or feeling like they want to cry (Pelowski, 2015).

We typically feel confused when our expectations are violated, and when we are confused, we tend to withdraw from the situation that caused us to feel that way. What is remarkable about awe is that although it, too, is evoked when our expectations are violated (and is often accompanied by feelings of confusion), rather than prompting withdrawal, feeling awe motivates people to engage more fully with the circumstances that evoke it. The sense of awe deepens our desire to better understand the world and ourselves and fosters novel ways of thinking (De Cruz, 2024). It helps us be less persuaded by weak arguments (Griskevicius et al., 2010) and to remember details better than other emotional experiences (Danvers & Shiota, 2017). Whereas a general positive mood signals that the environment is safe and predictable, thereby allowing us to rely on heuristics and internalized knowledge, feelings of awe discourage and reduce reliance on heuristics and increase new information intake. Note that this parallels the effects of slow and mindful observation that we discussed in Chapter 2; just as slow and mindful observation allows us to suspend our rote and automatic methods of engaging with the world and attend to its details more consciously and intentionally, so awe appears to induce people to attend to the details of their current environment. In these ways, awe may be a spur to acquire, refine, or extend our propositional knowledge, or to deepen our understanding of ourselves, or aspects of the world.

Supporting this suggestion is complementary evidence that experiencing awe can increase interest in science. For example, a study showed that people who experienced awe while watching a Planet Earth video reported being more aware of knowledge gaps they have in the world, agreeing more strongly with statements like "This activity makes me realize how much I don't know about nature" than participants who watched nature/animal videos overdubbed with funny commentary, which did not induce awe. They also agreed more strongly with statements like "Science magazines and stories are interesting" than the control group, suggesting a higher level of interest in science (McPhetres, 2019).

In addition to evoking epistemic emotions like awe, many artistic engagements also evoke negative emotions. Strikingly, people are often drawn to artworks that do this, apparently for this very reason. In our everyday lives, we typically aim to avoid negative experiences, yet in engaging with art, we often willingly feel sorrow, anger, or fear. We choose to listen to sad songs just to feel sad or nostalgic, or to cry, and we enjoy doing so. We choose to watch dramatic movies and to read literature that makes us feel a rollercoaster of emotions. We enjoy engaging with paintings that depict war or grotesque acts. We may even love to watch horror films in which people are brutally tortured and dismembered.

One reason we may be drawn to emotionally complex, including emotionally negative, arts experiences might be that they are *interesting* (Besser-Jones, 2024; Besser & Oishi, 2020). It is interesting to be able to explore and experience things that are outside our ordinary existence. Consider Georges Braque's invention of cubism, a style of painting in which an object is depicted on a two-dimensional canvas from multiple vantage points. It is challenging to engage with something that is familiar in some ways, but at the same time deeply strange and unfamiliar. As in experiences of awe, things we find interesting often lead us to allocate more of our attentional resources to them and to persist in our engagement with them. Although unfamiliarity can be challenging, grappling with the unfamiliar can serve as a spur to deepen our understanding through unsettling our certainty and encouraging us to see things in new ways. So, we may seek out and appreciate opportunities to experience negative emotions for the same reasons we seek out and appreciate opportunities to experience awe, or for the same reason that we carefully and mindfully observe things in our environment: Because doing so suspends our ordinary and automatic modes of engagement with the world and allows us to attend more carefully and intentionally to the world around us. This in turn facilitates our learning and drawing connections, in the ways we discussed in Chapter 1, which is part of living a cognitively richer life.

Another explanation, compatible with our discussion so far, for why we actively pursue negative emotional experiences through the arts is the "safety of fiction" theory, according to which the arts are a context for safely practicing feeling things without the consequences of those feelings in "real" life (Keen, 2006; Mar & Oatley, 2008; Zunshine, 2006). We can read a story that is horrifying and learn both about horrifying things and about how we might respond to such scenarios, without having to encounter a life event that is horrifying in that way. Reading Michelle Zauner's memoir *Crying in H Mart* may lead you to feel the intense grief that comes with experiencing the death of a parent, without actually having to lose one. Listening to the Beatles song "While My Guitar Gently Weeps" can be a context for rehearsing feelings, identifying, coping with, and regulating intense feelings associated with loss, disappointment, and distance from those you love. These "rehearsals" can happen at a safe psychological distance. Some also suggest that these rehearsals are good for our longer-term ability to navigate challenging life events, and so they facilitate our wellbeing. We will return to the relationship with wellbeing in Chapter 6.

One worry we may have about the idea that we can gain experiential knowledge from emotionally charged art experiences, including negative ones, concerns whether the emotions that we feel in response to art are the same as, or even relevantly comparable to, those we experience in real-life scenarios. Do horror films really make us feel *fear*? And, is that fear the same fear that we feel when we are alone and hear a strange noise? Is the sadness we feel when we listen to George Harrison's melancholy observations – *I don't know why nobody told you how to unfold your love* – the same sadness that we feel when our partner breaks our heart? If art-evoked emotions are fundamentally different in some way from their "genuine" counterparts – perhaps more detached, or aestheticized, or less intense – we may be dubious about the suggestion that we are truly *learning* something important through engagement with them.

Empirical researchers have approached these questions by assessing how people's reactions to art relate to the components of emotions outlined above. This involves identifying how relevant cognitive appraisals can occur in the context of arts engagement, by asking people to self-report their subjective emotional experiences, by measuring their physiological responses during experiences, and by measuring brain activity. Evidence from this research supports the position that people experience "real" emotions when they engage with art (Juslin & Västfjäll, 2008). Subjective first-person reports suggest that we feel a range of emotions across a range of arts experiences, including both basic emotions and complex emotions. Physiological responses to music and to visual art seem to parallel physiological responses to other everyday emotions, including heart rate changes, breathing changes, skin temperature shifts, feeling chills, crying, laughing, smiling, frowning, and furrowing our brows. Evidence suggests that brain regions that are typically implicated in emotional processing and reward are also engaged during art appreciation, including the thalamus, hippocampus, amygdala, prefrontal cortex, orbitofrontal cortex, midbrain/periaqueductal gray, insula, and nucleus accumbens (Koelsch, 2014; Vessel et al., 2013; Zatorre et al., 2007). There is also specific evidence that brain regions implicated in feelings of sadness are engaged when people report feeling sadness in response to art and music (Brattico et al., 2011).

Still, there is debate on this point; the nature of emotional responses may differ across specific art forms (i.e., music, theater, literature, visual arts); and there remains room for further empirical research across different arts. Moreover, philosophical questions about how to disambiguate emotions may not be settled by empirical information. While the evidence above suggests that people do feel emotions when engaging with art, it does not fully address the question of whether the emotions are the same as those experienced "in real life," particularly because the subjective experiences and physiological changes in response to art are often accompanied by *different* actions and behaviors than with those experiences in "real life." Although people may get goosebumps, feel tingling in their spines, startle easily, and even scream when watching a horror movie, they very rarely (if ever!) run out of the theater as they would if really encountering a ghost

(Walton, 1978). Some research suggests that negative emotions like sadness are "unadulterated" in the context of the arts, in the sense that they are experienced in greater isolation from other responses. For example, real-life sadness is often accompanied by stress and anxiety, but emotions evoked by sad movies or plays are more "purely" sad, or even accompanied by positive emotions (Goldstein, 2009; Sachs et al., 2015; Winner, 2018). This has led some researchers to suggest that the emotions we feel in the context of art are of a special kind, "aesthetic" rather than "utilitarian" (e.g., Menninghaus et al., 2019; Scherer & Zentner, 2008).

Even if the emotions that we experience in the context of artistic engagement are in important respects different from the emotions we feel in response to experiences outside the context of artistic engagement, the evidence above suggests that they play a parallel role in getting us to suspend our ordinary routines and focus on the object of those emotional responses carefully and mindfully. If emotions that are aroused by artistic engagement are introspectively indistinguishable from other emotional responses, if they evoke parallel physiological responses, and if they are accompanied with parallel neurological signatures, then it is plausible that they play a parallel functional role, including a role in honing our abilities to attend to, notice, and learn from features of our environment.

Here, we have suggested that through their emotional power, the arts are epistemically rich environments: spaces where our emotional responses and experiences fuel reflection, exploration, and cognitive growth. This connection between emotional depth and meaning-making provides a compelling foundation for the development of emotional intelligence, to which we turn next.

Defining "Emotional Intelligence"

Historically, in both philosophy and psychology, emotion and cognition tend to be conceptualized, studied, and discussed as distinct domains. Emotion was thought of as an a-rational, sometimes disruptive force, whereas cognition was positioned as grounded, deliberate rationality. Despite this history, decades of research show that emotions are integral to how we think, remember, make decisions, and relate to others. Emotions are not separate from thought; they shape, guide, and enrich cognition. Emotional intelligence, a concept that bridges these historically distinct domains, refers to a set of interrelated cognitive skills involved in perceiving, interpreting, and regulating emotional information, both in oneself and in others, including our ability to perceive and express emotions, to understand and reason with emotions, to regulate one's emotions, and to be attuned to and empathetic toward others' emotions (Mayer & Salovey, 1997).

There are two common approaches to understanding the nature of emotional intelligence: ability models and "mixed models" (Mayer et al., 2000). Ability models treat emotional intelligence as a set of mental abilities that can be objectively measured, trained, and improved. These models understand the development of emotional intelligence as the progression of interrelated skills. These skills include, first, perceiving and recognizing emotions in facial expressions, voices, music, literature, visual artworks, or one's own internal states. Once identified, emotions can be harnessed to prioritize and guide attention and support effective problem-solving. The metacognitive and reflective processes of understanding our emotions, including their causes, trajectories, and how they mix and shift, are built on these abilities to perceive, recognize, and harness emotions, and are a foundation for emotional growth and wellbeing. Assessment of one's development of these skills typically takes the form of measuring performance on objective tasks, like emotion matching, but it can also involve self-report insofar as they measure the respondents' perceived cognitive abilities (Lyusin & Ovsyannikova, 2016).

Mixed models of emotional intelligence include personality traits and motivational traits as components of emotional intelligence, in addition to cognitive abilities. For example, mixed models include traits such as optimism in characterizing emotional intelligence. These approaches are sometimes criticized for making the concept of emotional intelligence too expansive or too broad, insofar as they often overlap with constructs like creative intelligence, social intelligence, and aspects of the Big 5 personality inventory. Moreover, mixed models also tend to rely on self-report questionnaires for assessment. For these reasons, we focus primarily on the ability model, while acknowledging areas where mixed models provide valuable complementary evidence.

It is worth noting that there are several well-known critiques of emotional intelligence as a psychological construct. The critiques are rooted in questions about how meaningfully emotional intelligence differs from related concepts like social intelligence, and in concerns about its practical utility, as well as its validity. With respect to the latter, even the supposedly objective, performance-based tests have been criticized for relying on subjective scoring criteria, including casting doubt on what counts as a "correct" response. Moreover, there are questions about whether the term "emotional intelligence" is apt, as the abilities it encompasses (e.g., recognizing emotions) may be more accurately understood as basic perceptual skills. While we use the term "emotional intelligence" in this chapter to characterize the suite of emotion-related skills that we are describing, we do so with caution and are not endorsing this concept as universally valid or uncontested. We are less concerned with making a case for the importance of the construct than we are with describing the plethora of evidence that suggests the existence of emotion-related skills that explain an important dimension of the epistemic and social value of the arts. In that sense, emotional intelligence is primarily used here as an organizing principle to capture the important set of emotion-related skills that we emphasize. In this section, we lay out these key skills and how they can be measured: emotion recognition, understanding emotions, and emotion regulation. In the next section, we explore empirical evidence that supports the claim that the arts are an important venue for and a mechanism by which these skills can be developed and honed.

Emotion Recognition and Perception

Emotion perception and recognition involve the ability to accurately identify and express emotional information in oneself, others, artworks, or language (Mayer et al., 2000). Success in doing so requires close observation of others across contexts. For a visual or language-based artwork, this would involve identifying the emotions that one perceives to be expressed in the work, be they directly demonstrated or described (e.g., in the facial expression of a painted portrait) or implied (e.g., a character's reaction to an event). With respect to ourselves, we must actively notice the subtle variations in our somatic and affective experiences – when our facial muscles slightly furrow, when parts of our body tense or relax – as well as the connection between these kinds of responses and what we are engaging with or thinking about. With respect to other people, we must be able to recognize their facial expressions, posture, and vocal qualities, connect these cues to what the individual reports feeling, and recognize relevant aspects of their situation or circumstances.

We can perceive subtle expression shifts in the faces of other people, sometimes signaled only with the eyes, that indicate significant emotional shifts. Research on body and movement dynamics suggests that specific postures and motion patterns are associated with basic emotions like sadness or happiness (Atkinson et al., 2004). For example, slow, slouched walking is more indicative of sadness, whereas quicker, upright movement tends to reflect happiness. Voices are another rich source of emotional information. Prosody – the patterns and intonations of our speech sounds such as the variation in frequency, intensity, timbre, and timing – can reflect and communicate emotional states (Banse & Scherer, 1996). Faster speech with high pitch variability and greater intensity tends to sound happier, whereas slower, more monotone, and quieter speech tends to sound sadder.

Moreover, embodied theories of cognition hold that our actions and movements affect how we perceive those same actions in others, and that perception of others' actions involves mental simulation. Consistent with this theory, individuals who suffer from facial paralysis have reduced sensitivity to others' facial expressions (Japee et al., 2023). Being incapable of physically smiling may lead to having more trouble recognizing subtle smiling shifts in others. Similarly, basketball players may be more adept than non-players at discriminating when a ball is inappropriately carried, or when a jump shot is especially difficult. In this way, the actions that we are able to and skilled at producing might provide us with increased perceptual capabilities to understand actions and intentions. We will suggest below that the embodiment of emotional intelligence is key to the value of the arts in its promotion. Through training and repetition, actors and dancers become acutely attuned to expressive subtleties in movement and gesture. Musicians learn to detect shifts in tone and phrasing that signal emotional inflection. Visual artists learn the connection between gestural strokes and their emotions.

To make out this connection, it is helpful first to describe how emotional sensitivity (i.e., the ability to perceive or recognize emotions) can be measured. As we mentioned above, self-reports can be useful. For example, we can ask people to fill out surveys in which they rate statements about their own emotional perception abilities. However, these tools are limited: Even if someone thinks they are good at reading and detecting others' emotions, they may not actually be good at it. Recognizing this, we focus more on evidence provided by performance-based measures of people's perceptual discrimination abilities.

One class of such performance-based tests targets an individual's sensitivity with respect to nonverbal emotion cues conveyed without the use of language, such as facial expressions, body language, or tone of voice. In the "Reading the Mind in the Eyes Test" (RMET), participants are shown an image of a human face cropped to include just the area around their eyes, and asked to decide how the person is feeling (e.g., scared, happy, sad, worried) based on that information alone. An auditory version of the RMET asks participants to listen to a sound and to select the emotion being expressed by that sound from a list of alternatives (e.g., happy, sad, depressed) (Juslin & Laukka, 2003). Multimodal tests, in which both visual and audio prompts are shown, are also common (Bänziger et al., 2009; Mayer et al., 2003; Nowicki & Duke, 1994). The Empathic Accuracy Paradigm (Ickes, 2001) shows a video of a person having a discussion with another person who is out of view. For example, a woman is talking to her husband for fifteen minutes. Participants identify what they think the woman was thinking or feeling "underneath" what she says throughout the fifteen-minute period. Responses are scored as accurate if they match the woman's reported thoughts and feelings gathered while making the video. This measure is more naturalistic than the RMET, which requires matching a single and often complex emotion term to a static image of the eyes. For children, these kinds of tests are typically altered to be more developmentally appropriate. For instance, the Emotion Matching Test asks children to watch a film and determine whether a specific emotion matched a protagonist's emotion.

Understanding Emotions

Whereas emotion perception refers to the detection and identification of emotions, understanding refers to the capacity to label emotions accurately, including grasping the nuances of complex emotions and mixed emotional states (e.g., bittersweetness, pride tinged with guilt), and comprehending the relationships between emotions, their causes, and their consequences (Mayer et al., 2000). Merely recognizing that someone appears sad, for example, does not mean that one understands why they feel sad, what triggered that sadness, or how that emotion might change over time. Emotion understanding thus entails reasoning about emotional experiences, identifying causes or precipitating events for the emotion, predicting emotional trajectories, and determining how emotions might affect behaviors and thoughts. Like emotion recognition, this facet of emotional intelligence enables us to identify patterns of emotional experiences in both ourselves and others. For example, grasping that a friend's irritation might be masking or underlying the anxiety they feel about an upcoming exam requires reading their subtle micro-expressions and contextualizing their responses using other information about their situation. Similarly, understanding your own feelings of restlessness might stem from a combination of work anxieties, lack of physical exercise, and joy about a dear friend moving back to town, requires reflection and contextualization.

This dimension of emotional intelligence is closely linked to empathy and to theory of mind. Theory of mind refers to the ability to attribute mental states, including emotional ones, to others. Affective theory of mind is a sub-skill specific to attributing emotional states to others. Relatedly, a defining feature of empathy is the ability to recognize how others are feeling and to understand others' intentions. Empathy is similarly often studied and defined with respect to subcomponents, including a cognitive and affective component. Cognitive empathy, much like the affective theory of mind, refers to perceiving and knowing what others are feeling. In contrast, affective empathy typically refers to having emotional resonance with someone else, such that an individual feels another person's feelings (e.g., feels pain when observing someone else in pain). Empathy is often treated as a trait, but it can certainly be trainable and malleable, and it can vary in a state-based way (Schumann et al., 2014).

As with emotion recognition, measuring emotion understanding can be carried out using a variety of self-report and performance-based tools. Self-report questionnaires targeting empathy ask respondents to assess themselves on items like: "I am good at predicting how someone will feel"; "I can tell if someone is masking their true emotion"; "I find it easy to understand others' feelings when they are distressed." As above, though using self-reported experiences can be suggestive, it cannot tell you whether someone's self-assessment is accurate. Thus, self-report measures can and should be complemented with measures that can assess the skill more directly.

Our ability to accurately infer another person's mental and emotional states is often assessed using theory of mind and perspective-taking tasks. A commonly used task for children is the "Sally-Anne" task, which evaluates their ability to not only recognize another person's mental and emotional state, but to reason about it by using knowledge of their own mental states to make inferences about what they will do or think. In this task, the child watches as "Sally" hides a toy in her basket and then leaves the room. While Sally is away, another character, "Anne," moves the toy out of Sally's basket and puts it in their own. When Sally comes back into the room, the child is asked whether Sally knows if her toy is now in Anne's box. Success on this task requires the child to reason based on what information Sally has, not on what information the child has themselves.

The Emotion Understanding subtest of the Mayer–Salovey–Caruso Emotional Intelligence Test extends assessments of this perspective-taking ability to specifically emotional states. The subtest utilizes two types of assessments: one in which the participant has to determine how two emotions might "blend" or mix together, and one in which the participant must infer someone's emotional response based on a described scenario (e.g., "Sarah was afraid she was not able to complete the tasks she had been assigned and became concerned with her job evaluation. When her supervisor brought her an additional assignment, she felt _____." The response options available are: overwhelmed, depressed, ashamed, self-conscious, and jittery) (Mayer et al., 2003). Note that while multiple answers are plausible, the correct answer is often scored by comparing the individual's choice to the most common response given by a reference group of participants, sometimes referred to as a "normative" sample.

Other tests that target emotion understanding are emotion labeling tasks and vocabulary tasks. Participants may be asked to define specific emotion terms, to distinguish between emotion terms such as guilt and shame, and to match emotions to their causes. A related approach is to test for alexithymia, an experience in which individuals have difficulty recognizing, describing, distinguishing, and processing emotions, both their own and those of others. Individuals who experience alexithymia might feel anxious but struggle to name the emotion, to connect it to the "why," instead suggesting they feel "off" or focusing on physical sensations like feeling jittery. Such individuals also seem to have a reduced capacity for fantasizing, for imaginative thought, and for symbolic thinking, and often see themselves as less creative than others, not only artistically, but in an everyday problem-solving sense (Fuchs et al., 2007). Although alexithymia is described as a personality construct and often assessed in a personality context, evidence that some situational contexts can affect alexithymia and that it is exacerbated by depression suggests that people can experience it as a discrete state (Taylor & Bagby, 2000).

Emotion Regulation

Once we recognize and understand emotions, we can learn to successfully regulate them. Emotion regulation refers to "the processes by which individuals influence which emotions they have, when they have them, and how they experience and express these emotions" (Gross, 1998, p. 275). It involves the capacity to monitor one's emotions, to remain open and accepting of one's feelings, and to apply an appropriate and adaptive strategy for managing the feelings and the corresponding behaviors to promote wellbeing. One cannot regulate and manage emotions if they cannot perceive, express, and understand them, and our response to what we perceive someone else to be experiencing can vary depending on our capacity to regulate our own emotional states (Gross, 1998; McRae & Gross, 2020).

Emotion regulation is not simply a matter of dampening negative feelings or enhancing positive ones. It could also involve managing or mitigating positive emotions; for instance, holding back laughter when a child says something in a serious tone that one finds cute, or calming oneself when overexcited in order to focus properly. It can also involve amplifying negative emotions, such as deliberately invoking seriousness or urgency before a high-stakes meeting, or evoking anger in advance of a protest. Effective emotion regulation is about flexibly modulating emotional responses in a way that appropriately fits the context (Aldao, 2013). Ineffective emotion regulation, or dysregulation, is characterized by inflexibility or one's adopting fixed strategies, such as always suppressing negative emotions.

The key strategies that people employ to regulate emotions include: behaving in a way that increases the likelihood that you will experience an expected set of emotions (i.e., situation selection), changing aspects of a situation that you are already in so that its emotional impact is altered (i.e., situation modification), redirecting your focus so as to modify your emotional response (i.e., attention deployment), and modifying your interpretation or appraisal of a situation to affect the emotional response (i.e., cognitive change) (Gross, 2015). These strategies can be deployed intrinsically and extrinsically: Intrinsic regulation refers to the processes we use to regulate our own emotions, while extrinsic regulation refers to those processes we employ to regulate others' emotions (i.e., soothing a baby, cracking a joke to make our friends feel better). These strategies can operate consciously, by our own deliberate volition, as when we intentionally take a walk to calm down, or outside of our awareness, as when we automatically close our eyes or turn away from something scary, upsetting, or disgusting (Gross, 2015).

Emotion regulation can be measured in a host of ways. Typically, self-report questionnaires are used to assess both regulation capacity and the specific regulation strategies someone employs. The Emotion Regulation Questionnaire (ERQ) (Gross & John, 2003) assesses the extent to which people employ cognitive reappraisal and expressive suppression by asking people to rate their agreement with questions like "When I want to feel more positive emotion (such as joy or amusement), I change what I'm thinking about." And, "I control my emotions by not expressing them." The Difficulties in Emotion Regulation Scale (DERS; Gratz & Roemer, 2004) is a comprehensive measure targeting emotional arousal, awareness, understanding, and acceptance of emotions, and one's ability to act in a healthy way regardless of the intensity of the emotional state they are experiencing. Questions include participants' responses to statements like: "I experience my emotions as overwhelming and out of control"; "When I'm upset, I have difficulty getting work done."; "When I'm upset, I believe that my feelings are valid and important." Similarly, the Emotion Regulation Skills Questionnaire (ERSQ; Grant et al., 2018) contains several subscales reflecting the authors' model of adaptive coping with emotions: emotional awareness, emotional sensation, clarity, understanding, acceptance, resilience, compassionate self-support, readiness to confront, and modification of negative emotions.

Beyond questionnaires, performance-based assessments are also widely used to test emotion regulation. For example, participants might be given scenarios intended to mirror everyday life experiences, such as actions one would take to stay in touch when a friend moves away, and their responses would be scored accordingly. Or, they might be given the Emotional Stroop Task, which is a modification of the standard Stroop Task. The standard task asks participants to name the color of the ink a color word is displayed in. On some trials, the ink and the word match (i.e., "blue" appears in blue ink). On the critical trials, the ink and word do not match (i.e., "blue" appears in red ink, and the correct response is "red"). The participant's goal is thus to suppress or inhibit the word that they read. In the Emotional Stroop Task, some of the words are emotionally charged – death, germs, battle – but the task remains to name the color. Performance on the task aims to reveal the extent to which the emotional content of a word interferes with color naming, thus assessing the participants' capacity for emotion regulation with respect to their ability to disengage from the emotional content of the word to quickly and correctly name the color. Another common performance-based measure involves assessing physiological responses to emotional stimuli. Researchers may present participants with a highly emotionally charged stimulus (e.g., a photograph of a dismembered body) and assess a variety of physiological measurements such as skin conductance, heart rate variability, or brain activity, as a proxy for their emotional regulation capacities.

The Arts and Emotional Intelligence

We turn now from the central competencies of emotional intelligence – emotion recognition, emotion understanding, and emotion regulation – to the growing body of empirical evidence that suggests engagement with the arts can enhance these key competencies. We organize this discussion into two parts: The first focuses on practices of making art, and the second on those of appreciating art.

Art Creation

Theater and performance studies theorists have long argued that acting expands the actor's understanding of other people, as it involves emotion recognition and understanding, perspective-taking, embodiment, and compassion toward others (Kemp, 2012). Actress, playwright, and teacher Anna Deavere Smith characterizes the practice by saying that "the spirit of acting is the *travel* from the self to the other" (Smith, 2015, p. xxvi). One of the main goals of an actor is to communicate and embody their character through language and nonverbal cues, and they do this through understanding and inhabiting aspects of their character's individuality or personal identity, including their characteristic or specific speech patterns, their movements, their behaviors, or their attitudes. Connecting to a character does not necessarily mean the actor must convince others that they *are* that person, but acting does require feeling connected to the person portrayed in some way, accepting them as they are, and consistently maintaining that connection and embodiment.

Doing this requires enormous training, practice, and skill. Verbatim acting, an approach developed by Smith, exemplifies the specific way in which acting can foster emotional understanding. Smith's performance strategy involves interviewing real people and studying their language and speech with the goal of embodying them in performance. This approach is premised on the idea that the actor can distinctly access a person's "essence" through their words and speech patterns. As Smith explains, "If we were to inhabit the speech pattern of another, and walk in the speech of another, we could find the individuality of the other and experience that individuality viscerally" (Smith, 2015, p. xxvii). Important to Smith's approach is that she invites both the audience and the individuals she interviews and portrays in her shows to participate in a post-performance conversation, in order to further understand the similarities and differences between herself and the person portrayed. Smith distinguishes between mere imitation or mimicry and something like genuine other-understanding. In performing a character, she notes that she can never *become* the other person; she can only reveal their likeness by also honoring their differences. To do this, the actor must engage in perspective-taking, exercise affective theory of mind and cognitive empathy, and employ flexible modes of thinking (which we explore in more detail in Chapter 4).

Notice that theater, along with dance and music, is a highly embodied practice. Bodily awareness and control are central to their performance. As we noted, actors must practice moving their bodies and faces in subtle ways to express nuanced emotional states. Similarly, dancers move their bodies in precise and expressive ways that explicitly convey emotions, and musicians learn to move their bodies to apply just the right amount of pressure to create specific sounds. As mentioned above, embodied theories of emotion posit that this motor expertise enhances one's ability to perceive and discriminate between the learned motions and their associated meanings, so that learning to perform emotionally expressive movements sharpens perception of emotionally expressive movements in others.

Empirical research supports the idea that artistic practices can shape emotion recognition. In one set of studies, professional ballet dancers viewed video clips of people performing gender-specific ballet moves. The key findings show that brain regions relevant to perceptual discrimination responded differently to those ballet moves the individuals were trained in executing (i.e., male dancers skilled at performing male-specific moves), in contrast to those moves that they were highly trained in seeing but not executing (i.e., male dancers skilled at seeing but not performing female dancers' moves) (Calvo-Merino et al., 2005, 2006). More recent research shows that compared to nonexperts, ballet dancers more accurately categorize emotion-expressing ballet video clips and have stronger emotional responses to those clips (Christensen et al., 2016).

Other research shows that adolescents enrolled in acting classes have better emotion recognition skills and higher cognitive and affective empathy, both compared to themselves before they began acting, and compared to peers in control groups (Goldstein & Winner, 2012; Goldstein et al., 2009). Children and adolescents participating in intensive acting classes (compared to those participating in visual arts classes) also show greater improvements in adopting effective self-regulation strategies, including understanding and processing their emotions (rather than suppressing them), and effectively managing distress (Goldstein & Lerner, 2018; Goldstein et al., 2013; Maierna & Camodeca, 2021). Other research points to additional social benefits from intensive acting curricula, including better collaboration, increased sense of togetherness and friendship, higher integrity, and greater self-confidence (Hughes & Wilson, 2004; McCammon et al., 2012; Yassa, 1999).

Music and dance have also been shown to cultivate emotional intelligence. Research on the benefits of music training shows that it can cultivate one's ability to detect and recognize emotion in music and in other sounds, including speech and voice (Martins et al., 2021). In one study that followed children enrolled in either formal music instruction, sports, or another nonmusic-based after-school program, music training specifically improved their pitch-matching ability (i.e., their capacity to accurately match the vocal sounds one heard to the correct sound), as well as their performance on a visual and auditory emotion-matching task (Villanueva et al., 2024). Music training also fosters one's ability to infer an infant's distress from auditory evidence (Parsons et al., 2014). It may even help reduce age-related declines in emotion perception and in auditory perception more generally. People's ability to identify negative emotions, although not positive emotions, starts to decline in middle age. This is likely due to a host of variables, including increased familiarity with witnessing the negative emotions of others (perhaps, especially for parents) potentially leading to desensitization. But music training seems to mitigate these losses (e.g., Lima & Castro, 2011). Similarly, in a systematic review of multiple studies, dance participation improved all three relevant emotion-related skills for children: emotion recognition, emotion understanding, and effective adoption of emotion regulation strategies (San-Juan-Ferrer & Hípola, 2020).

With respect to empathy specifically, actors tend to rate themselves as more empathetic than a control sample on self-report measures (Nettle, 2006), visual artists rate themselves as more empathetic than nonartists (Goldstein et al., 2009), and dancers score higher than nondancers on self-reported emotional sensitivity (Izountouemoi & Esteves, 2023). Higher scores on trait empathy questionnaires also correlate with both physiological and behavioral responses to art. Individuals who experience emotional contagion – the "catching" of an emotion – react more strongly and more aptly to both visual art and to music. For visual art, individuals high in trait empathy smile more when they engage with art that expresses positive emotions, and frown more when they engage with visual art conveying negative emotions (Gernot et al., 2018). Similar findings have been reported within music. People with higher empathetic capacities also seem better able to understand and interpret emotional expressivity and intentionality in music (Balteș & Miu, 2014; Wollner, 2019).

There is also evidence that art-making practices can reduce alexithymia over time. In a cross-sectional study with a sample of over 5000 adults, alexithymia scores were independently negatively correlated with creative achievements across a variety of arts forms in both men and women, including visual arts, music, theater, and writing (Lennartsson et al., 2017). Professional artists had lower alexithymia scores than amateur artists, who had lower scores than nonpractitioners. Engagement in cultural activities, such as visiting museums, also predicted alexithymia. We do not know if participating in the arts activities caused the alexithymia to reduce over time, or if the reduction in alexithymia encouraged more participation in arts activities, or if a third variable mediated this relationship. However, a randomized control study with women experiencing burnout suggests that arts activities may play some causal role in reducing the severity of alexithymia (Viding et al., 2015). Women who participated in different monthly creative activities (dance, theater, drawing, and vocal improvisation) over a period of three months had reduced alexithymia scores after the initial three months and maintained that reduction in a follow-up that occurred another three months later. In contrast, those in the control group drawn from the program's waitlist did not show reductions in their alexithymia. This is consistent with research showing that mindfulness interventions, which bear significant similarities to arts interventions, lead to improved emotional clarity and self-awareness (Cooper et al., 2018).

In addition to the research that aims to establish directly the relationship between arts practices and elements of emotional intelligence, there is indirect evidence that points to emotion-related skill acquisition through the arts. For one, arts experts within their respective domains – be they musicians, visual artists, or art historians – demonstrate more granularity or differentiation in their emotional responses in their domain than do nonexperts (Barrett et al., 2001). Art practitioners can name, differentiate, and experience a wider variety of precise, finely distinguished emotions while they are appreciating art in their expert domain. Musicians listening to music report more granular emotions in response to the music than do nonmusicians (Kantor-Martynuska & Bigand, 2013; Kantor-Martynuska & Horabik, 2015). Moreover, musical expertise is associated with different neurophysiological responsiveness to dissonance (Dellacherie et al., 2011) and to violation of harmonic expectation, indicating increased emotional response (Steinbeis et al., 2005, 2006). Nathaniel Barrett and Jay Schulkin (2017) propose that people who can experience more finely differentiated emotions in music may actually enjoy negative emotions in music more than nonexperts, because they can differentiate those feelings from the more "normal" negative feelings they encounter in real life. Likewise, individuals who have higher visual art knowledge and a deeper understanding of art history experience tend to describe more nuanced negative emotions (but not more nuanced positive emotions) while examining paintings than individuals with lower levels of knowledge about the relevant art (Fayn et al., 2018). And, similarly, individuals with more visual arts mastery tend to enjoy negative content in visual art more than nonexperts do (Leder et al., 2014), as well as enjoy more abstract art than nonexperts (Furnham & Walker, 2001; Pihko et al., 2011). Per Barrett and Schulkin's proposal, this may be due to greater emotion recognition and regulation on the part of the art experts. It is also consistent with research showing that visual art experts have different, less extreme physiological responses in their facial muscles to artworks featuring negative content than non-experts (Leder et al., 2014).

There is considerably more room for empirical research across all arts domains with respect to emotional intelligence. First, research within some art domains is scant. Much of the art-making research on the suite of skills related to emotional intelligence has focused on theater, dance, or music; less work has been done on visual art, writing, poetry, and other arts practices. Moreover, although studies point to positive findings within theater, music, and dance, there is also research showing mixed and sometimes null results (Stutesman & Goldstein, 2023). For example, while short-term music-training interventions seem to improve performance on an auditory emotion recognition task relative to a visual art intervention, longitudinal assessments have shown that musicians with six or more years of training are no better at vocal emotion recognition than a control group (Mualem & Lavidor, 2015). Studies examining children's emotional development can be especially mixed. (See Stutesman & Goldstein, 2023, for review.) The differences in findings could stem from a number of sources, including the type of arts practice studied, the type of student studied, their age and motivations for engaging in the arts practice, the timeline of the interventions, and the measurement strategy.

In her latest book on the importance of acting and theater for our lives, Thalia Goldstein examines how and whether acting classes train what she identifies as eight broad "habits of mind": body awareness and control, playfulness, imagination and visualization, considering and understanding others, flexibility and openness, thinking collaboratively, decision-making, and metacognitive reflection (Goldstein, 2024). Goldstein suggests it would be fruitful for empirical research to use mixed-methods approaches to examine these habits of mind more closely, and we agree that such an approach would be useful across all arts domains. As she aptly writes:

> What students are learning, pragmatically and practically, is how to act. But what they are taking away is deeper, psychological, and possibly transferable when they leave the theater. From Shakespeare to devised works, formal performances to site-specific improv games, the Acting Habits of Mind underlying training open doors to bigger and better thinking for all who choose to walk through. (p. 8)

Similarly, we think that examining how arts classes across domains actually function (rather than how we hope or speculate they function) through the lens of the identified habits of mind can be an especially useful framework for empirical research.

Art Appreciation

As we saw, much of the existing research on the relationship between art-making and emotional intelligence concerns the performance-based domains of theater, dance, and music. In contrast, the literary arts are a primary focus of empirical research investigating a connection between art-appreciating and emotional intelligence, especially the emotion recognition and perspective-taking competencies.

The relationship between fiction exposure and social cognition begins to develop in early childhood and continues into adulthood. In a study of four- to five-year-olds, those who read more stories with caregivers, and who have exposure to a diverse array of children's storybooks, perform better on perspective-taking tasks like the Sally-Anne task than children with less exposure to storybooks, even after controlling for age, parents' income, and parents' education levels (Mar et al., 2010). The fact that reading stories can support success in these tasks suggests that reading fiction may contribute to perspective-taking development by giving children more opportunity to hear about and work through others' perceptions, beliefs, desires, and goals. With respect to adults, there is growing evidence that lifetime exposure to narrative fiction predicts better emotion recognition skills and better capacity to understand others' emotions and experiences. In a 2017 meta-analysis, Micah Mumper and Richard Gerrig evaluated 36 studies that reported on the relationship between reading habits and perspective-taking, many of which used both self-reports and the RMET test. Frequent leisure reading of fiction or nonfiction was associated with better scores on the RMET test across many of the studies.

Moreover, more fiction reading was also associated with increased self-reported empathy and feelings of empathy that people tend to experience toward others (Mumper & Gerrig, 2017).

While these results are suggestive, experimental research randomly assigning participants to specific reading interventions provides more evidence for causal relationships. Researchers have asked groups of participants to complete a series of tasks both before and after reading a specific story to assess how the story reading impacts their performance. In one set of studies, David Kidd and Emanuele Castano (2013) compared how well people did on the RMET as well as other theory of mind tasks after they read either a short story that they classified as "literary fiction," a short story they classified as "popular fiction," or a short nonfiction story. Across several studies, participants who read the "literary" short story performed better on the RMET than those who read nonfiction or popular fiction. RMET scores were also predicted by reading exposure, consistent with the correlational studies discussed above. There are also existing studies that seem to contradict these findings and the hypothesis that stories enhance empathy (Wimmer et al., 2021). Moreover, several researchers have failed to replicate Kidd and Castano's results (e.g., Panero et al., 2016).

In attempting to make sense of these mixed findings, it is important to note that the reported socio-cognitive effects of fiction reading and of reading in general are small (Dodell-Feder & Tamir, 2018). That they are small does not mean that they are not real. The small size of the effect could be because the tests used to measure both reading habits and emotion recognition are not as sensitive as we might hope. Researchers assess story exposure, for example, in a fairly indirect way because "exposure to narrative" over the course of someone's entire life would be impossible to directly measure. Take the Author Recognition Test (ART), which asks people how many authors they recognize from a long list of (real and fake) author names. The psychologists who created and validated this scale suggest that this measure is well correlated with people's reading habits, and many researchers have replicated the validity of this test as a good predictor of reading exposure. However, one can also easily imagine cases where reading habits are not well-captured by this test. People who are avid readers may have a poor memory for authors and titles. People who do not read fiction at all may still recognize many authors for a host of reasons (e.g., education, exposure to media). For instance, Clair reads little fiction (she estimates less than once a month, or less than 5 novels a year), but recognizes nearly double the number of fiction authors on Raymond Mar and Marina Rain's (2015) list of 110 fiction authors as Sasha, who reads fiction nearly every day and about 25 novels a year. Sasha's mom, an avid reader who often finishes 100 fiction books a year, only recognizes 10 more authors than Clair does. We raise this not to discredit the many careful research studies using the ART, but to suggest that there is still work to be done to develop empirical methods that can contribute to theories about how arts engagement develops perspective-taking skills. The psychological tests that are applied to measuring reading habits, general art engagement, and perspective-taking are all indirect (by nature), and are thus quite broad-stroke in what they measure.

There is also research to support the notion that visual arts appreciation can foster emotional intelligence. In one study, researchers trained medical students to look at patients' faces by first examining portrait paintings by various artists at the Frick Museum in New York. The reported results were qualitative in nature. Museum staff and medical faculty observed marked improvements in students' description, interpretation, and presentation skills. For example, in the pretest, which occurred before the museum workshops, students described a photograph of a middle-aged woman by focusing on objective features they noticed, like her facial features, grooming, makeup, and jewelry. In the posttest, however, they described the same photograph with more precision and felt comfortable making inferences based on those observations, including remarks that the subject appeared sad, anxious, worried, and perhaps ill.

The training also got students to practice emotion recognition skills in various contexts that were outside of their domain of focus (Bardes et al., 2001). Similarly, there is increasing evidence that medical and nursing students who are trained to engage with and enjoy the visual and literary arts exhibit greater empathy and better emotional understanding of their patients, and thus provide better patient care compared to peers who study traditional medical science alone (Charon, 2001; Chen et al., 2017; Hardy, 2017; Xue et al., 2023). Outside of medical contexts, young children participating in multi-week, guided, museum-based interventions demonstrated improved emotion understanding of people described in story vignettes they had not heard before (Ebert et al., 2015). Other research has found similar results in children, although the emotional intelligence improvements do not necessarily last over time in the absence of continued practice (e.g., Hoffmann et al., 2021).

Finally, the connection between mindfulness practices and emotional skills, particularly emotion regulation, also provides some indirect evidence for how arts engagement may contribute to emotional intelligence. As we described in Chapter 2, mindfulness is a practice that asks the individual to purposefully and nonjudgmentally focus on the present moment (Kabat-Zinn, 1994), and arts engagement manifests many elements of mindfulness. At its core, mindfulness meditation can be conceived as a family of complex emotional and attentional regulatory strategies (Lutz et al., 2008). Research shows that even brief mindfulness interventions can foster improvements in emotion labeling, decrease our emotional reactivity, improve emotional clarity and granularity, and facilitate recovery from negative emotions (see Guendelman et al., 2017 for review). One study also suggests that beyond the traditional emotion regulation strategies (i.e., distraction, suppression, cognitive reappraisal), mindfulness also fosters increased compassion and acceptance of all emotions (Lam et al., 2024). Taken together, these mechanisms – heightened awareness, attentional modulation, and compassionate care – underscore why mindfulness meditation is a robust approach to cultivating emotional intelligence. Similarly, engaging with the arts by practicing careful observation or by incorporating mindfulness may be a highly effective way to develop emotional skills.

Despite these promising results, there are theoretical challenges for experimental work in this area. Most importantly, skills are developed over time, often over not only years but decades or a lifetime. Skills certainly cannot develop over the course of one encounter. We should hardly expect to become a better ukulele player after practicing the ukulele for one hour. Similarly, we should not expect that reading one short story, viewing one artwork for ten minutes, or listening to one piece of music will change something as complex and socially embedded as our emotion recognition and empathy skills. At the same time, it is difficult, if not impossible, to isolate the effect of someone's engagement in a specific social practice over the course of their life from the countless interactions, experiences, and complicating events that occur concurrently. Even longitudinal studies that would recognize the development of these skills over longer periods of time will likely not be able to have true control groups that allow us to make stronger causal claims. Moreover, research in this area generally describes and studies near transfer effects. Far transfer effects do not appear frequently in the literature, either because they are not often studied or because researchers have not found these kinds of effects.

Summary

Throughout this chapter, we have suggested that the arts can be a mechanism for exploring and understanding our own emotions and those of others. We have described a wide array of basic and complex emotions that people experience when engaging with the arts and how those emotional experiences might contribute to emotional intelligence, and we have surveyed substantial evidence pointing to the importance of the arts in promoting such development. However, we must also caution readers about drawing any causal conclusions at this stage of research. As we have discussed, there are wide gaps to fill. One thing is certain, though: The connection between arts engagement and the development of emotion-related skills is complex and nuanced.

CHAPTER 4

The Arts, Open-Mindedness, and Creativity

Starting Point

Origami, the traditional Japanese art of paper folding, is often admired for its simplicity and beauty. Its practice involves a sophisticated form of material thinking, that merges tactile exploration with mathematical precision. It is an art form that demands patience, attention, spatial reasoning, and a tolerance for trial and error. Among the most influential folds studied by both origamists and scientists is the Miura-Ori fold. Invented by origamist and astrophysicist Kōryō Miura, the Miura-Ori folding pattern is celebrated for its elegance and ingenuity. The design forms a pattern of interconnected parallelograms that contract and expand in a single fluid motion that produces a rhythmic, sculptural effect. What makes this fold especially captivating is its "shape memory": When unfolded, the paper retains an "imprint" of its folded shape such that it can be much more easily refolded into its small shape (see Garcia, 2017, to try making your own).

Although the fold originated with the practice of origami, its influences extend far beyond paper. In 1985, Miura proposed that the fold be used as a method for more easily expanding and compacting spacecraft solar panels – an application that was realized in 1995. Since that time, Miura's folding pattern has found its way into fields as diverse as biomedical engineering, architecture, and furniture design. It is even used to create emergency shelters, an application in which the ability to expand and contract surface area efficiently is especially crucial. The appeal of the fold lies not only in its functional properties but in the kind of thinking it represents, namely: flexible, interdisciplinary, and attuned to both form and function.

A contemporary artist and designer whose work exemplifies this fusion of artistic and scientific thinking is Tine De Ruysser. She adapts a variation of the folding pattern to a variety of materials such as wood, metals, and plastics. Her work includes transformable wearable and sculptural

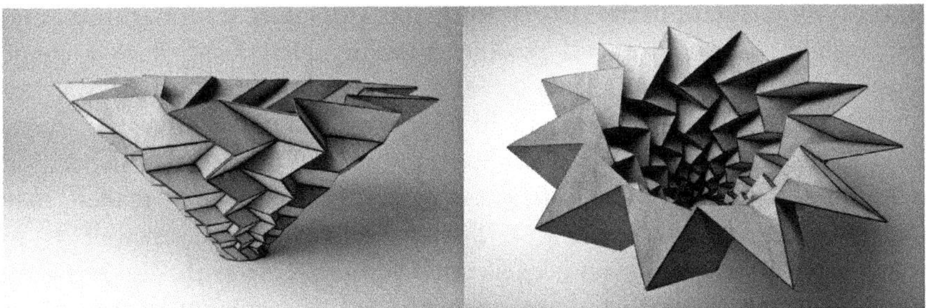

Figure 4.1 Tine De Ruysser (2010). Cone – side view (left) and top view (right). Plywood and polyester.
Courtesy of Tine De Ruysser.

pieces: avant-garde bracelets that unfold into bags, foldable bowls, and shoulder capes. Her designs draw on the spatial principles of the Miura-Ori fold, but reimagine its possibilities in the context of fashion, the body, and everyday utility (Figure 4.1).

What makes these contributions so remarkable is not just their aesthetics or their utility, but the *kind of thinking* that made them possible. For both Miura and De Ruysser, innovation involves moving beyond conventional solutions, preconceptions, disciplinary boundaries, and assumptions about materials. They think in ways that are playful, nimble, and flexible, as well as rigorous. These present powerful examples of creative, flexible problem-solving that are grounded in openness to unfamiliarity and ambiguity.

Throughout this chapter, we use the term *open-minded engagement* to describe the kind of thinking Miura and De Ruysser demonstrate. As we will see, open-mindedness is a highly complex disposition that draws on a host of cognitive capacities, including attention and observation (Chapter 2), emotional intelligence (Chapter 3), and skills involved in creative cognition, including cognitive flexibility, curiosity, divergent thinking, and metacognition. Our goal is to explore more fully the role that open-minded engagement plays in the arts and, as in Chapters 2 and 3, to propose that the arts are a venue for developing and refining the various cognitive skills that underlie open-mindedness.

Defining "Open-Minded Engagement"

Open-minded engagement is a complex disposition that draws on a set of cognitive skills involved in being receptive to diverse perspectives, in approaching unfamiliarity, uncertainty and ambiguity with curiosity, and in engaging in creative and flexible thinking. Describing it as a single disposition is not meant to imply that it is a simple or singular process, nor to imply that it is not, itself, part of larger constructs. For example, open-minded engagement is related in important ways to the broader disposition referred to as openness, or openness to experiences (which readers may recognize as part of the Big 5 Personality Inventory), as well as to constructs like curiosity and intellectual humility. As with our focus on emotional intelligence, we use open-minded engagement as a way of organizing a host of related skills that reflect how many scholars explain the value of the arts in their own lives, be they creators or appreciators.

Jason Baehr offers the following definition of open-mindedness: "an open-minded person is characteristically (a) willing and (within limits) able (b) to transcend a default cognitive standpoint (c) in order to take up or take seriously the merits of (d) a distinct cognitive standpoint" (Baehr, 2011, p. 202). Central to this conception is the ability to think beyond or outside of the heuristics and assumptions that one brings to a given context, and being able to entertain the validity, strength, or plausibility of positions and ideas other than one's own.

Being able and willing to take up and evaluate another's perspective, admit the possibility of being wrong, and potentially change one's own mind as a result, requires flexible, nimble, imaginative, and creative thinking. In this way, creativity is especially relevant to open-minded engagement. Creativity refers to a capacity to generate novel and interesting ideas, solutions to problems, or ways of expressing oneself, that often involves bringing seemingly disparate ideas together or combining prior knowledge in new ways. Creativity involves a host of processes including divergent thinking (i.e., the ability to generate many ideas), convergent thinking (i.e., the ability to bring ideas together), inhibitory control (i.e., the ability to block out irrelevant information), problem finding and solving, and cognitive flexibility (i.e., the ability to shift our attention, to shift tasks, or to shift perspectives). To engage open-mindedly, we need to be capable of working outside of normal routines, of conceptualizing problems in unique ways, of thinking expansively and nonrigidly – all hallmarks of creativity.

Try the following task: *Take three minutes to list all the different possible uses you can think of for a brick.*

How many did you think of? Most of us will probably have lists that contain things like: building homes/structures, paperweights, or perhaps even weapons. But you may have also come up with more unusual responses: as a color sample, say, or as a counterweight for a pulley system, or as a bridge for mice to cross a small stream. Responses on a task like this – known as the "Alternative Uses Test" (AUT) – that are less usual, as measured by how many other people who take the task also give that answer, are considered to be more creative answers, and producing a greater number of less usual responses is a way of exhibiting creativity.

There is reason to think that open-minded engagement is related to performance in creative tasks like these. Research suggests that people who score higher on tests assessing trait openness and open-mindedness have less self-censure and self-doubt, and also tend to generate more ideas in tasks like the one described above. They also tend to generate less usual and more disparate ideas without self-judgment (Kaufman et al., 2016).

Importantly, mental flexibility of this kind and creativity are not *fixed* traits but can be practiced and developed over time. In one set of studies, college students spent five to ten minutes imagining that school was cancelled for a day and writing about what they would do, think, and feel on that day. One of the participant groups was asked to do this task by imagining the seven-year-old version of themselves getting a day off from school, whereas the other group simply imagined a cancelled day on their current campus (Zabelina & Robinson, 2010). Getting participants out of their typical mindsets by asking them to adopt the seven-year-old version of themselves was a way to encourage open-minded thinking. Whereas the control group often wrote about sleeping extra hours and catching up on homework or studying, the "child mindset" group wrote about playing, being spontaneous, and doing things they enjoy (e.g., going out for ice cream, playing with friends, petting dogs). After the ten-minute reflection, participants completed an AUT, such as the "uses for a brick" test described above; additionally, individuals rated their own open-mindedness on a questionnaire (a version of the openness to experience scale). The most original ideas on the AUT came from the students who imagined their seven-year-old selves on the previous task, and those who scored highly on a separate trait open-mindedness test. Intriguingly, those who were less open-minded according to the trait test still performed highly on the creativity task *if* they were also in the child mindset group.

Getting outside of routine habits of mind, as in the study above, relies on the ability to slow down our attention and to employ observation skills of the kind we discuss in Chapter 2. Psychologists refer to the cognitive bias that inhibits our ability to break out of automated habits of mind as "functional fixedness." Overcoming this bias is required to succeed on these kinds of tasks. Often, the first things that come to mind during creative thinking tasks are the most typical or obvious examples. Imagine being asked to draw an "alien animal" that lives on a different planet. Most people will draw creatures with features typical of animals that live on Earth: eyes, arms and legs, and symmetrical features (Ward, 1994). However, when encouraged to slow down and put more effort into the task, people tend to be more creative. In Ward's studies, the encouragement to slow down led people to make more unusual drawings of the animals, or that blended the typical features in new ways, or that did not resemble animals on Earth at all. This finding is consistent with other research on brainstorming that shows that earlier in the brainstorming process, people rely more on easily accessible ideas that are more obvious and less original; later on in the process, more original ideas emerge (Nijstad et al., 2010).

Open-minded engagement is not only about foregoing our routines and preconceptions but doing so in the service of entertaining and taking seriously different perspectives or alternatives. This often involves perspective-taking, the cognitive process of considering people's thoughts, feelings, and desires, including not only accurately recognizing others' emotional experiences (as in Chapter 3), but also imagining ourselves in their shoes. However, one's beliefs and feelings about what someone else is thinking and feeling can only be (at best) an approximation of the other person's mind. To truly take them seriously, perspective-taking must be complemented by perspective-getting: listening to their viewpoints, asking questions, feeling comfortable with uncertainty, and jumping to fewer conclusions about their mental states (Eyal et al., 2018).

Moreover, although people who are open-minded are open to listening to other people's viewpoints, to questioning their own beliefs, and to revising their own beliefs, true open-mindedness does not mean openness to everything that comes along. As Jack Kwong explains, development of the trait is difficult and complex because it is not a mere willingness to entertain all novel ideas. Rather, it involves,

> know[ing] how to interpret and evaluate novel ideas in a serious manner, how to assess them vis-à-vis [our] own beliefs, how to detect and counter obstacles such as prejudices and biases, and when, or when not, to open up to novel ideas... (Kwong, 2019, p. 512)

For the trait to be genuinely useful for expanding our knowledge or understanding, our ability to assess others' ideas must be sufficiently nuanced to discern what is appropriate to be open to in the first place, including being sensitive to how people attempt to manipulate and control information. People must be *critically* open, not open to anything and everything.

Open-Mindedness through Arts Engagement

The arts are an especially good context for fostering open-minded engagement. In conceptualizing arts engagement this way, we are especially influenced by Yuriko Saito's *The Aesthetics of Care*, in which she argues that caring about and for others and the material world requires "open-minded responsiveness," such that one can "experience others for who they are, apart from their value as a means to satisfy [one's] own interest or expectation" (Saito, 2022, p. 35). To value and respect another person, we must learn how to recognize them as independent from us, as their own beings, and not simply a canvas on which to project our own worldviews, hopes, or dreams. Similarly, to appropriately engage with and understand a work of art, Saito argues that we should approach the work as its own thing, and not merely some material for the projection of our own beliefs, worldviews, or fantasies about what it is and what it says. To engage with art is to be open to what it is saying, on its own terms, in its own way.

Approaching both art and the world in this way encourages not only playful engagement, but a curiosity about the world and other people that is (often) experientially rewarding in its own right. Arts engagement is fun and stimulating, and it invites us to think in ways that are not routine. Moreover, *not*-knowing is often part of the fun of arts engagement. Songs, paintings, and dances are puzzles that we can wrestle with and return to see in new and different ways. They are valuable contexts for the development of open-mindedness because they can make being confronted with differences (from one's expectations, from one's experiences) rewarding and engaging.

Art Creation

As we have already alluded to, open-minded engagement is foundational to how artists create. For artists, being open-minded means remaining responsive to the demands of the creative process: letting questions and themes emerge that may not have originally been intended, shifting direction mid-process, or abandoning preconceptions when the work calls for it. Doing so can allow artists to move beyond stylistic conventions, materials, and disciplinary norms, and to embrace more experimentation, play, and risk-taking. Open-mindedness in this context also means cultivating a kind of resilience in navigating uncertainty, ambiguity, and creative blocks. Rather than seeing uncertainty or mistakes as threats, artists who engage open-mindedly can come to see them as critical to their success and growth. Popular accounts from artists and writers underscore the importance of embracing uncertainty in one's creative practice. As David Bayles and Ted Orland put it in *Art & Fear: Observations on the Perils (and Rewards) of Artmaking*, "[u]ncertainty is the essential, inevitable, and all-pervasive companion to your desire to make art. And tolerance for uncertainty is the prerequisite to succeeding" (Bayles & Orland, 2010, p. 21).

Although the empirical literature does not show conclusively that art-making causes open-minded thinking, several related areas of research suggest that artists not only practice this kind of thinking, but also that doing so is valuable to their artistic practices. A strong relationship has been shown between the personality trait of openness to experience and creativity across a wide range of domains (Feist, 1998; Kaufman et al., 2016; Puryear et al., 2017). "Openness to experience" encompasses a wide range of predispositions and behavioral and cognitive-motivational tendencies, including intellectual curiosity, proneness to imagination and fantasy, aesthetic appreciation and sensibility, and creative variety-seeking (e.g., Christensen et al., 2018, 2019; Kaufman, 2013). In fact, openness to experience is commonly called the "creativity trait" by personality psychologists, because it strongly predicts performance on divergent and convergent creative thinking tasks (Dollinger et al., 2004; Silvia et al., 2008), predicts the number of real-world creative achievements someone may have (Kaufman, 2013; Kaufman et al., 2016), and predicts engagement in everyday creative behaviors (Silvia et al., 2009). The trait is often divided into two facets: intellect and openness. Intellect refers to curiosity, abstract thinking, and a preference for engaging with intellectual ideas. Openness refers to aesthetic appreciation, a tendency to engage with fantasy, and receptivity to cultural diversity (e.g., Christensen et al., 2019; Connelly et al., 2014; DeYoung et al., 2007, 2012; Nusbaum & Silvia, 2011). The intellect facet has been more strongly associated with scientific achievements and general intelligence, whereas the openness facet has been most strongly associated with arts-related behaviors and creative thinking (Kaufman et al., 2016).

Because openness to experience is such a broad trait, researchers have attempted to home in on specific behavioral and cognitive-motivational tendencies that might lead to flexible, creative thinking. One study found that the variety of creative experiences that people voluntarily engage in predicts their capacity for flexibility and originality (Koutstaal et al., 2025). That is, people who actively try out a wide range of creative activities, whether in traditional arts domains like visual arts, music, literature, and theater, or in other creative domains like sports, science or technology, tend to come up with more original and flexible ideas, regardless of their personality traits. This suggests that the trait may lay the foundation for an individual's interest in or motivation to seek out or continue in various pursuits. Actually engaging in a variety of creative pursuits matters much more, though, for the relevant creative outcome (in this case, increasing one's capacity to generate many original and useful ideas).

Ambiguity tolerance, referring to one's comfort with and even attraction to ambiguity, novelty, disorderly situations, and what is unfamiliar, is another relevant trait for art-making (Stoycheva, 2025). It is typically measured using self-report questionnaires (e.g., Budner, 1962; Caulfield et al., 2014; Lauriola et al., 2016). Example items include: "There is a right and a wrong way to do almost everything."; "A person who leads an even, regular life in which few surprises or unexpected happenings arise really has a lot to be grateful for."; and "I generally prefer familiarity over novelty." People with higher tolerance for ambiguity agree less strongly with statements like these than people with lower tolerance for ambiguity. Importantly, ambiguity tolerance, though generally stable, can be malleable to exposure, even over the course of relatively short-term interventions (Endres et al., 2015).

Because the creative process often unfolds without clear answers or endpoints, and it demands that artists persist in the face of confusion, disorder, and unfamiliar terrain, we should expect a relationship between art-making and high ambiguity tolerance. Margaret Chisolm and colleagues (2021) suggest that:

> tolerance of ambiguity and full engagement [with art] together nurture an appreciation for avoiding premature closure and embracing radical openness (i.e., not being overly attached to or protective of one's own first ideas, not ruling out others' perspectives or differential diagnoses precipitously). (p. 1103)

This tolerance is also tied to playfulness in creativity, where a playful disposition relates to the tendency to perceive ambiguous situations positively (Tegano, 1990). While there are few studies that specifically and directly examine ambiguity tolerance and art-making, research suggests an association between the trait and real-life creative achievements in job settings, and between the trait and a host of creative thinking skills, including generating original ideas, generating meaning, expressing ideas symbolically, and redefining ill-formed problems (Stoycheva, 2025). In this way, ambiguity tolerance appears to be not just a prerequisite for successful creativity but also an outcome of the creative process that can be strengthened or developed.

This understanding of ambiguity tolerance aligns closely with empirical accounts of creative self-regulation. Self-regulation is a broad psychological concept that refers to one's ability to modulate emotions, thoughts, and behaviors in pursuit of long-term goals. Emotion regulation is a subset of self-regulation, focused specifically on how people influence their emotional experiences and expressions. Zorana Ivcevic and Emily Nusbaum (2017) identify six key self-regulation strategies: understanding the unpredictable nature of the creative process, adjusting one's approach, setting appropriately ambitious goals, flexible planning, persistence in the face of obstacles, and effective emotion management. These strategies include both attitudes about one's self and one's work, and cognitive and social skills of the kind that have been our primary focus in this book. Among these strategies, tolerance – or at least acceptance – of ambiguity in the creative process features prominently. More recent work reinforces this idea. As Katya Stoycheva (2025) argues, successful lifetime creativity and learning depend on one's capacity to endure ambiguity, to commit to engaging in novel and complex creative pursuits, and to remain cognitively flexible.

Experiences of ambiguity are by their nature often unexpected and unusual, or otherwise violate our expectations. They call for cognitive flexibility (Ritter et al., 2012). Cognitive and perceptual flexibility typically refer to processes that allow us to shift between tasks, perspectives, interpretations, or strategies. They involve the ability to dynamically adapt our thinking in response to new information. For example, focused attention is often required to find appropriate solutions to problems, but in some contexts, defocused attention is critical to doing so. Not all problems are solved by attending closely to specific details; some are better approached by broadening the scope of our attention. This de-focusing might be especially useful during brainstorming and ideation (recall the brick task above). When we are stuck or fixated on a single solution, broadening our attention so we can enter a more associative, free mode of thinking will help us to consider more peripherally related things (Gabora, 2010).

Art-making, too, demands cognitive flexibility, as it involves a push-and-pull between focused and defocused attention, between conscious and unconscious processing, between persisting in a given task and exploring new possibilities, and in adjusting attentional control based on the needed context. There is evidence that especially creative thinkers are curious information seekers who have the capacity to persist in tasks, have the capacity to engage executive control and delay their gratification, and have both high risk tolerance and high ambiguity tolerance (Sternberg, 2006). There is also evidence that flexible cognitive and attentional control is a characteristic of especially creative thinkers who have recognized real-world creative accomplishments, including individuals who are successful artists, musicians, poets, scientists, and mathematicians (Carson et al., 2003; Zabelina & Robinson, 2010).

Research exploring the brain dynamics underlying creative cognition supports the notion that imaginative thought involves increased push-and-pull communication between the brain networks involved in self-generated thought (the default mode network) on the one hand, and those involved in executive control (e.g., attentional control networks, prefrontal cortex) on the other. When creative cognition is goal-directed, such as in a study where professional pianists were asked to improvisationally express a specific emotion on the piano, both self-generated thought and cognitive control networks dynamically cooperated (Pinho et al., 2016). In contrast, when artists do not have an explicit task goal, they rely more on brain networks supporting spontaneous and self-generated cognition, with attenuated executive control network activity. This has been shown with improvisational jazz musicians and with improv rappers (Beaty et al., 2018). Interestingly, people who score high on the openness facet of openness to experience tend to spend more time during their resting state (i.e., when there is no task) recruiting the default network. Moreover, research suggests that people with greater openness to experience have a stronger ability to flexibly and efficiently toggle between these networks, fostering their ability to direct spontaneous thoughts toward creative ends (Beaty et al., 2018).

This way of describing flexibility in relation to open-minded engagement echoes our discussion of attentional flexibility in Chapter 2. There, we suggested that arts engagement is associated with, and may lead to, increased attentional flexibility. For example, we reviewed evidence that visual artists are better able to flexibly control and deploy their attention than are control groups (e.g., Chamberlain & Wagemans, 2015). While we initially discussed this as evidence that the arts help cultivate refined observational skills that enable artists to notice what matters in a given moment, both during and beyond the act of making, we can also interpret it as a sign of refined capacity for open-minded engagement. Specifically, artists may be more attuned to the demands of the task, less fixed on one way of looking, and more capable of flexibly and dynamically shifting their attention.

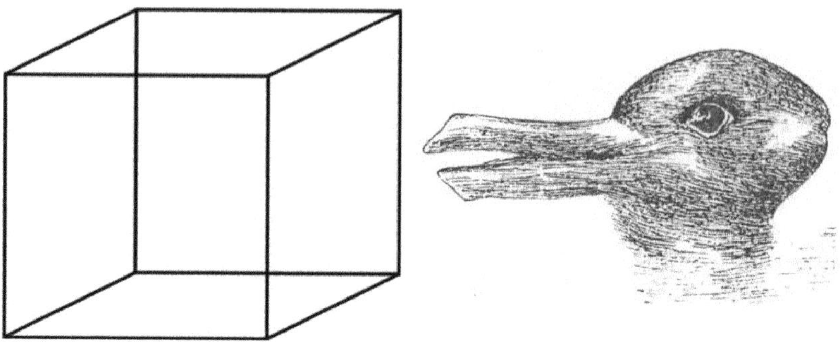

Figure 4.2 Ambiguous perceptual images. The Necker cube (left) and the "duck/rabbit" illusion (right).

In line with this, research suggests that visual arts training can foster perceptual flexibility, or the ability to see things in different ways. In one study, researchers compared visual arts students to nonarts students with respect to their dynamic interpretations of bistable visual illusions. For example, the famous Necker cube can be seen with either the left square or the right square as the face of the cube closest to the observer. The "duck/rabbit" illusion can be interpreted as a duck when the protrusions on the left of Figure 4.2 are viewed as a beak, or as a rabbit when they are viewed as ears.

Most people can see both interpretations of ambiguous figures relatively easily, especially with some directed probing. Research with visual artists shows that artists spontaneously and intentionally shift their interpretations more easily, but there is no difference in the ability to hold onto a single interpretation. Moreover, artists performed worse on a different inhibitory control task in which they were instructed to report the shape of a central figure (i.e., a right-pointing arrow) that was flanked by distracting figures (i.e., left-pointing arrows). This suggests that artists' attention, at least for this task, was "leakier" or more diffuse because it let in more distracting information. As we noted earlier, diffuse attention can be useful for divergent thinking, as it fosters more perceptual exploration and novelty (Chamberlain et al., 2018).

In another study using the Necker cube, researchers assessed whether spontaneous and intentional switches happened more frequently for people who had greater openness to experience and whether they could hold on to a single percept for a longer period of time. They also measured cognitive flexibility in a number of ways, including a self-report questionnaire, and both the AUT and a more "perceptual" AUT, in which participants had to generate several interpretations of what an abstract figure could be. The study showed that openness to experience predicted intentional Necker cube reversals, but that this relationship depended on cognitive flexibility. That is, cognitive flexibility acted as a kind of gatekeeper that enabled more open individuals to intentionally shift their perceptual interpretations and to hold onto the task-directed single interpretations. This finding underscores that personality traits like openness to experience do not operate in isolation, but instead, interact with cognitive skills like flexibility to shape how we experience the world (Koivisto & Pallaris, 2024).

A different study explored the relationship between openness to experience and cognitive flexibility using a paradigm called binocular rivalry, in which different images (e.g., house, cat) are shown to each eye. Phenomenologically, one's perception usually switches between seeing the image shown to the left eye and seeing the image shown to the right eye. Sometimes, though, perception is "mixed," such that a fused image appears to the viewer. Interestingly, people with greater openness to experience "see" far more mixed percepts than do less open people (Antinori et al., 2017). In a separate study, more open people tended to also experience more mixed emotions in their daily life, which again suggests that openness is linked to experiencing a more complex and a more diverse range of experiences (Barford & Smillie, 2016). While these studies are not directly related to the arts, they do hint at a relationship between the two, as openness and creative arts are intertwined in the ways we outlined above. Together, they highlight how flexible attention and cognition contribute to the cognitive architecture supporting open-minded engagement.

Factors affecting openness have also been studied through the absence of the trait, rather than its presence. For example, a high need for cognitive closure (NFC) hinders cognitive flexibility and creativity. NFC is typically understood as a kind of preference (specifically, a preference for order and predictability), along with ambiguity *in*tolerance, and a propensity to be strongly decisive while processing information (Webster & Kruglanski, 1994). Situational contexts like time pressure can affect NFC (Kruglanski & Webster, 1996), but NFC is also considered a dispositional trait that tends to remain relatively stable across many contexts (Webster & Kruglanski, 1994). A heightened need for closure leads people to become more reliant on early information cues when they make decisions. This means that they produce fewer internally generated hypotheses, which in itself impedes the rationality of their judgments (Mayseless & Kruglanski, 1987). Given this bias, it is not surprising that high NFC has been associated with fewer creative behaviors and a lower number of creative outputs (Rocchi, 1998; cf. Chirumbolo et al., 2005), and that creativity suffers when NFC is manipulated through increased time pressure (Chirumbolo et al., 2004). Whereas people who display high NFC seek fast resolution to problems, questions, or tasks, artists' practices often involve (either explicitly or implicitly) delaying closure and revisiting their work and ideas – sometimes so much so that they never consider a work finished. In fact, art-making as a practice seems to encourage the opposite of NFC. In this way, creative practices may actually offer a counterbalance to closure-seeking tendencies, and perhaps, with enough practice, a means of retraining them. Indeed, there is evidence related to art appreciation (discussed below) that makes precisely this point.

A thread that emerges across this empirical study of openness to experience and its related cognitive skills and competencies is that the process of creating art requires and reinforces cognitive flexibility and ambiguity tolerance. These are not best thought of as traits people are just born with. A more precise and instructive framework is to think of them as habits of mind and skills that are cultivated over time. Artists develop open-minded responsiveness, perhaps even a kind of open-minded resilience, through their sustained practice. So, while art creation is surely a place for artists to express their ideas, their emotions, or their identity, it is also a training ground for developing the skills necessary to be open-minded.

Art Appreciation

Art appreciation, like art creation, has long been recognized as a social practice that is especially well-suited to cultivating open-minded engagement. As we have already discussed at length, the arts do not reward quick judgments, nor do they offer clear-cut answers. Rather, the arts invite us to sit with ambiguity, to explore multiple interpretations, and to attend closely to perspectives other than our own. Whether encountering unfamiliar imagery in painting, emotionally complex narratives and fantastical stories in literature, or abstract movement and gesture in contemporary dance, appreciating art involves an active openness and suspension of certainty. De Ruysser's folding art, for example, shows us that materials like metal or wood that we might typically associate with rigidity and stability can be reimagined and fluidly folded and unfolded. Moreover, appreciating art allows us to step outside of ourselves, to displace the self, which thereby expands our perspectives. Iris Murdoch refers to this aspect of arts engagement as "unselfing," the reward for which is that you can "transcend selfish and obsessive limitations of personality and can enlarge the sensibility." Similarly, Elain Scarry argues that appreciating beauty involves "radical decentering" that involves letting ourselves learn and change through engagement with the other, such that "we find we are standing in a different relation to the world than we were a moment before." John Dewey echoes this in his view, contending that "works of art are means by which we enter, through imagination and the emotions they evoke, into other forms of relationship and participation than our own" (Saito, 2022, p. 37). Consistent with these philosophical accounts, a growing body of empirical research points to art appreciation developing and enhancing our capacity for open-minded thinking.

Openness to experience, in particular the openness facet described above, strongly predicts whether people are interested in art, whether they tend to experience beauty in response to art, how much they enjoy abstract art or genre-bending artworks like surrealism, their ability and interest in engaging with the ambiguity inherent in art, and the complexity and range of their emotional responses to art (e.g., Oleynick et al., 2017; Silvia & Nusbaum, 2011; Silvia & Sanders, 2010; Terracciano et al., 2003; cf. Chamorro-Premuzic et al., 2009; Swami et al., 2010). Additionally, research suggests that art appreciation can foster open-mindedness by providing individuals with opportunities to engage in abstract thinking, critical thinking, and meaning-making. In one study, researchers investigated how appreciating art in a museum involves abstract thinking (Mikalonytė et al., 2026). They asked visitors to examine fifteen different pottery objects in a museum context, and to either rate each object on how beautiful they found it, or to engage in a more basic perceptual task by matching the real object to a simplified line drawing. They reasoned that judging the beauty of the objects would reflect a deeper form of aesthetic appreciation, one that involves more interpretation and meaning-making, and would therefore elicit more abstract thinking than the perceptual task. To measure the extent to which abstract thinking was elicited, participants completed a questionnaire in which they chose between an abstract and a concrete description of an everyday action. For example, participants chose whether reading is best described as "gaining knowledge" (abstract) or as "following lines on print" (concrete), whether making a list is best described as "getting organized," or as "writing things down," or whether greeting someone was best described as "saying hello" or "showing friendliness." Responses were scored as involving more abstract thinking when the participant chose the "why" description (e.g., getting organized) over the concrete "how" description (e.g., writing things down). The results showed that participants who rated the objects' beauty gave more abstract responses on the questionnaire, and this was particularly true for those who also regularly engage in creative pursuits, whether through museum visits or art-making of some kind. This suggests that aesthetic appreciation promotes higher levels of conceptual thinking for individuals who are already creatively inclined. Moreover, compared to perceptual matching, aesthetic appreciation led to higher reports of transformative and self-transcendent feelings such as feeling enlightened, awed, moved, transformed, interested, happy, excited, absorbed, and stimulated.

These findings are consistent with research exploring the neural mechanisms of art appreciation. When people view artworks by adopting a more "pragmatic" or everyday mindset, they tend to focus on more concrete, object-based, visual features that activate brain regions involved most in object recognition and perceptual processing. However, adopting an "aesthetic orientation," one that is characterized by openness, receptivity, and active meaning-making, recruits brain areas associated with higher-order self-referential processing and with the evaluation of internally generated information (e.g., Cupchik et al., 2009; Vessel et al., 2013). This suggests that the mindset with which we approach an artwork is important. Aesthetic engagement that allows us to challenge our preconceptions, to engage in processes of interpretation and to make meaning, and to engage in abstract thinking (rather than mere looking or perceptual exploration) supports open-mindedness by activating higher-order cognitive processes.

Art appreciation also seems to foster ambiguity and uncertainty tolerance, and the ability to weigh multiple perspectives, though the research on this connection is still emerging. In one study, medical students who participated in a 90-minute art discussion reported increased acceptance of the idea that art could have multiple possible meanings and interpretations, and no single "right" interpretation (Bentwich & Gilbey, 2017). In another study, medical students completed a six-week course titled "Observation and Uncertainty in Art and Medicine" held in part at the Metropolitan Museum of Art (Gowda et al., 2018). The course aimed to strengthen students' observational skills through engaging with visual artworks, while encouraging them to reflect on and better understand their own cognitive biases and their ability to navigate uncertainty. The measured gains in ambiguity tolerance and reflective capacity were apparent but modest – likely because the sample size was small, because there was self-selection into the course, and because students already had relatively high scores to begin with. However, the participants' written reflections told a deeper story. Many described becoming far more comfortable with not having all the answers and becoming more aware of how their own interpretations might differ from others. As one student put it:

> Med school is a long journey through accepting uncertainty... I think this whole year for me has been a long process of being comfortable with being uncomfortable. I can't know everything... I can't do everything I need to do. I don't have the time. And accepting that, moving on and not letting it cause so much anxiety. This class added to that. (p. S11)

Another wrote: "An expression on someone's face that I interpreted as sad, somebody else interpreted as frustrated... It made me realize how singular my own perspective is and how important it is to really consider multiple interpretations" (p. S11).

A key takeaway from these and similar findings (e.g., Hitsuwari & Nomura, 2023; Klugman et al., 2011) is the powerful role the arts can play in developing the skills associated with openness and cognitive flexibility. In a complex field like medicine, which itself is often described as both a science and an art, the ability to remain open, responsive, and flexible is paramount. Unfortunately, modern medical training (and education more broadly) can sometimes emphasize certainty and efficiency at the expense of reflection and ambiguity. Engaging with the arts offers an opportunity to reset this balance, by reminding clinicians of the importance of the interpretive and humanistic aspects of their work. Psychologists have made similar claims about training in their field, suggesting that exposure to fictional literature "can balance practitioners' extensive content knowledge with the development of meta-cognitive habits that favor improved information processing ... [that] in turn, may have applications in professional fields" (Djikic et al., 2013, p. 153).

As with art creation, several studies have explored how an individual's need for closure may affect their art appreciation experiences. For example, individuals with high NFC dislike abstract artworks more than their low NFC counterparts, but they like figurative artworks, in which the meaning and artistic intent is less ambiguous, to the same extent as their low NFC counterparts (Ostrofsky & Shobe, 2015; Wiersema et al., 2012). Recall, high NFC individuals prefer to quickly reach closure in their decisions, whereas low NFC individuals postpone judgements for longer periods of time. This suspension of judgment is important to art appreciation. Spending more time with art is not only related to increased preferences for particular kinds of art or artworks, but also to increased understanding of the artist's intentions or the meaning of the artwork, increased likelihood of reporting that the experience was transformative in some way, and sustained interest in the arts (Sherman et al., 2025). In a study in which participants were shown a series of paintings and asked to view and evaluate key dimensions of them, higher NFC individuals made quicker art preference judgments than lower NFC individuals, thereby understanding the art less well (Ostrofsky & Shobe, 2015).

More experience with the arts and the encouragement to engage in art appreciation practices may be viewed as an antidote to these outcomes for higher NFC people. In one study, participants who were asked to read a fictional short story were subsequently measured as having a lower need for closure than those who read a nonfiction short story, suggesting that even a brief exposure to fictional literature can increase our flexibility (Djikic et al., 2013). They also show that this effect is especially strong if you are an avid reader – irrespective of whether you tend to read fiction or nonfiction. This suggests that with respect to NFC, everyone benefits from reading fiction, especially if you read a lot. They suggest that reading literature – and perhaps we can expand this to other domains of art appreciation – "may offer a pedagogical tool to encourage individuals to become more likely to open their minds" (p. 153).

Summary

In this chapter, we explored how open-minded thinking is engaged and developed through the arts. We identified open-minded engagement as being receptive to and embracing of new ideas, values, beliefs, lifestyles, and cultures, but in a critical and bounded way. We suggested that one's willingness to entertain novel views involves engaging cognitive processes like perspective-taking and perspective-getting, ambiguity or uncertainty tolerance, as well as mental flexibility. We identified the arts as an especially important set of practices to develop open-mindedness, and surveyed empirical evidence that links aspects of openness, specifically ambiguity tolerance and mental flexibility, to arts engagement. Coming into an art interaction with a rigid set of beliefs about what the art should and can tell you, and what you might and might not feel, will thus only get you so far. In contrast, if you can embrace and accept that you may not quite know what could happen, pause on projecting your preconceptions, be open to what the artwork is saying to you on its own terms, you will surely engage more fully, come to understand more about the artworks and artist themselves, and deepen your own capacity for continued openness.

What seems clear is that open-minded engagement is epistemically and personally valuable, particularly in the context of art-making and art-appreciating. Open-mindedness fosters our ability to think about and experience things in ways that are not given by or possible within the worldview, assumptions, or starting points that we came to the relationship with. Being open pushes us to understand and think in new ways, or to think differently about ourselves and the world. This experience is not always (or often) a pleasant one. It can be hard to be confronted with things that challenge your understanding or sense of self; it can be difficult to let hard truths be asserted.

Stepping back from our discussions here, and in Chapters 2 and 3, we see that people engage with art and value art for many reasons. First, it is enjoyable, restorative, and emotionally provocative. It also helps us to engage with emotions that can be challenging and confusing, it exposes us to a diverse array of perspectives, and it helps us to see things anew, to understand people anew, and to foster feelings of connections to others, the world, and to ourselves. In these ways, the arts help us to practice and deepen both our observational capacities and our open-minded thinking. Implicit in this is that the arts, or arts practices, become indelibly linked to our senses of self, to who we think we are, and to how we identify in relation to others and to the world. In Chapter 5, we explore the relationship between the arts and self-identity more deeply. Whereas in this chapter, we primarily explored how open-mindedness is a cognitive disposition or set of skills or competencies, Chapter 5 explores the importance of what comes from this kind of engagement, including moments in which people feel changed by or transformed by art.

CHAPTER 5

Self, Identity, and Transformation

Starting Point

The arts are intimately linked to who we are as people. As Dominic McIver Lopes writes: "Nobody needs to be told their aesthetic pursuits express who they are, endow their life with meaning, bring them happiness, or fulfill their personal ideals. The puzzle is *how* our aesthetic pursuits can be so important in these ways" (Lopes, 2018, pp. 216, emphasis added). This chapter takes up that puzzle by asking how the arts relate to our sense of self. Whereas the previous chapters explored how the arts help us to think, know, understand, or learn better, this chapter explores how the arts can serve as a medium for becoming – and, at times, recovering – ourselves.

In March 2010, Serbian-born performance artist Marina Abramović embarked on a three-month-long, life-changing journey at the Museum of Modern Art (MOMA) in New York City. During her provocative and controversial performance, *The Artist Is Present*, Abramović sat motionless in a chair across from museum visitors for eight hours a day, six days a week. Visitors were invited to sit with her one at a time in silence for as long as they wanted. Over the course of the performance, Abramović sat with more than 1,500 different people. Most people sat gazing into her eyes for at least ten minutes. Many sat with her for hours at a time. One visitor even sat across from her for the entire day. Visitors experienced a range of emotions; many were moved to tears after a ten-minute encounter. Photographer Marco Anelli documented the entire performance and published the collection of all 1,545 portraits in his book *Portraits in the Presence of Marina Abramović* (Anelli et al., 2012; Figure 5.1).

What drew so many people to wait for hours to get a chance to sit across from Abramović, or to sit for such prolonged periods in silence across from a stranger? Abramović herself said that "Nobody could imagine ... that anybody would take time to sit and just engage in mutual gaze with

Figure 5.1 *The Artist Is Present* (2010), by Marina Abramović. Museum of Modern Art, New York, NY, USA.

me... It was [a] complete surprise ... this enormous need of humans to actually have contact" (*Marina Abramović*, 2010). In a documentary on her work, Abramović recalls, "There's so many different reasons why people came to sit in front of me ... some of them are angry, some of them are curious ... so many people are in so much pain ... very soon, I'm just a mirror of their own self" (Akers & Dupre, 2012).

People's responses to Abramović's work highlighted the connection they felt to her, the dynamism of emotions they confronted, the surprising sense of timelessness they experienced, their appreciation for an opportunity to reflect on their thoughts and feelings and to heal in someone's presence, and the general transformative nature of the encounter. Artist Yazmany Arboleda described the unique value of the experience, writing: "In a world in which looking at your watch, your phone, or your computer screen is as regular as breathing, it is rare to have this space where time no longer matters" (Arboleda, 2010). Art journalist Rebecca Taylor wrote of the surprising intimacy of the experience:

> We sat absolutely still in deafening silence, exchanging energy, and just being with each other. I've heard it said that couples married for decades

> can sit in silence and understand one another perfectly, but I'd never imagine that sort of intimacy could be possible between two total strangers. It is. (Taylor, 2026)

While visitor Paco Blancas, who sat with her fourteen different times, called the experience: "transforming. . . – it's luminous, it's uplifting, it has many layers, but it always comes back to being present, breathing, maintaining eye contact. It's an amazing journey to be able to experience and participate in the piece" (Stanley, 2010).

Sitting across from the artist and engaging in mutual gaze, you must be (and can only be) present as yourself. There are no phones, no distractions, and no other people; there is no conversation to deflect away from your own thoughts and experiences. There is nothing to do other than just be in the space with Abramović. This gives participants a chance to explore and reflect on crucial aspects or dimensions of what they are experiencing, of who they are, and the way they relate to other people. It is not surprising then that people report "being seen" or "feeling seen," and that the context brings up complex emotions that participants can (and do) reflect on, either in the moment, as part of the experience, or afterward. Abramović herself discusses how challenging the performance was for her, and not only, or even primarily, in the physical sense of needing to sit still for so long (Akers & Dupre, 2012). Rather, one of the biggest challenges she faced was that by offering her own eye contact and vulnerability, she absorbed and relayed back others' emotions. She found herself not only being a vessel for revealing others' emotions, but also experiencing them herself, and thus feeling transformed in both emotional and physical terms.

Building on the insights from Abramović's work, we begin this chapter by exploring the notion of self-identity and how we can think of the self as inherently "aesthetic." We then turn to questions of transformation to consider how transformation through arts engagement can happen for individuals and for our communities, and what such change tells us about the connection between identity and art.

Aesthetic Selves: The Relationship between Art and Self-Identity

A central claim of this chapter is that our identities are substantially formed by our aesthetic engagements, not just as hobbies, but as integral expressions of who we are and who we understand ourselves to be. Consider Ted Cohen's reflection on a memorial service he attended for a friend:

> The program for the service was a number of remembrances and two musical selections. The musical selections, performed by a string quartet,

> were chosen by someone who had known my friend and knew that both were favorites of his. Why is this music appropriate? There are a number of answers, good answers, to this question. I draw your attention to one. My friend has died and is not present. I listen to music I know he cared for. It is a fact about my friend that he cared for this music, perhaps even a constitutive fact about his sensibility: it partially defines who and what he was. It is, thus, an entrance into that sensibility. I sit listening, not merely thinking that this music meant something to my friend, but bending my imagination to the task of *reaching* and *comprehending* an aspect of my friend which responded to this music, that is, feeling what it was to be my friend. (Cohen, 1993, p. 154)

Cohen is present with his friend and accesses him through listening to music that he loved. The music and the fact that he loved it are part of his friend's sensibility: the distinctive set of things he cared about, how he responded to the world, and what he found interesting, engaging, funny, and beautiful. That these things are true of someone does not go away when they die. Their sensibility, and our ability to access it and them through the arts, remains.

This notion of a sensibility is tied deeply to what it means to be who you are, that is, to one's sense of self, and even to what it means to be a "self" in the first place. As with the nature of art (discussed in the Introduction), there is almost nothing uncontroversial that can be said about the nature of the self. For that reason, we will move away from discussions of the self directly, to focus on the notion of having a "sense of self."

The American Psychological Association Dictionary defines an individual's sense of self as "(a) a set of physical, psychological, and interpersonal characteristics that is not wholly shared with any other person and (b) a range of affiliations (e.g., ethnicity) and social roles" (*APA Dictionary of Psychology*, 2018). A sense of self involves an individual's perception or understanding of their identity. We can distinguish at least two primary components of people's reflections on who they are: (1) a set of characteristics and traits, ranging from physical (i.e., height, eye color), to psychological (i.e., agreeableness), to interpersonal (i.e., aptitude with respect to communication of feelings), the particular constellation of which is specific to the individual; and (2) a host of affiliations with social groups (e.g., gender identity, ethnicity, sports team fandom) and social roles that one occupies (e.g., spouse, parent, student, employee). A sense of self is also tied to the notion of authenticity or individuality. It is about the particular and unique constellation of things that one cares about, attends to, and spends one's time doing. The preferences that one has, in large part, are what make a person the particular person that they are (Wiltsher, 2024).

The arts are foundational to these preferences, projects, and habits that we adopt and make our own.

This connection has been explored empirically by Joerg Fingerhut and colleagues (2021), who examined whether changes in one's music or visual art tastes might be indicative of a change in self-identity. Imagine that you are truly connected to the punk rock music scene. Now, imagine that you start attending the symphony and begin to develop an interest in classical music. Over time, your preferences shift so that you are now truly connected to classical music and prefer it to punk. To what extent would you have changed as a *person*? When asked questions like this, people agree that shifts in music preferences, particularly shifts that might be considered more radical, like preferring punk music to preferring classical music, change one's identity. Moreover, changes in preferences for visual art genres, and for development of novel aesthetic interests (e.g., becoming a visual art lover, or learning an instrument) seem to alter one's self in a significantly larger way than changing one's job, developing novel leisure interests (e.g., becoming a passionate hiker), or changing one's food preferences. In fact, people rank aesthetic pursuits as equally significant to their identity as morality, religion, and politics. For this reason, Fingerhut and colleagues argue that people see the arts as practices and activities that make them who they are.

They explain this partly by suggesting that our art preferences, or more basically, thinking of ourselves as art lovers, serve as social signals. Enjoying punk music and attending punk rock concerts, for example, signals much more than your taste for specific sound profiles. It also signals to others your likely political and economic beliefs, the kinds of people you are likely to spend time with, the places you tend to go, or the kind of food you might like to eat (and, when we were younger, even the kind of cigarettes you smoke). So, although Fingerhut and colleagues' studies focused nearly exclusively on what we may describe as people's discrete musical preferences, it may be that these seemingly discrete musical preferences are indicative of a whole set of related "preferences" that are part of people's social status. As Fingerhut and colleagues (2021) state:

> the construction of [self] identity includes our relationship to cultural artifacts ... [the arts] are not merely forms of entertainment but also constitute important values we care about and that are central to us. Hence, we are *aesthetic selves*: central aspects of our identity are constituted by cultural and art-related preferences. (p. 2)

This may be why people think preference-related changes are identity shifting. Note that this set of studies was somewhat indirect, in that they asked people to intuit and predict how their identities would shift because of taking on new aesthetic interests. But, additional research corroborates the claim that when people discuss important and memorable aesthetic experiences, they do so in ways that indicate the arts have become intertwined with how they understand themselves as individuals. Some researchers even suggest that aesthetic experiences are a linchpin for self-discovery, self-actualization, and strengthening our sense of self (Magon & Cupchik, 2023). For example, research shows that music plays a powerful role in evoking autobiographical memories and in reinforcing personal and social identity across cultures. In Western contexts, the music one listens to from adolescence to early adulthood is often linked to self-defining memories and experiences and to our social and relational self. Many couples and friends suggest that they have special songs that remind them of positive memories in their relationship, and that strengthen feelings of connection and intimacy. Similarly, in Indigenous cultures worldwide, music is experienced as autobiographical, telling personal stories of individuals' various experiences of pain, healing, and joy. (See Thompson et al., 2023 for review.) For these reasons, music has also been used therapeutically to treat a variety of self-related neurological disorders and symptoms, with great success. For people with Alzheimer's and other forms of dementia, for example, music is often used to trigger personally meaningful memories, helping patients to at least temporarily remember aspects of their lives that are less accessible to them in the absence of the music. Music appreciation also helps people with dementia feel better overall, such that during and immediately after music therapy or after group music-making sessions, individuals with dementia are less agitated, in a better mood, and better able to communicate their emotional experiences (Baird & Samson, 2015). In all of these ways, music helps people reaffirm and reconnect to their own sense of self.

In a recent study, researchers conducted interviews in which they asked people with various degrees of arts expertise (ranging from professional artists to only some interest) to describe their most salient experiences either making art or engaging with art across various forms (e.g., visual arts, dance, music, literature; Wilt et al., 2025). The findings reveal a set of core relationships between the arts and people's self-identity, such that salient experiences with art (both making and appreciating) increased people's feelings of being authentically themselves, revealed important aspects of their identities, and fostered the development of what they called their authentic selves. As one participant shared:

> [Art has] allowed me to connect to my deeper self for sure, and ... it allowed me to reach this level of being myself, that is very hard to become, because you always feel, I don't know, you feel the pressure of being

> understood by whatever is your environment, whether it's your friends, family, people that's at your work. And so, yeah, somehow you, this deeper part of you is more advanced than your conscious self. It precedes you. So, you have to catch it back, and then it also allows you to go further in life.

Additionally, people described art as a pathway toward authentic emotional awareness and expression, as important to realizing their connections and relationships to others, and as critical to enhancing their understanding of what it means to be fully present in the world. This is illustrated by another participant's reflections:

> I think I just fully came to realize how important my loved ones are to me. I don't know about anything beyond that... The [artwork] served as an opportunity to help me connect with others on a deep, emotional level and help them understand their emotions too. I think it helped me understand that I'm very much a people person.

These descriptions suggest that aesthetic experiences and aesthetic pursuits or practices have very explicit and direct existential importance to us. Engaging with the arts is bound up with our identities; it helps us gain clarity about who we are as unique selves and how we relate to others.

Another way to see how the arts shape our sense of self is to examine how our relations to the arts and aesthetic practices are affected when we lose someone, or we experience challenges or threats to our sense of self. Art therapy done in clinical contexts as well as nonclinical art engagement interventions have long been used to help people recover or negotiate a challenge to their sense of self. Creative art therapy involves creative arts activities like drawing, dancing, or singing, often employed in service of helping patients to better regulate their emotions, to understand and modify disordered self-image, or to foster self-compassion (e.g., Haeyen & Heijman, 2020). The central goal of an art therapist is to help individuals who are struggling with challenges like health crises (e.g., cancer diagnoses), physical or emotional trauma, grief or loss, or serious mental illness, to "express themselves in ways beyond words or language" ("What Is Art Therapy?," 2022). Unlike traditional artistic creation, which focuses on the artistic process or the aesthetic quality of the output, creative art therapy prioritizes interpretating and analyzing the creative process, as well as the personal meaning gained from the artistic process. In this way, art therapy is focused on the elements of art creation that contribute to healing, and the art therapist provides opportunities for patients' stories to be heard and appreciated, helps establish an environment of safety, and helps elicit meaning from the patients' experiences (Nelson et al., 2024).

Work in creative art therapy suggests that arts interventions may be an especially important means by which individuals' autonomy – their ability to make decisions for themselves and feel affirmed in doing so – can be enhanced, developed, or otherwise healed. Consider how many choices are made in the course of creating a painting: What is it about? How big is it? Exactly what colors will you use? Exactly where will each specific shape/color/line go? When is it done/should you keep working? The answers to these questions must come from you as the artist. There is no other source for answering the questions – it is *your* painting, you must decide what it is, how to execute it, and when it is done. In this way, the decisions made in creating the painting are personal: They reflect *you*, *your* aims, *your* sensibility, *your* taste, *your* vision.

Evidence suggests that creative art therapy can support healing one's sense of being an autonomous being, capable of making decisions that reflect a self that matters. In an art therapy program with incarcerated teenage boys that focused on painting, the participants reported that the program boosted their self-confidence. Because the participants were being recognized and affirmed for making something of value, their sense of self-worth was enhanced (Persons, 2009). Similarly, Linda Kelemen and Liat Shamri-Zeevi (2022) report that an open-studio art therapy project for teens with mental health conditions supported the participants' identity development by emphasizing autonomy support, through asking the participants to make choices and then affirming those choices. Some have even described the decision-making process involved in art-making as being absorbing in a way that they found therapeutic, as with a participant in Marie-Christine Ranger and colleagues' (2023) study of women with cancer:

> The facilitator said, "Okay, we're going to start, and we have two hours," and at one point I thought, "Boy, is it really going to take that long to do this?" But by the time I kept looking at the clock, I thought, "Wait a minute, I might run out of time here." So it was really amazing, but I think it was because I was making so many little decisions and thoughtfulness about what I wanted this piece to be and it was an expression of me. I mean, that was really unique. Very unique. (Lynn, S1I, p. 4)

Research shows that art therapy offers even more than autonomy; it also provides a vital space for individuals to redefine, renegotiate, and recraft their identity. This is especially relevant for individuals experiencing significant life shifts, such as new mothers, who often grapple with a fractured or shifting sense of self, or even feel a loss of their former identity. A review of arts-based interventions for new mothers identified creative expression as a powerful means for women "to explore important aspects of the motherhood experience including, complex emotion, identity and bonding with the unborn child" (Crane et al., 2021, p. 325). Similarly, in a study of an arts-based intervention for trans youth, creative activity was an especially important mechanism for engaging with and documenting the participants' self-reflection, and for engaging each participant as a unique individual. As the authors describe this:

> It also allowed youth to express who they are beyond the silo of (trans) gender identity, which is often reductively filtered through an exchange of language. For these participants, art provided a forum for others to see them in expanded form, not strictly contained within the bounds of verbal conversation and its attendant identity category of trans* youth. (Asakura et al., 2020, p. 1069)

These arts-based interventions create a mechanism or space for participants to be themselves, in the full sense of what that means, by calling on them to make decisions for themselves that express or reflect that they are a person, with a distinct point of view, and that this expression and existence is valuable or important.

As indicated earlier in this chapter, grief is also an especially robust area of study relevant to the relationship between creative art therapy and self-identity, with more than 80 percent of trained art therapists working with bereaved individuals (*American Art Therapy Association I. Newsletter, XK,* 2007, p. 23). Traditionally, psychologists assumed that everyone experiences grief in more or less the same way, by moving through standard stages. However, more recent empirical evidence suggests that this is not the case, and evidence supports a shift toward recognizing multiple complex trajectories of grief (Beaumont, 2013). Among a number of empirically validated frameworks developed to characterize the current approach to the bereavement experience, two are most well entrenched: the dual-process model and the meaning reconstruction model (Weiskittle & Gramling, 2018). The dual-process model approaches grief as a process of moving back and forth between dealing directly with the loss – such as expressing emotions related to death and engaging in continuing bonds with the deceased – and finding one's way in a now-changed personal and social landscape, through trying out new roles and orientations to one's environment. From the perspective of the dual-process account, creative art therapy is thought to be effective for bereaved individuals because the process promotes expression and exploration of feelings, which are a central part of many individuals' grieving processes (Green et al., 2021).

The meaning reconstruction model, on the other hand, approaches grief as a process of restoring aspects of one's self-understanding and understanding of the world in the wake of the loss. Theorists suggest that there are two narrative processes involved in grief that constitute meaning-making. The first involves processing the *event story* of the death, and the second involves a healthy engagement with the *back story* of one's relationship to the deceased person (Neimeyer & Thompson, 2014). The *event story* involves seeking to understand the loss itself – to make sense of it – reflecting on, perhaps, why it happened, how it fits into the larger picture of our lives, how it shifts our sense of how the world works, or otherwise what it means for us. Whereas the *back story* involves grappling with how the loss or death shakes the very foundation of our network of bonds and meanings that constitute our understanding of ourselves as related to others.

Art therapeutic approaches to support bereaved individuals' meaning-making tend to use narrative therapeutic responses, including narrative storytelling or creative writing. Writing "found poems" or "rescued speech poems" from the conversations of people who had lost a partner, for example, helps facilitate the bereaved's meaning-making with respect to the loss (Penwarden, 2022). This has been extended to the visual arts modalities as well through activities like body-mapping, photography, and storyboarding (Beaumont, 2013). Participants highlight how important art therapy is for their sense of self, their ability to understand how their identities were challenged by their loss, and how it provided a context for moving forward and reintegrating back to a fulfilling life (Nelson et al., 2024). For example: "Art therapy helped me grieve all the things I didn't realize I had given up; my sense of self, loss of identity, my own life and agency" (p. 10).

Transformed by Art

That we are aesthetic selves, such that the arts constitute our identity, and help us re-find or renegotiate how we see ourselves, illustrates a broader phenomenon: the power of art to foster transformation. This underscores the discussion we began this chapter with in which "transformation" was a recurring theme of people's experiential accounts of Marina Abramović's performance piece. Indeed, it is actually quite common for people to describe arts experiences as transforming in some way. Consider Randy's first personal account of experiencing the musical *A Chorus Line:*

> When I look back at it now, it's crazy how this visceral moment in "A Chorus Line" just changed my life forever... We find out who we are.

> We find out who other people are. We find out who we want to be, who we strive for by opening ourselves up to the arts. You know, whether it's going to the theater, going to the ballet, going to the opera, going to a museum, it's very effective, it's very moving, and that's the beauty of the arts. You know, it affects us in many different ways that we don't always realize until, sometimes, years later. But those tiny little seeds are planted, and if you just let them grow, it'll change your life. It did mine, for sure. (*How Art Changed Me*, 2024)

This description is rich with suggestions about what self-transformation looks like. It may be an insight, perhaps into who we are, or who others are; it may provide us inspiration, an ideal, or an aspiration to strive towards; or, it may be the planting of a "seed," an interesting idea that roots itself inside our psyches to grow and develop over time. The philosophical and psychological literature is still relatively underdeveloped with respect to conceptual resources for explaining this rich and striking experience that Randy describes. However, a promising approach has been to examine people's experiences with art under the umbrella of "transformative experiences" (TEs).

Scholars define TEs as enduring and potentially irreversible changes in individuals' self-identity, self-concepts, worldviews, relationships, and personality that are brought about by a unique or salient event (Chirico et al., 2022; Miller & C'de Baca, 2001). Although any kind of experience could conceivably be transformative, people tend to cite religious, spiritual, or mystical experiences, near-death experiences, experiences with psychedelic drugs, traumatic experiences, having children, and, most relevant to us, aesthetic and arts experiences (Chirico et al., 2022). TEs leave people changed in two senses: epistemically and personally. Experiences can be *epistemically transformative* by providing new forms or degrees of knowledge or understanding. A frequent and favorite example of this kind of epistemic change is that of tasting a durian fruit (Paul, 2016). The overwhelming odor (some would say aroma) is utterly unique and difficult to describe using language to anyone who has not tasted it. Our typical way to describe things by using familiar language and referring to experiences we have already had just does not capture the experience. By tasting durian, we learn something new – we gain experiential knowledge, as discussed in Chapter 1 – that we could not have gained any other way.

Transformative experiences are also *personally* transformative; they change one's identity in a substantive way by shifting or changing one's core values, desires, or preferences. It seems to be this second sense of transformation that is important to explaining Randy's experience watching *Chorus Line*. What distinguishes a standard learning experience from one that is transformative, some philosophers argue, is that you cannot know, prior to undergoing them, how you will be changed by having done so. LA Paul, for instance, contends that when it comes to TEs, your previous experiences are insufficient evidence for how you will feel, or how your preferences and values will themselves be radically changed, by having the experience (Paul, 2016). In this sense, TEs are opaque to us. Randy did not know, and could not predict, how – or even that – seeing *A Chorus Line* would shift who he is and how he understands himself in such a significant way. TEs are experiences that we must choose to undergo, not just without knowing what they will be like, but also how we may respond to them, and how they might change us.

Havi Carel and Ian James Kidd argue that this core notion of transformative experience developed by Paul is, in fact, even broader because it includes experiences that are involuntary or nonvoluntary (Carel & Kidd, 2020). They give a litany of examples of experiences that can be transformative in the two ways described above, but which are not "chosen" in any meaningful sense. This includes: "serious accident, chronic illness, separation from a loved one, war, forced migration, poverty, famine, being the victim of a violent crime, suffering severe depression" (p. 202). The robustness of the non- or involuntary categories suggests that we must recognize and embrace the extent to which our knowledge and even *ourselves* (e.g., what we care about, what our preferences are, what we think of as most central to our identities) are radically contingent, vulnerable to change, and may be substantially out of or beyond our control. Although scholars have generally thought of TEs in the context of a single unique event, it is not only special, one-off experiences that can be transformative; the cumulative effects of quotidian experiences can be as well. The experience of not having enough to eat or being unsure of whether or when your next meal will come may not transform you in a moment or instant, but as a daily experience, they surely will. These kinds of transformative experiences are especially hard to study and have received much less scholarly attention than the core, one-off experiences.

Two important questions for our investigation are raised by this discussion. First, is arts engagement capable of being a transformative experience? Second, if it is, do these accounts of TEs satisfactorily capture or explain people's self-reports of having been transformed by a work of art? Nick Riggle introduces the concept "transformative expression" to suggest several specific ways in which art-making and art-appreciating might foster transformation of the self (Riggle, 2020). He defines transformative expression as a matter of a certain kind of activity becoming centrally important to your sense of who you are as a result of engaging in that activity. He gives the example of a makeover show. He imagines someone who prior to the show had no interest in changing her personal style, but through the process of the "makeover" comes to see styling herself in a new way as an important and especially meaningful thing that she can do for herself. Moreover, through such an experience, one's sense of self has been transformed.

Riggle argues that some artworks, or perhaps kinds of artworks, can *invite* transformative expression by "inviting a certain kind of uptake in participants, namely, engagement with the work through the kinds of actions the work requires"[1] (Riggle, 2020, p. 171). He suggests that this kind of invitation and aim is present as a significant tradition within twentieth- and twenty-first-century avant-garde art, and specifically what we may refer to as participatory art, including social sculpture and relational aesthetics. For example, Abramović's piece creates an environment or space in which reflection is encouraged. The table and her presence, and the directive of participating in an artwork in which you are implicitly asked to be present with the artist, do not tell you how to focus your attention, or aim to elicit specific emotions. The aim instead is to offer you time and space to open yourself up to yourself and others. In this way, the experience creates conditions for potential transformation, because of the importance of reflection and witnessing one's own experience and reaction.

Given these considerations, and the evidence in prior chapters that highlights relationships between the arts and epistemic change or improvement – including experiencing enhanced empathy, social awareness, and emotional development; enhanced critical thinking skills; increased tolerance for ambiguity, potential for belief revision, creative insights – it seems plausible that the arts are not only a common venue for TEs, but are a "potent catalyst for personal and societal change" (Pizzolante et al., 2024, p. 13).

[1] Riggle identifies and further disambiguates kinds of transformation an artwork may invite or otherwise aim to foster:

1. Replacement – the work aims to replace at least one core commitment with another.
2. Introduction – the work is designed to introduce a new core commitment.
3. Elimination – the work is designed to eliminate a core commitment.
4. Structure – the work is designed to restructure commitments...
   a. Core Restructuring – where the restructured commitments are core ones. b. Peripheral Restructuring – where the peripheral commitments are made core ones.
5. Group Transformation – the work is designed to cause a group of people to share commitments, where the pre-transformed group exhibits a plurality of commitments and is transformed into a homogeneity (Riggle, 2020, pp. 172–173).

Recall that, in Chapter 2, we highlighted the various ways mindful attention and observation are cultivated through arts engagement. Notice that *self*-awareness is a kind of mindful attention that enables us to recognize and reflect on our own thoughts and emotions, often in relation to others and society. Engaging with the arts can activate and deepen this awareness in a myriad of ways. Moreover, when appreciating art, we often actively tune in to our emotional responses. Recall again "The Panther" from Chapter 3: We not only attend to the emotions we perceive the creature experiencing, but also to the feelings those perceptions stir within us. This dual awareness invites introspection, reflection, and self-examination. Through the act of naming the emotions recognized in the subject and in oneself, we engage in an inquiry into our own mental states. We can notice how our mental states shift throughout the reading, the images and associations that surface, and how we interpret the work in light of our personal context. The emotional experiences we have while engaging with art, like awe, wonder, and nostalgia, are often triggered by things that are vast and beyond our initial understanding. These emotions disrupt our habitual modes of thinking, driving curiosity and self-exploration. However, they are also characterized by feelings of self-diminishment, smallness, and reduced self-focus, which may make it seem like they are not related to self-reflection. However, to make sense of the experience, we need to engage in self-reflection, a process that psychologists often call "cognitive accommodation," in which we ask questions like "What does this mean to me?" "Where do I fit in the bigger picture?" or "Why am I experiencing this sense of wonder?" In this way, art can become both a mirror and a medium for accessing and enhancing our self-knowledge. Importantly, this kind of self-reflection, prompted by deep emotionality and some kind of violation of our expectations, leads to a metacognitive reassessment of an artwork and, eventually, a transformation in the self. In this way, defamiliarization, "becoming unsettled," and self-reflecting are crucial to self-knowledge, self-discovery, and identity (Sherman & Morrissey, 2017).

Moreover, unfamiliar and uncomfortable arts contexts that push people out of their comfort zones but still encourage them to engage in open, reflective dialogue (centrally important to our discussion in Chapter 4) have been empirically connected to TEs (Tackett et al., 2023). Discomfort and disruption to one's self-schemas appear to be key triggers or preconditions for personal and epistemic change. The cognitive dissonance and misalignment between one's preexisting views or expectations and the current event or experience they are presented with contribute to the discomfort.

Art often explicitly aims to do just this: To disrupt one's "normal" way of being in the world by highlighting something they may have overlooked or ignored. Consider *What It's Like, What It Is #3*, an artwork by Adrian Piper included in the MoMA and the Hammer Museum's 2018 retrospective of her work. The mixed-media video installation featuring a Black man "standing" in the center of a strikingly white room reciting, "I'm not dirty, I'm not horny, I'm not lazy, I'm not evil, I'm not stupid, I'm not vulgar. . ." The room surrounding the man is intimate and small enough to see in its entirety from any one spot in it, but it feels expansive because of its whiteness (a metaphor that should not be lost on the viewer). There is ample space for the visitor to position themselves in several places around the room, including sitting comfortably on the seats of the surrounding "amphitheater."

Thinking of this space as an amphitheater is an intentional reminder that the man in the center is on display, not only in the artwork, but in the world, and being made to perform a fixed, stereotyped identity. The installation is intense, confrontational, and profoundly honest in its demonstration of the painful racism a Black man experiences daily. It is also cold, removed, and stripped down, an intellectual exercise for the viewer (Figure 5.2). In adjacent rooms at the retrospective, other mixed-media installations such as *Four Intruders Plus Alarm Systems* (1980) and *Art for the Art World Surface Pattern* (1976) present voices of how audiences may react (and perhaps have reacted) to viewing Piper's challenging pieces (e.g., whispering "I feel attacked by this piece, where I don't feel attacked by blacks at all" or "My housekeeper and I have a wonderful relationship").

Piper's work calls on visitors to be open to the artwork in the ways we discussed in Chapter 4, to contemplate the information they are receiving, to welcome or at least accept the discomfort it produces, to reckon with their own complicity, to consider the complexity of their responses to gaining this new (or deepened) perspective, and to consider how to refine their biases and prejudices. Doing this kind of reflection can be consciousness-altering, leading to what many might characterize as a TE.

Indeed, when TEs occur, the confusion, discomfort, and anxiety one feels in response to art are often accompanied by "self-transcendent emotions" like feeling moved, touched, or in awe, including having a sense of self-diminishment and smallness, and feeling of oneness and connection with others and the world (Mikalonytė et al., 2026). Other common emotional experiences include increased curiosity, gratitude, and compassion, and physiological states like having chills or feeling like crying (Pelowski, 2015; Pizarro et al., 2021; Pizzolante et al., 2024). People who report these feelings during museum visits also indicate higher self-

Figure 5.2 Adrian Piper, *What It's Like, What It Is #3*, 1991. Video installation. Video (color, sound), constructed wood environment, four monitors, mirrors, and lighting. Dimensions variable. Installation view from Dislocations, The Museum of Modern Art, New York, 1991–1992.

Photo credit: MaliOlatunji, courtesy of the Museum of Modern Art, NY. Collection of The Museum of Modern Art; acquired in part through the generosity of Lonti Ebers, Marie-Josée and Henry Kravis, Candace King Weir, Levy' Gorvy Gallery, and with support from The Modern Women's Fund.

awareness and suggest that the feelings fostered the subsequent epiphanies and insights they uncovered (Pelowski, 2015; Pizarro et al., 2021; Pizzolante et al., 2024). Most crucially for transformation, moments of insight represent an acute awareness of something new that the individual was previously unaware of, encourage one to then articulate what it is that they learned, and in doing so involve profound changes to one's self-identity that are enduring rather than momentary (Chappell, 2019; McDonald, 2008).

Randy's description of *A Chorus Line* aligns with this pattern: The insight moment was preceded by the tiny seeds that were planted prior, and an acute and sudden knowledge that came about in a singular "visceral moment" while watching the musical. As a result, he was changed. Similarly, in her piece "The Painting That Changed my Life," Kerry Folan writes about the challenges associated with her encounter with contemporary artist Amy Pleasant's painting *After the Death* (Folan, 2017). In her initial look at the painting, she was utterly confused, writing, "The effort was pointless, like staring at the empty boxes of a crossword puzzle I had no hope of solving . . . my article was going to be a disaster." But, after giving herself more time, she began to feel understanding emerge:

> That first whiff of insight is such a specific, powerful high. That moment when the confusion subsides and the observer floods with wonder, washed with a wave of understanding. It doesn't last long – in the next moment, intellect wrestles inspiration into coherence and logic takes over... For a few seconds at the beginning, there is just the pure joy of enlightenment.

Folan's TE can be described as her understanding something new about grief *and* acceptance of her own way of grieving following the death of her father from her engagement with Amy Pleasant's painting. She writes:

> I connected with the painting's insight... The painting insisted on the mundanity of death, and of grief. The stark truth that someone else's death will always be, by definition, anticlimactic – that there will always be an after to a death because the laws of time require that our own story continue while theirs fades into the past.

Theoretical models of the cognitive processes of reading fiction and literature also support this understanding of what it means for literature to be transformative. Reading literature or narrative fiction can promote transformation through several interrelated mechanisms, including by prompting self-reflection and expanding one's conception of possible selves (Djikic et al., 2009; Green & Appel, 2024; Kuiken et al., 2004).

Unlike much of our everyday reading for information (i.e., news stories, email), narrative fiction often provides an opportunity to grapple with complex characters, ambiguity, and emotional dynamics; to understand an event or story from different perspectives; or to experience the defamiliarizing of central story elements. Martha Nussbaum argues that fiction, when well written, can *teach* us how to see the world in a rich, nuanced, and complex way, including the experiences of others (Nussbaum, 1985). In the previous chapters, we have identified a set of cognitive skills whose development may represent the kind of learning she describes in her argument. What we focus on here is how narrative, and narrative fiction specifically, invite a kind of self-reflection that may lead to transformative experiences. Notice that fictional stories (whether or not they are told through books or literature "proper") are social in nature, and involve understanding other people's emotions, goals, and beliefs, as well as how people relate to one another. Relatedly, literature invites us to engage in self-referential thought, considering how we might act in the same scenarios presented, recognizing something in ourselves more acutely, or by having to switch periodically between adopting the positions of alternative selves. These processes seem to encourage both momentary increases in self-awareness and shifts in identity and self-concept.

In one study, participants who read a short story by Anton Chekhov reported greater shifts among multiple personality traits than those who read a story with similar content but lacking Chekhov's literary and stylistic features. The trait changes were especially pronounced in individuals who had the strongest emotional responses to the story (Djikic et al., 2009). Similarly, being transported into a literary text – "losing oneself" – is also (perhaps paradoxically) connected to enhanced self-awareness. This immersive experience, also called narrative transportation, allows individuals to momentarily set themselves aside and enter the narrative world. Yet, in doing so, they return to themselves with renewed self-awareness. This is a feeling people often describe about powerful art experiences: that they have to lose themselves to find themselves (Magon & Cupchik, 2023).

Emotional absorption in a literary work can open space for reflection and meaning-making, leading to increased self-awareness and self-discoveries that may have lasting changes on our identity (Shedlosky-Shoemaker et al., 2014). Absorption also expands people's notions of possible selves (Slater et al., 2014). Michael Slater and colleagues suggest that, while in many cases this expansion of the boundaries of self while reading is temporary, it *can* be personally and epistemically transformative. For instance, self-altering literary reading is especially likely to occur during life crises (e.g., Tangerås, 2018), which is consistent with our discussion above on the role of art therapies in identity (re)discovery. Additionally, when the fictional narrative holds personal significance – say, a favorite book an individual reads and rereads over the course of their life – the "extra voice" of the characters or author may become integrated into the self and persist over time as part of the person's internal dialogue and sense of self (Brokerhof et al., 2018). Empathy, aesthetic sensitivity, curiosity, interest, and openness also seem to strongly contribute to an individual's capacity and motivation to connect deeply with an artwork, and to experience TEs because of art engagement (Pizzolante et al., 2024).

Finally, the first-person accounts throughout this section resonate with our discussions in Chapter 3 of the value of awe. Insofar as the arts are a context in which we are likely to, and encouraged to, feel things like interest, curiosity, (productive) confusion, awe, and wonder, they are a context that may initiate a process of learning, growth, or change that ultimately leads to our holding different beliefs and values than those we had before. Because they are enjoyable, in the sense that they are positive emotional experiences, and intellectually engaging, in the sense that they encourage continued attention and development, they are especially well suited to triggering epistemic and personal change.

Aesthetic Selves and Community

An important way the arts contribute to identity formation is by fostering our connection to other people. We derive meaning in our lives through being connected to and in relationship with others, and the arts offer a powerful domain for deepening those connections. One way that people describe their life as being a good one, or an experience contributing in a positive way to their life, is to say that it is "meaningful." Philosophers have written a great deal about the meaning of life, and we will not survey that literature here, but we follow Susan Wolf (2010) in recognizing that meaningful lives have both a subjective and an objective component, and meaning arises from the connection between the two. The objective things we do and care about – marriages, children, careers, volunteering, travel, learning to play the guitar, baking pies, making pasta – play a critical role in the meaning of our lives. But, to actually contribute to *meaning* in our lives rather than being just something we do, we have to actually care about and be personally fulfilled by these activities, relationships, and projects, and we must also be successful in actually carrying them out.

Many of the things that we pursue and participate in as candidates for meaningful projects involve connections to others. Affinity or affiliation – understood not as mere membership in a group, but a kind of active association and connection with other people – is an important element in meaning and in our sense of self. For example, volunteering in your neighborhood every two years as a poll worker may contribute to living a meaningful life. The value of volunteering is objectively grounded in the importance of living in a community characterized by respect for self-determination. We can gain fulfillment by engaging in this project through its capacity to be about, for, and with other people. Nancy Sherman argues that we specifically derive value from such projects because they create a *shared* world. She contends that engaging in mutual pursuits, expanding and extending beyond the self to see oneself as being part of the broader community, is key to flourishing. There is a pleasure that one feels in mutual interaction, and this pleasure entails a sense of "common good." These goods are thus valuable not only because of the pleasure we gain from them (i.e., our fulfillment and satisfaction from engagement), but also in the shared journey or social connection they foster (Sherman, 1993).

With these preliminaries in place, we can see why the arts are an especially rich context for meaning and affiliation. As Dominic McIver Lopes explains:

> [a]esthetic engagements, from listening to music to pie baking . . . contribute to meaning. Genuinely feeling fulfilled comes from an agent's recognizing that they are making positive contributions to an endeavour that is bigger than them. Aesthetic projects fit the bill perfectly. To engage aesthetically is to participate in an aesthetics practice where there are standards of goodness independent of individual attitudes, where personal achievement supports the achievement of other participants in the practice, and where there is an opportunity to contribute to a group with a continuing history and tradition. (Lopes, 2018, p. 211)

Recognizing the arts as *social practices* (as we explain in the Introduction) allows us to see how they play this important role in human life. This is not to say that everyone has to have an arts practice in order to have a meaningful life. Instead, it suggests that when we look for what makes lives meaningful, we will likely encounter the arts in great numbers and in significant depth, because, by their nature, they are contexts for meaning. First, arts practices (both creation and appreciation) are complex: You can get better at them; getting better at them constitutes making something of value; and we subjectively care about them, are engrossed by them, and attached to them. Second, they are, at their core, shared. Not only are the practices and techniques learned, passed down, and developed interpersonally, but the works themselves are often in conversation with others and extensions of those conversations. In this way, third, they are tied to feeling part of "something bigger than yourself," namely, being in common pursuit with others (either locally, or over the span of many generations).

We suggest that this "doing things in common" contributes to our sense of fulfillment from the arts. As Erin Westgate and Shigehiro Oishi explain this "[e]ngagement in the arts, music, and literature may also spill over into social capital . . . through artistic activities that act as markers of shared identity (e.g., street art, folk music)" (Westgate & Oishi, 2022, p. 4). Louis Tay and colleagues (2018) refer to these as socialization mechanisms that foster flourishing. Writers bond in writing groups, painters and visual artists form cooperatives, and people come together to consume the books, artwork, and music they produce, leading to vibrant book clubs, lively art shows, and tight-knit music scenes that blend enjoyment of the arts with social bonding. Such sharing can intensify positive feelings (Boothby et al., 2014) and may itself serve as a powerful grounding for our sense of self.

It is not only through making together that the arts can connect us in meaningful ways. The PPE Portrait Project launched by Mary Beth Heffernan in 2014 was created with the aim to help mitigate the stress and anxiety felt by those being treated for Ebola. Because Ebola is highly contagious, healthcare providers must wear full protective equipment (PPE), covering their entire body, faces, and head, when treating patients. The PPE looks incredibly alien, and interacting with someone in full PPE is alienating to a patient, who is already experiencing a great deal of physical and emotional pain as a result of their disease. Heffernan photographed members of care teams and created a way for them to share their faces with their patients by affixing their pictures to their PPE. In doing so, she opened a path of social connection between patients and providers and provided a way for patients to feel less alienated by their providers.

The project took on new life in 2020 during the COVID-19 pandemic, when the entire world, not only care providers, shifted to a "masked" culture seemingly overnight. Heffernan's project expanded to a host of healthcare institutions within the US and Canada and received widespread recognition and attention for collaboration between medicine and the arts, especially with respect to identifying a role for artists' expertise in humanizing medicine (Figure 5.3).

Heffernan's work is informed by research on the psychological distress caused by source isolation, which refers to the removal or separation of a patient with an infectious disease from others, including healthcare workers. It is also informed by theories of human connection and community developed through her arts practice, which has engaged questions about photography, representation of the body, and vulnerability. As Heffernan describes the creation of the portraits:

> The portrait you wear for a vulnerable patient is always and only your own image, preferably made expressly for this purpose, offering the expression you wish the patient could see. It is a unique currency; it does not instantiate varying degrees of worth or a hierarchy, like ID badges. PPE Portraits, like faces, are of equal worth, of an equal but immeasurable value that one exchanges with another to affirm their mutual humanity. (Bryan-Wilson & Heffernan, 2020)

Importantly, the PPE Portrait Project is social practice art, or social sculpture. The work of art is not best understood as the photograph on the PPE itself, but instead, the experiences between the artist, the healthcare worker, and the patients that are created through the making and

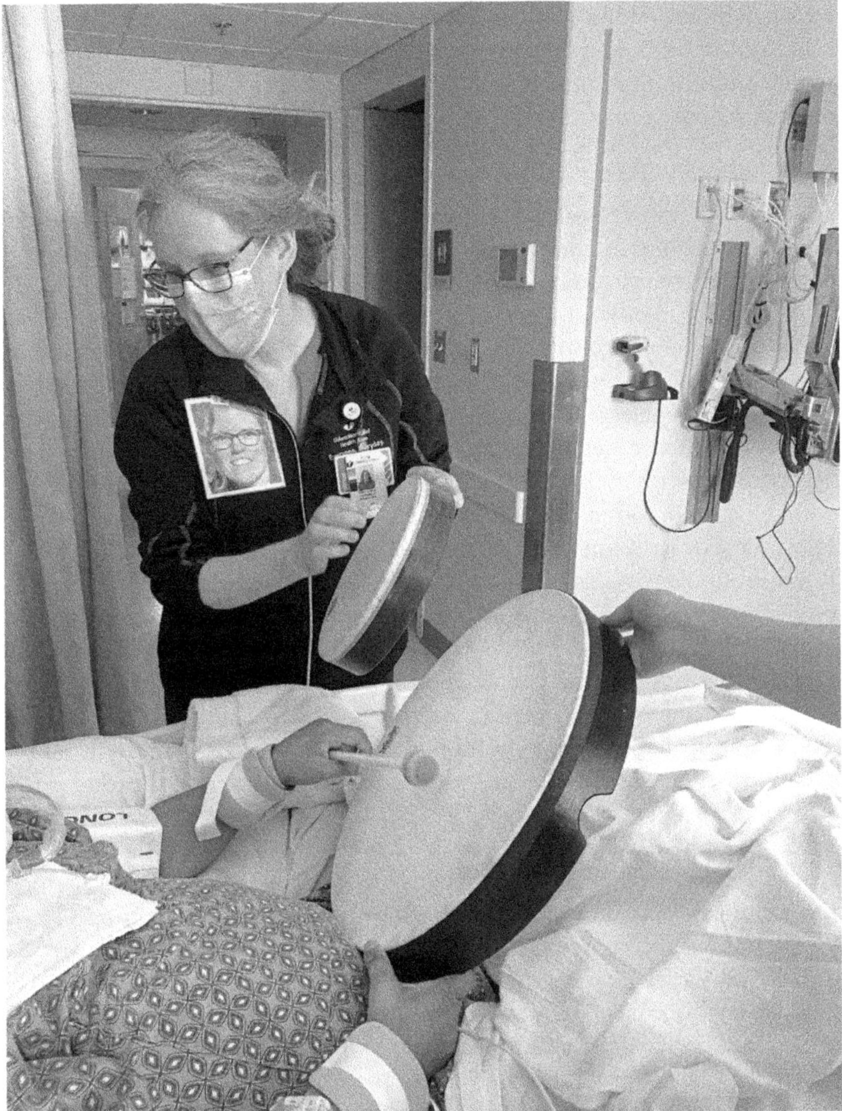

Figure 5.3 Mary Beth Heffernan (2020). PPE Portrait Project.
Courtesy of Mary Beth Heffernan.

wearing of the portrait. In fact, Heffernan describes it as a "theater for two" (Bryan-Wilson & Heffernan, 2020).

Moreover, affiliation or connection with other people may itself constitute a form of transformation of the kind described above in our discussion of TEs. Often, shifts in our moral attitudes and attachments to others stand out to us as especially important to who we are and how we view the world. Insofar as the arts are a context for deepening these associations and affiliations, they may also be a means for transforming our beliefs and attitudes in ways that we recognize as true revisions, expansions, or developments in who we are. Next, we discuss evidence showing how engaging in arts activities promotes social affiliation and prosociality – increased feelings of connectedness to others, as well as cooperating and helping each other – and community transformation.

A growing body of empirical research demonstrates that the arts enhance our connection to diverse groups of people, foster cooperation, encourage us to accept differing viewpoints and to reduce our use of stereotypes, and lead us to engage in helping behaviors. Children who sing and dance together in groups are more cooperative (rather than competitive) with each other, while playing subsequent games, than those who engage in other group activities, including art-making (Good & Russo, 2016; Kirschner & Tomasello, 2010). Children enrolled in structured group music classes report feeling closer to and more connected to one another (Rabinowitch et al., 2013), report having higher self-esteem (Costa-Giomi, 2004), are more socially inclusive (Welch et al., 2014), and are better at self-regulation tasks that involve self-control and inhibition, compared to groups of demographically similar children who do not experience structured early childhood music classes (Rabinowitch et al., 2013; Schellenberg et al., 2015; Winsler et al., 2011). Beyond early development, in a 2010 study, Peter Miksza showed that high school students who participated in group music-making in school were more concerned than their peers with what they called "social ethics," which included building friendships, helping others, and correcting social inequalities (Miksza, 2010).

One potential reason group music-making could have such affiliative benefits is that music-making inherently involves coordination, cooperation, and moving in synchrony with others in a group. Music has a specific property that researchers call "rhythmic entrainment," a process through which music's external rhythm changes our own "internal" rhythms, such as by making us move or clap to the beat, or by "capturing" or synchronizing our heart rate. Entrainment also leads to temporal and affective coordination across people. For example, moving synchronously with others increases our sense of connection to them. People who walk or dance in step with each other, clap to the same beat, or even simply tap a button at the same rate tend to report liking each other more, tend to cooperate better, and tend to help each other more in subsequent tasks (Wiltermuth & Heath, 2009).

Although music is not the only stimulus that promotes movement synchronization, it may be an especially strong stimulus for promoting social affiliation, cooperation, and empathy because of this natural tendency to bounce and move to music. When a toddler is bouncing synchronously with another person in the room to music, the toddler is more willing to help that person and their friends than if they were bouncing asynchronously (Cirelli et al., 2017). In this way, collective music-making (and dancing) is connected to social cognition, and this connection is developed in early childhood, likely playing a strong role in our identity formation and social bonds. Music psychologists argue that music's capacity to entrain our bodies' rhythms is an important mechanism for social bonding. It's a simple and effective way to connect to and coexist with people who may have radically different views from you and may be especially useful for promoting compassion in times of great conflict (Cross, 2014; Hikiji, 2005).

Relatedly, exposing children to literary stories about friendship between characters who are within and outside of their typical identity groups, or about characters from their own culture having positive interactions with characters from different cultures, improves children's attitudes toward stigmatized groups (e.g., disabled individuals; refugees; immigrants) by decreasing stereotypes (e.g., Cameron et al., 2006; Vezzali et al., 2012). In a series of studies with children, one group read a passage from *Harry Potter and the Chamber of Secrets* wherein Draco Malfoy, a schoolmate of Harry who is depicted as a negative character throughout the series, insults Hermione, one of Harry's best friends, by calling her "filthy little Mudblood." (The insult refers to her parents not being wizards.) The children also read Hermione's reaction (a feeling of humiliation that she feels despite being the most talented young witch in the school), and they read about the angry reactions of Hermione's friends. Following this reading, researchers held a discussion with the children about prejudice. In the control condition, children read passages from *Harry Potter* unrelated to prejudice (namely, a passage in which Harry buys his first magic wand, and one in which Harry plays a wizarding game called Quidditch, where they fly on brooms). Children who read and discussed prejudice, primarily those who identified more with Harry, showed improved attitudes toward immigrants. (Interestingly, identification with Voldemort, the evil antagonist in the series, was also independently associated with more negative out-group attitudes; Vezzali, Stathi, et al., 2015.)

In the same article, researchers reported on additional experiments with young adults. For teenagers, reading *Harry Potter* novels was similarly associated with improved attitudes toward a stigmatized group, primarily among individuals who identified with the main character. This was even true for undergraduates, who are clearly older than the main characters within the series. Both reading the books or watching the film adaptations was positively associated with increased self-reported perspective-taking skills, and with improved attitudes toward out-groups. This was especially true not for those who identified with the main young characters (as few did), but rather for those who identified less with Voldemort, the adult antagonist. Since this series of studies, a wider research program has shown that prejudice and intergroup anxiety can be mitigated and reduced by both direct and indirect vicarious contact (Di Bernardo et al., 2017; Vezzali, Hewstone, et al., 2015). In fact, indirect contact with others, through the arts (whether that be via music, literary texts, or visual art), seems to be as effective as direct positive, social interaction with others. How long these effects last is still a subject of debate and continued research is needed (Pelowski et al., 2024).

Seeing live theater similarly impacts people's understanding and acceptance of others. Steve Rathje and colleagues (2021) conducted a large-scale study in collaboration with multiple theater companies, investigating people's sociopolitical attitudes, beliefs, and actions before and after seeing a play. Specific sociopolitical issues they examined ranged from participants' views on same-sex couples raising children, to their views on racial discrimination, income inequality, welfare, corporate regulations, wealth redistribution, and affirmative action. The specific set of views the researchers were interested in varied depending on the play participants attended. The study investigated participants' emotional connection to other people (e.g., "I have tender, concerned feelings for people who are less fortunate than me"), their connection to people like the ones who were being depicted in the specific play (e.g., "I have tender, concerned feelings for factory workers in Detroit."), their altruistic charity behaviors (i.e., both interest in charity and actual donations they were asked for), and how immersed they were in the play. The study showed that attending plays helped increase people's understanding and acceptance of groups depicted in them. Moreover, the plays led to changes in people's sociopolitical attitudes, such that they were more open to the complicated views highlighted in the play. People also donated more money to charities – both related and unrelated to the show's context – after seeing the play. These results are consistent with prior research done with smaller samples in which individuals who saw a play about the Holocaust had greater care for individuals who are suffering than a control sample (Harvey & Miles, 2009). Similarly, audience members reported more positive attitudes about hunting after watching a musical about hunting (Heide et al., 2012).

Rathje and colleagues (2021) also found that people's attitudes were most likely to change if the viewers' attitudes were more dissimilar to those expressed by the play. More conservative people who saw the Pulitzer Prize-winning play *Sweat*, which explores the lives of factory workers in the town of Reading, Pennsylvania, were especially likely to report changes after the show. This is likely because individuals who are engaging with views already very different from their own have more room for change, especially on these metrics.

Other research suggests that both making art and appreciating art relate to increased helping behaviors, including offering to help strangers, more volunteering, and more contributing to social organizations and charities (Leroux & Bernadska, 2014; Polzella & Forbis, 2014; Van de Vyver & Abrams, 2018). This has been called the "virtuous circle" of arts engagement and prosocial behavior, wherein art engagement leads to more prosocial behavior (i.e., more volunteering and more giving), even sometimes multiple years later. This prosocial behavior then feeds back into increased engagement with the arts (Kou et al., 2020; Van de Vyver & Abrams, 2018). Interestingly, the correlations with prosocial behaviors have been shown to be stronger for art appreciation activities (i.e., visual art viewing, music listening, performing arts attendance, and reading literature) than for art-making activities (i.e., writing, performing arts, and visual arts; Kou et al., 2020) .

Finally, returning to our discussion of awe, recall that it is an inherently relational emotion that fosters feelings of collective oneness and of self-diminishment, and fosters bonding with others. Awe can influence people's attitudes and behaviors, specifically, increasing their expression of devotion and loyalty to leaders and to a (relevant) collective, as well as increasing prosocial behavior. In Paul Piff and colleagues' (2015) paper, awe experiences induced in a number of ways across several experiments were associated with making more socially oriented decisions, acting more generously, reporting more prosocial values, and decreased feelings of individual entitlement. In one part of the study, participants read scenarios like "You've waited in line for 10 minutes to buy a coffee and muffin at Starbucks. When you're a couple of blocks away, you realize that the clerk gave you change for $20 rather than for the $10 you gave him. You savor your coffee, muffin, and free $10." They then rated how likely they would be to engage in the described behavior (i.e., not returning the excess $10). People who experienced awe chose to behave in a way consistent with accepted moral norms more than those who were induced to feel other pleasant emotions like pride. Relatedly, a study by Eftychia Stamkou and colleagues (2023) showed that children who watched awe-inspiring videos acted in more prosocial ways (i.e., they donated more of their reward from participation in the study) and were more generous with their time than children who watched either joy-inspiring or emotionally neutral videos. Together, these findings show that awe functions partly to bond individuals into a social collective.

Art-connected transformation does not only happen within individuals, but often and perhaps even more powerfully, within or for communities. The cases here are far too numerous to survey in their entirety. We focus instead on community participatory arts practices and how they help us to envision and create more just communities. Additionally, we describe the emerging role of arts practices in peacebuilding as examples of transformation that can occur within communities. In both cases, such artistic practices are part of the larger ecosystem of socially engaged art practices and of community-building more broadly (Lombardo & Novak, 2024).

Community arts, sometimes referred to as participatory arts, participatory community arts, or community arts and cultural development (CACD), are characterized by dialogue and co-creation of artworks, wherein the artist works deeply and in collaboration with community members. Diverse arts modalities are used as spaces for a variety of community members to work together, to express their individual and collective identities, and in doing so to promote the broader wellbeing of the community. They are especially powerful for communities that feel some element of social, political, and economic exclusion and oppression (Sonn & Baker, 2016). Indeed, they are often practiced *in response* to oppression, as a means for giving voice to marginalized peoples.

Practitioners often take social change or community transformation to be a primary goal and outcome of this kind of arts practice. Social and community change is brought about and exemplified in the many opportunities for connection that participatory arts afford: Creating spaces for being together, facilitating formal and informal discussions, and active collaborative participation are all important aspects of a participatory arts practice that foster identity development of individuals that are simultaneously potentially transformative for the communities of which they are part. Yael Harlap highlights and formalizes seven specific goals of social change that many arts organizations and artists engaging in community arts practices aim at in their efforts to achieve both individual empowerment and broader community transformation (Harlap, 2006, p. 255). These include:

1. working toward equity and justice;
2. raising consciousness and awareness;
3. fostering individual empowerment and participation;
4. bringing people together and building relationships among individuals and groups;
5. creating dialogue;
6. giving voice and telling stories;
7. creating new visions and opening new imaginations for what the world could be.

Researchers have identified four large-scale processes that participants in these kinds of practices experience. The first is the process of *connecting*. Through community arts, participants can "forge connections with teaching artists, their own pasts, and emotions, as well as with other participants as they develop and expand their talents and techniques." The second is the process of *expressing*. Arts-based workshops demonstrate the value of participants' own experiences and voices and provide a welcoming and safe environment to express those voices. The third is the process of *learning*. Community arts "emphasize experiential learning to facilitate the participants' attempts to understand a variety of issues." The fourth is the process of *discovering*. The process of making art together "provides an opportunity for personal inquiry and reflection and, thus, creates the potential for increased self-awareness" (Morris, 2019).

Theorists cite different mechanisms to explain why and how the arts play this important role in individual and community transformation. Those adopting a liberation psychology lens suggest that community arts practices are a context for "conscientisation" or critical consciousness. They argue that as tools for dialogue and active engagement, community arts practices facilitate individuals' understanding of the ways in which larger processes of oppression or dehumanization operate in their lives and in their communities. As such, the practice can reveal new possibilities for action and identification. It can also create new self-understanding, enhancing one's self-esteem and self-confidence. It may also be that these individual and collective changes come about through community art's capacity to create opportunity for all participants to be equal stakeholders in a jointly held vision that aims at that change (Clennon et al., 2016).

Building on these insights and successes, in recent years, practitioners and theorists have called on those organizing efforts aimed at transitional or restorative justice to include participatory arts as explicit elements of the peace-building process (Fairey, 2018). These arts practices are seen as spaces in which communities can come together to articulate their different points of view, to hear and understand those experiences, and to collectively imagine potential futures. They argue that it is integral to the nature of the arts that we find in them a mechanism for not only discovering ourselves but articulating and voicing ourselves to others. The arts allow us to see and hear other people, especially about things that are hard to find the words to explain, or that are emotionally difficult and charged. The arts invite imagination and collective deliberation in a way that few other human practices do, hence positioning them to productively and meaningfully move forward in a way that can inform who we are as individuals and as communities. As Sherin Shefik describes it, "participatory art is a context-specific, collaborative and bottom-up process that can contribute to individualized and collective healing, make the invisible visible, extend social responsibility, restore collective memory, repair the social fabric, reclaim truths and foster collective change" (Shefik, 2018, p. 314).

One powerful example of an individual and community transformative arts practice is Tanisha Hill-Jarrett's "Radical Imagination." Hill-Jarrett's research is centered on understanding how psychosocial stressors and structural racism and sexism impact Black women's cognitive aging. She has shown that the risks of Alzheimer's disease and related dementias are highest for older Black women, and that this could be explained by psychosocial stressors, including economic instabilities, accelerating health declines. Her commitment to making wellness and brain health accessible to communities in need is demonstrated in her scientific and clinical practice, and perhaps most directly in her community-facing work.

Hill-Jarrett developed "Radical Imagination" to create a culturally relevant community-participatory creative arts programming for older Black women in the San Francisco Bay Area. Hill-Jarrett invites Black women to a ten-week program through which they learn about brain and mental health, and participate in art-making, co-creation, storytelling, and photography. According to Hill-Jarrett and colleagues, the work is "grounded in principles of Afrofuturism and radical healing . . . [to allow] participants [to explore] past narratives of Black women and [create] a collective vision for a future centering Black women's needs" (Hill-Jarrett, 2025). Afrofuturism is core to this work, which refers to an

> epistemology and form of artistic expression that explores the African diaspora experience through alternate realities and futures using imagination,

> technology, and mysticism ... [and] has been used by Black American artists, activists, scholars and others as a framework to reclaim and unveil lost histories ... and reimagine the future through a lens of hope where Blackness is integral and all Black people are safe. (Hill-Jarrett, 2023, p. 3)

The program thus centers the creation of counter-narratives, inviting participants to construct alternative narratives of themselves to those imposed by the dominant cultural surround, and to work through those narratives through artistic co-creation and dialogue.

One artistic outcome of the program was a photoshoot, interview series, and exhibition, designed by Hill-Jarrett and photographed by Austin James. The aim of the exhibit and an example photograph (Figure 5.4) are described as follows:

> Thirteen aging Black women considered "what it means to manipulate time in ways that defy Western frameworks of time, labor, and capital ... [sharing] stories of resistance and counternarratives that highlight ways they have reclaimed time to age well. Through *remembering* (and intuitively reconnecting with their true history), *reclaiming* (time and the Black woman image), and *reimagining* (Black women narratives + a socially transformed future rooted in equity), this series places Black women as

Figure 5.4 "Dorothy," by Austin James (2023). Photograph and interview series. *Other Side of Time* project.
Courtesy of Austin James.

> the central story writers of their existence and the future. The women consider what it truly means for Black women to defy the social construction of time and exist on "the other side" – in an alternate space that promotes Black women's self-determination, health, and joy. (*The Other Side of Time*, 2023)

Participants report increased feelings of hopefulness about their ability to shape the future and interest in future investment in similar practices, and they felt strongly that they learned about themselves, others, and their communities on a range of dimensions. An especially powerful and important consequence of this work is its fluid connection to health and wellbeing. Jarrett-Hill writes that invoking the Black radical imagination has a host of positive brain health effects, especially for this demographic, who are at an increased risk of neurodegeneration partly due to social identity–related determinants of health, which are addressed through the community-building and identity-strengthening aspects of the work.

Summary

In the arts, we find, express, or explore who we are. In another vein, the arts reflect our sensibilities. They reflect what we like and care about, and how what we like and care about has shaped who we are as individuals. We value our attachments to cultural objects and participation in communities of practice that create them. We locate ourselves with respect to them and rely on what we listen to, what we like to read, the foods we eat, etc., to ground and organize who we are. Although it would be going too far to claim that the arts *uniquely* play this role in our lives, as we have argued, they are exceptionally well-suited to this kind of work.

Moreover, the close connection between the arts and emotion allows creative expression and appreciation to be a vehicle for processing complex emotions, especially those that might destabilize our sense of who we are, or that arise as we navigate difficult questions about identity. The arts, in many guises, are a vehicle for expressing ideas and experiences beyond words, allowing people to have a voice when they otherwise might not. The recognition of others' perspectives is foundational to what it means to appreciate art. As such, the arts are a context for enhancing self-respect and self-esteem, not only by enabling one to "put oneself out there," but also by enabling one to do so in a way that is recognized by others. Finally, the creation of artworks requires processes of decision-making that enhance people's sense of their own agency and autonomy, and confidence in their ability to contribute things of value to the community.

We have suggested that meaning and fulfillment are central to developing and maintaining a sense of self, and that the arts – as inherently social practices – are an especially rich context for this development. Artistic engagement necessarily involves a kind of shared or common pursuit through which individuals can find, express, and locate themselves. As we saw in Hill-Jarrett's work, this connection between the arts and wellbeing also extends to mental and physical health itself. In Chapter 6, we take up the question of the relationship between the arts and wellbeing more fully.

CHAPTER 6

Wellbeing, Flourishing, and the Arts

Starting Point

We spend a significant amount of time engaging in creative activities such as singing, dancing, performing, writing, painting, or sculpting, and in appreciating art through reading, looking at paintings or sculptures, listening to music, or watching plays and dance performances. We also devote significant money to cultural and creative activities: In 2021, museums added $9.4 billion to the United States economy, while performing arts companies and presenters added $30.4 billion, and publishing added $127.3 billion (*The U.S. Arts and Cultural Production Satellite Account (1998–2021)*, n.d.). Throughout our discussion, we have indirectly argued that this investment of time, money, and attention is "worth it" for a number of reasons. Engagement with the arts helps us cultivate a host of critically important cognitive and socioemotional skills. Moreover, the arts contribute to how we understand who we are, both as individuals and as communities. People's motivations for engaging with the arts surely vary based on their needs, desires, and values (Falk & Dierking, 2013), and many cite the social and epistemic benefits we have discussed in depth thus far. However, we have not *yet* directly addressed what is perhaps the most intuitive and universal answer to the question of why the arts matter: Art brings us joy, happiness, or wellbeing.

Consider the craft of "yarn bombing," also sometimes referred to as "guerilla knitting." Perhaps you have stumbled across a tree, a telephone pole, a bench, or a bicycle rack that is unexpectedly "dressed up" in colorful, vibrant yarn. Yarn bombing is a creative and whimsical practice thought to have emerged in 2005 when Magda Sayag, a Texan shop-owner, made a yarn cozy for her shop's door handle in an effort to add color and joy to her urban landscape. This practice became increasingly popularized on social media. While some yarn bombers see themselves as "craftivists," merging "their craft and activist interests to fight for a better

Figure 6.1 Photographed by Bill Longstaff in Tomkins Park, Beltline (Connaught), Calgary. He writes: “These trees were yarn-bombed by Ujamaa Grandmas, a group that raises money and awareness for the Grandmothers to Grandmothers Campaign of the Stephen Lewis Foundation which helps support grandmothers and children in Sub-Saharan Africa suffering from the effects of the HIV/AIDS pandemic.”

world, often by knitting or crocheting political statements as a form of protest,” most people who yarn bomb and create the local, guerilla installations do so just for fun, as way to bring unexpected delight to others in their community and as a way to beautify their community (Figure 6.1; Mann, 2015).

Yarn bombing is *fun*, and we miss something important about the nature of the arts and why they matter if we do not adequately recognize that they are sources of pleasure, play, and positive feeling. In this chapter, we aim to show that the arts contribute to living a flourishing life not only by making us think deeply, honing our cognitive skills, and making our lives more interesting and richer with experiences, but also by making our lives happier and healthier. As is our practice throughout the book, we begin by examining the question of what it could mean to "live a good life," before turning to various strands of evidence showing the arts as expansive sources for wellbeing in our lives.

Wellbeing

Traditionally, theories of wellbeing are divided into two camps: subjective and objective (Lin, 2022a, 2022b; Tiberius, 2006). According to subjective theories, an individual's wellbeing is a matter of the quality or nature of the *experiences* and other relevant mental states of the individual whose life it is. Subjective theories are further divided according to what kinds of mental states are taken to be at the core of wellbeing, and how they are conceived to be related to wellbeing. Some subjective theories are *experiential*, holding that the quality of the experiences we have forms the basic building blocks of wellbeing. For example, hedonists claim that the mental states relevant to wellbeing are pleasure and displeasure; mental states like anxiety, fear, sadness, and physical pain make your life worse because they are experiences of displeasure. What makes your life go well, according to this view, is having a high proportion of experiences of pleasure to experiences of displeasure. Another experiential theory is the psychological richness account recently proposed by Lorraine Besser and Shigehiro Oishi (2020). According to their view, what is relevant to your wellbeing is not just the amount or intensity of the experiences of pleasure and displeasure that you have. Instead, a good life is one in which these experiences are varied, novel, or otherwise "rich;" wellbeing consists in the variety and diversity of experiences you have, not just in their affective character. What is characteristic of the subjective-experiential camp, on either approach, is that wellbeing is about what life is like from the inside, for the person living it.

A different kind of subjective theory is *evaluative*. Theories of this kind hold that an individual's wellbeing is determined not by the experiences themselves, as experiential theories hold, but instead by a normative judgment about one's experiences. The most robust set of theories in the subjective-evaluative camp is desire-satisfaction accounts, according to which wellbeing is a matter of whether and to what extent one's desires are fulfilled. Rational choice theory and neoclassical economic theory tend to favor desire-satisfaction accounts of wellbeing. Alternatively, life-satisfaction accounts, rather than focusing specifically on desires or preferences being met, view wellbeing as consisting in a broader endorsement or judgment that one's life is going well overall. The value-fulfillment account is yet another kind of evaluative theory of wellbeing, one which contends that what matters to wellbeing is whether you are living according to your own values, achieving the goals that you care about (Tiberius, 2018).

In contrast to subjective theories, *objective* theories of wellbeing, also referred to as *eudaimonic* theories, claim that there are things beyond an individual's own internal states that contribute to how well their life is going. The term *eudaimonia* can be found in Aristotle's *Nicomachean Ethics* and is often translated as "flourishing." These theories suggest that flourishing depends on a set of objective features: They are *not* about how the individual who has them feels, or what the individual thinks about them, but instead, about the kind of being that one is (e.g., human, squirrel, oak tree) and whether and to what extent the relevant features are present or part of one's existence. For instance, flourishing for a tree might entail features like efficiently undergoing photosynthesis. Whereas, for a human, flourishing might include things like one's ability to act autonomously, to have meaningful relationships, to learn, to contribute to one's community, or to have a purpose in life. These are the kinds of things that can be present or absent in one's life, regardless of what experiences one has or what judgments one makes about them (Figure 6.2).

We have not included health on the above list of features potentially contributing to objective wellbeing. The relationship between health and wellbeing depends on the definition of health itself. For example, the constitution of the World Health Organization (WHO) begins by defining health *as* wellbeing. They write: "Health is a state of complete physical, mental and social well-being and not merely the absence of disease or infirmity" (*Constitution of the World Health Organization*, n.d.). The WHO definition is a positive definition, articulating what health is the *presence* of (namely, wellbeing), rather than what it is the *absence* of (namely, disease). (See Larsen, 2022, for discussion.) Alternatively, one could choose to understand health as a subjective state (i.e., as the *feeling* of being healthy), or as a separable component of objective wellbeing (i.e., as one of the things that contributes to wellbeing).

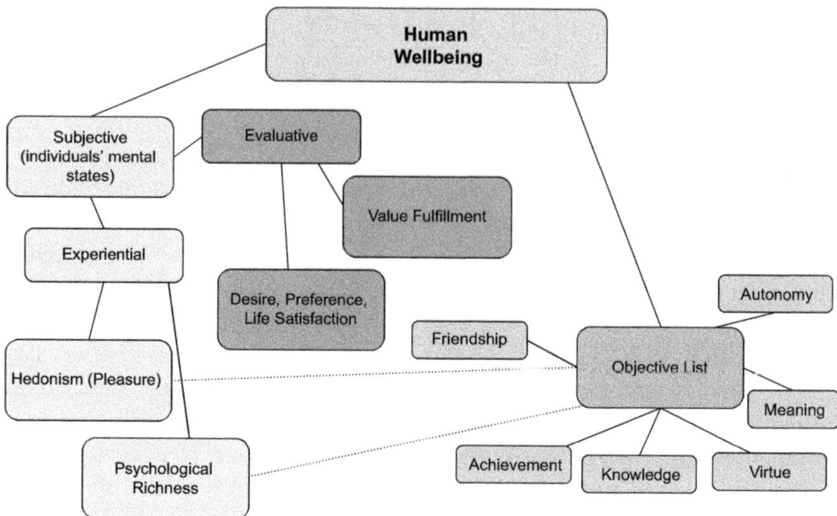

Figure 6.2 Theories of wellbeing.

As indicated above, our goal is not to endorse a particular view of wellbeing or the relationship between wellbeing and health. To understand the value of the arts and the role they play in living a good human life, it is more productive to recognize that each theory of wellbeing highlights discrete dimensions according to which we (rightly) judge that our lives are going well or poorly. Instead of engaging with the debate about what it *really* means to be happy (or healthy), we will follow our usual practice of being pluralistic and recognizing that each of these theories captures something that we care about. We care about what our lives *feel* like. We care about whether we can achieve what we set out to do and whether we are able to live according to our values and deeply held principles. We care whether our lives are rich and interesting and rewarding. We care about whether we are psychologically, socially, and physically healthy. And, we care whether our lives are characterized by features like having knowledge, friendships, autonomy, and meaning. All these ideas contribute at one time or another to our motivations for engaging with the arts.

There are good reasons for thinking that the arts can contribute to living well across all of these different dimensions, and the connection between arts engagement and wellbeing – whether we mean subjective, objective, or both – is a focus of many recent theoretical papers, books, empirical investigations, and clinical interventions (e.g., Fancourt & Finn, 2019; Tay & Pawelski, 2022). As Erin Westgate and Shigehiro Oishi (2022) argue, we should expect direct affective benefits from art appreciation and creation. We should also expect more long-term effects, as a result of fostering skills and abilities that contribute to how we understand ourselves and what we care about. There are also indirect benefits of engaging in social activities that promote connection to the broader community, and that we enjoy participating in. In what follows, we begin by focusing on subjective wellbeing (SWB) and the evidence suggesting engagement with the arts contributes to it. We do not here distinguish between experiential and evaluative accounts, as a great deal of the empirical literature uses measures that are relevant to both, including a number of physiological measures that people tend to associate with the concept of health rather than that of wellbeing. We then turn our attention to recent work on the relationship between the arts and health, before returning to how our arguments throughout bear on the question of the relationship between arts engagement and objective wellbeing.

The Arts and Subjective Wellbeing

To investigate SWB, researchers often use qualitative interview approaches, survey questions, and physiological measurements. Participants might be asked to reflect on their momentary experiences and to indicate the range of emotional experiences they are having while engaging with art, especially how happy, relaxed, or satisfied they are, as indicators of wellbeing. Those momentary measurements can be complemented with physiological measurements, such as cortisol or blood pressure. Participants may also be asked more longitudinal questions about their overall life satisfaction or their overall physical and psychological health.

Researchers have marshaled a wide variety of evidence related to how art appreciation might foster SWB. People participating in arts activities, such as reading, listening to music, theatergoing, or visiting museums, tend to report greater overall happiness and life satisfaction than people who do not engage in these activities (Blessi et al., 2014; Brajša-Žganec et al., 2011; Wang & Wong, 2014). What specific type of engagement is needed, and how much of it is needed, to achieve these outcomes is not quite clear. While we may assume that more arts participation is better for overall wellbeing than less participation, even somewhat infrequent participation seems to be associated with higher life satisfaction (e.g., Wheatley &

Bickerton, 2017). Moreover, variety with respect to arts experience may also matter (Westgate & Oishi, 2022). More work is required to disentangle the *quality* of one's engagement from the *quantity* of engagement. If you visit a museum once a year, but do so in a way that is engaged, reflective, and thoughtful, or if you read one really good book a year, it may be just as impactful on your wellbeing as going to museums regularly.

Furthermore, as we have seen in previous chapters, one issue with interpreting the results of these studies is that many of their methodologies are correlational or cross-sectional in nature, making it difficult to distinguish between various alternative explanations of the results: whether it is the arts participation that led to positive changes in wellbeing, whether happiness leads people to participate in more arts activities, or the role of other factors such as physical or financial accessibility. Longitudinal research and experimental research, in which researchers randomly assign individuals to engage or not engage with art, can more robustly demonstrate causality. Such longitudinal work similarly shows that participating in cultural and aesthetic activities is linked to positive or higher SWB, pointing toward a causal link between art engagement and SWB (Węziak-Białowolska & Białowolski, 2016). Moreover, promising experimental findings seem to demonstrate that art activities, like visiting art museums and cultural centers, lead to various specific wellbeing improvements. For example, an experience-sampling study from the United Kingdom in which participants tracked their momentary happiness at random points in time showed that live performances (e.g., theater, dance, concerts) and museum and library visits were rated as among the happiest activities that people engaged in throughout their week, coming in second to intimacy/sexual activity (Bryson & MacKerron, 2017). These cultural arts activities ranked higher than being out in nature (e.g., birdwatching, walking/hiking) and other types of leisure that we engage in, such as sports or exercise. This is consistent with previous research, which suggests that people choose to visit museums and to engage in nature-based activities like walking in a park specifically for improving their wellbeing and restoring their capacity for engaging in everyday life (Scopelliti & Giuliani, 2006). Additionally, art museum visits affect physiological markers of wellbeing including lowering cortisol, reducing self-reported stress, and reducing blood pressure (Clow & Fredhoi, 2006; D'Cunha et al., 2019; Grossi et al., 2019; Mastandrea et al., 2019).

Moreover, when researchers interview museum visitors after they have completed their visits, many tend to describe their experiences in terms of elements of experiential SWB (e.g., Packer, 2008; Sherman et al., 2025).

Visitors emphasize the restorative nature of museums, including feeling unhurried, peaceful, relaxed, invigorated, thoughtful, and rejuvenated as a result of their visit. They also suggest feeling self-reflective, more attentive to the natural world around them, and inspired to create art and to improve the world in some way. These positive states contribute to what visitors reflect on as a renewed capacity to deal with anxiety and the challenges of everyday life in more positive ways. Visitors also connect these experiential SWB states to developments that we may associate more with either evaluative SWB or even objective wellbeing, such as experiencing personal growth, an increased sense of purpose in life, positive social relations, and self-acceptance. Interestingly, research suggests increases in SWB-related measures are especially strong for people who report having a deepened understanding of the artwork and the artists' intentions. When people do not understand the art or its meaning, they become more withdrawn, confused, bored, and restless (Sherman et al., 2025).

Beyond visual art, there is extensive research supporting the connection between listening to music and SWB. Music is perhaps an even more ubiquitous art form in our everyday lives than the visual arts, as people listen to music while driving, while walking, while exercising, while cooking, and even while showering. People most commonly report listening to music because it influences their emotions and mood in some positive way (Rickard, 2012). Adolescents listen to music for multiple hours a day, and describe it as the indoor leisure activity they engage with most and most prefer (e.g., North et al., 2004). Music seems to enhance SWB, especially when people are purposeful and frequently engaged with it, in contrast to passively listening or listening to music they do not freely choose (e.g., North et al., 2004). Both adolescents and adults often use music as an everyday emotion regulation strategy (Saarikallio & Erkkilä, 2007), particularly by choosing music that is aligned with the emotions currently felt, or with the emotions that they want to feel (Thoma et al., 2012). Outside of everyday listening, music is also used in work or educational contexts to promote collaboration and SWB (Rickard, 2012) and in medical contexts as a way to promote calm, decrease stress, and manage pain (McCaffrey et al., 2020).

What remains to be understood are the mechanisms that explain these effects. Further research is required to establish *how* arts experiences foster feelings of happiness, restoration, calm, and increased satisfaction with life; how and why they reduce stress; and why they are effective emotion regulation tools, including the specific circumstances under which these effects are most likely to emerge. The answers here will be complex. We suggest that any explanation will concern the specific mental states evoked through arts engagement. Below, we focus on "flow" states as an example of how this may be investigated.

The term "flow" was coined and described by Mihaly Csikszentmihalyi (1982) and can be likened to being "in the zone." A flow state occurs when people become fully immersed and present in what they are doing, directing all their attention to the task at hand. People experiencing flow states tend to lose their sense of time while concentrating on the task, and often retrospectively report some kind of time distortion, such as feeling that time had slowed down or that it had sped up. Their concentration also means feeling less self-conscious, feeling more confident in their ability to tackle the task, and feeling more generally energized and capable. Csikszentmihalyi suggests that flow states are most likely to be experienced when the activity is sufficiently challenging, but not overly so. A task too challenging means we may not have the capability to complete it, whereas a task too simple may not be interesting enough to warrant immersive engagement.

A defining characteristic of flow is that it is rewarding and positive, even an "optimal experience." When people talk about being in a flow state, they describe the activity as intrinsically motivating and as worth doing for its own sake. They find the task deeply enjoyable and feel encouraged to press on with the task at hand. Physiological evidence confirms that evidence of flow experience can also be found in the body. In a 2010 study on expert pianists, researchers found that increased states of flow were associated with physiological markers of enjoyment and reward, including decreased heart rate, deeper breathing, and increased activation of muscles associated with smiling (de Manzano et al., 2010). This reward signal associated with flow states may contribute to promoting increased practice and thus to generating higher quality creative products. Moreover, having more frequent flow experiences is associated with increased perceived quality of life (Csikszentmihalyi, 1996). There is extensive evidence that flow states are related to positive affect, and experiencing flow seems to also impact wellbeing beyond the immediate effects of a given flow experience. For instance, individuals may seek out flow experiences as a self-regulation or coping mechanism to reduce their anxiety overall, or to reduce creativity-related performance anxiety more specifically (Collins et al., 2009; Moral-Bofill et al., 2022). Although people can experience flow across several domains (e.g., sports, chess playing), the arts may be an especially common way to induce flow states; both art creation and art appreciation may induce elements of flow states as described above.

The Arts and Health and Medicine

In 2019, WHO's Health Evidence Network published a landmark review of more than 900 research studies examining the effects of art engagement on a variety of health benefits (Fancourt & Finn, 2019). The review included experimental studies examining whether and how a broad range of arts interventions might affect clinical populations, as well as more correlational studies examining population-level associations between arts engagement and reduced incidence of ill-health. Daisy Fancourt and Saoirse Finn found that art engagement was related to wide-ranging health benefits including promoting social determinants of health (such as reduced loneliness, increased connectedness, improved quality of life), acting as a buffer against age-related cognitive decline and against mental and physical illness, and fostering the management and treatment of a variety of serious mental illnesses and neurodegenerative diseases such as Parkinson's, dementia, Alzheimer's, schizophrenia, chronic pain, anxiety, and depression.

This report spurred a revolution of sorts. Previously, the notion that the arts can contribute to healthcare was known but under-examined, under-specified, and unfortunately, often treated nonseriously by clinicians (Fleming & Collins, 2024). With the more recent support of the WHO and funding agencies like the US's National Institute of Health, The Sound Health Network, and The National Endowment of the Arts, physicians, scientists, therapists, artists, educators, philosophers, and policy experts have begun to more fully combine their efforts to more systematically and collaboratively consider whether and how the arts can support more holistic patient care. As a result, the last decade has seen a meaningful uptick in research studies in this area. Although we cannot exhaustively survey *all* the work done in the area around the arts and health (as that could constitute its own book!), we describe some of what we believe are the most exciting ways in which the arts have been incorporated into therapeutic and medical contexts to help people live healthier, fuller lives.

Anxiety and Depression

Anxiety is one of the most pressing mental health concerns across the world, with about 30 percent of the global population experiencing an anxiety disorder at some point in their lives (Kessler et al., 2005). Anxiety is often comorbid with a variety of other health conditions and may become clinically relevant for individuals suffering from a range of traumas, especially for vulnerable populations such as children. Individuals who have anxiety disorders report lower quality of life than those who do not, including lowered feelings of control and self-efficacy, decreased social contact and support, and lower SWB (Cramer et al., 2005). Moreover, individuals with anxiety disorders have difficulty with emotion regulation. In some cases, this means experiencing more intense emotions, fear and anticipation for specific emotions, trouble understanding their emotional responses, or inadequate emotional responses (A. Abbing et al., 2019).

The most traditional approaches to treating anxiety are cognitive behavioral therapy (CBT) and pharmacological interventions. However, art therapy is also an increasingly common, potentially effective complementary approach, particularly because talking-based therapies like CBT can sometimes increase anxiety and the reliving of trauma. In contrast, art therapy can allow patients to distance themselves from the anxiety, and "to deviate from 'the thinking-mode' into a 'feeling-mode' . . . to support the individual to obtain 'profound connection to embodied experiences' . . . to become aware of the anxiety feelings and responses in the body and learn to influence (downregulate) these feelings, by practicing and experiencing" (A. Abbing et al., 2019, p. 3). Art therapy may also be effective in fostering improved emotion regulation skills. As we described in previous chapters, the arts are an important tool for fostering and promoting emotional intelligence in healthy individuals. Artistic exercises, such as expressive writing or drawing, employed in a clinical setting can similarly foster self-insight, offer novel emotion regulation strategies, and decrease emotional distress (Pennebaker, 1997).

There is good reason to think that art therapy, even when done in a relatively passive way, can reduce anxiety in nonclinical populations. As we have already discussed, art engagement can be relaxing and fosters a host of positive emotions. Museum visits can lower cortisol, a stress hormone, and can foster feelings of relaxation (Mastandrea et al., 2019). Additionally, creative activities done for therapeutic purposes (or at least not done for the sake of the product) are often stress- and anxiety-reducing. Undergraduates' pre-exam anxiety can be managed and reduced via art-making, and prisoners' prerelease anxiety can be mitigated with arts interventions (Jakobsson Støre & Jakobsson, 2022; Walsh et al., 2005; Yu et al., 2016). Although the evidence is still limited in scope and rigor with respect to clinical populations, art therapy seems to effectively reduce anxiety. In one randomized controlled study of anxiety disorders in adult women, ten to twelve sessions of art therapy led to a significant decrease in anxiety symptoms, a significant improvement in quality of life, and increased accessibility to emotion regulation strategies, including accepting one's emotions. Importantly, these improvements were long-term and remained at the three-month follow-up. Moreover, the largest improvements occurred in patients with the highest pretreatment anxiety scores (A. Abbing et al., 2019). In a separate case study of an adult woman with anxiety, similar effects were reported a year after treatment (A. C. Abbing et al., 2019).

Hospital settings are another common area where anxiety runs high, due in part to the features of the hospital environment itself. In hospitals, patients are confined to sterile rooms, exposed to constant beeping sounds and emergency notifications, and regularly confronted with the illness and pain of other patients, as well as experiencing a constant explicit attention to their own health, at a time when they are most vulnerable and least able to care for themselves. Research in environmental aesthetics into the cognitive and affective importance of preserving green and natural spaces bears out the idea that our environment shapes our capacity for healing, by promoting SWB through increased positive emotions and reducing negative states like stress and anxiety. According to attentional restoration theory, exposure to natural environments can help people restore and rejuvenate attentional capacities (Kaplan, 1995), can relax and reduce stress, and can aid in healing (e.g., Ulrich, 1981, 1984). A stroll through a garden can be especially psychologically and physiologically meaningful in a hospital situation, and exposure to art can have similar effects. Artworks both in patient rooms and in waiting rooms affect people's satisfaction, comfort, and health outcomes (Caspari et al., 2007; Harris et al., 2002). Aesthetic elements like wall color, the presence of artworks, and the type of artworks displayed contribute to patients' experiences, partially in their capacity to draw out momentary positive emotions in patients, distract them from their current stressors, and improve their overall mood as a result (Ullán & Belver, 2021). In one study, children who were randomly assigned at the time of admission to the hospital to either a room with an aquatic window mural or a tree window mural had less stress (indicated by better physiological markers such as heart rate and blood pressure) relative to those assigned to the room with no mural present (Pearson et al., 2019). Although more research in this domain is needed to address the mechanisms by which the aesthetic dimensions of the clinical environment may foster therapeutic benefits, the basic conclusion is that the mere presence of art can create a positive, pleasant, and engaging environment, which means better and potentially faster healing.

The arts have also been incorporated into hospital settings through active arts participation, including more targeted art therapy sessions. Participating in arts activities while in the hospital has been linked to improved health outcomes. In their review of the literature, Ana Ullán and Manuel Belver (2021) describe studies showing that children who participated in visual arts activities during their time at the hospital experienced reduced anxiety, had better moods, felt more equipped to identify and express their emotions, were more accepting and positive about their treatments, and had reduced pain symptoms. In this way, arts participation can, at the very least, indirectly support health by providing patients with an activity that promotes their wellbeing.

Like anxiety, depression is a leading cause of mental illness globally. Art therapy, coupled with pharmacological treatments, can also provide patients with relief from the symptoms of their depression, in particular for those with depression associated with loneliness and isolation. This effect is particularly pronounced for the elderly population. A 2019 study assessing mortality risks among older adults found that engaging in receptive art activities (e.g., art museum visits, concert and theatergoing) on a relatively frequent basis (i.e., every few months or more) was associated with a 31 percent lower risk of dying, independent of demographic, socioeconomic, health-related, behavioral, and social factors (Fancourt & Steptoe, 2019). The arts have thus been suggested as a buffer against the multifaceted risks of aging, including depression, loneliness, diminished quality of life, and neurodegeneration. Art museum visitation has been consistently associated with increased social inclusion (Herron & Jamieson, 2020), reductions in social disconnect (Koebner et al., 2019), and feeling better equipped to connect with others (Roberts et al., 2011). Even online art engagement has been associated with reductions in loneliness (Trupp et al., 2022). Museums and galleries have successfully developed programs that positively impact community engagement and improve social functioning, connectedness, and hopefulness among individuals with depression (Irwin et al., 2022).

The arts also indirectly contribute to good patient outcomes by destigmatizing depression and mental illness more generally. Stigma related to mental health is one of the largest barriers to receiving treatment and is associated with worse outcomes for those who need services. Factors that contribute to increased stigma include a lack of knowledge about the nature of the mental illness, a lack of knowledge about how to access adequate care and treatment, a perceived sense that other people discriminate against people with mental illness, and one's own implicit biases

(Henderson et al., 2013). There is a growing body of research that suggests arts engagement may reduce stigma by increasing knowledge about mental illness (e.g., a play may follow a character diagnosed with depression and schizophrenia), emphasizing the value of treatment and social support, and fostering empathy and social cohesion (Jeffers et al., 2022). In at-risk communities where stigma may be highest, such as among young people, the arts may be especially helpful because they foster broader community wellness (Gaiha et al., 2021). In one community-partnered participatory research project, people attended one of two arts events (a spoken word and comedy show or a photography exhibit) held during the Pan African Film Festival as part of Black History Month in February 2005 in South Los Angeles (Chung et al., 2009). The spoken word events included a broader discussion about depression and featured poems read by community members about their own personal experiences with depression and stress. Attendees filled out a survey related to their experiences. After the events, attendees reported high levels of collective efficacy, noting that they felt hopeful that the community could make progress on improving access to care for clinical depression and an interest in advocating for those resources in their community specifically.

Together, these findings point to roles for art, art therapy, and aesthetically valuable environments in promoting mental health insofar as they foster community and cultural identity, self-expression, self-understanding, and emotion regulation, each of which is a protective factor or buffer against mental health symptoms and distress.

Acute and Chronic Pain

Pain is defined by the International Association for the Study of Pain (IASP) as "an unpleasant sensory and emotional experience associated with actual or potential tissue damage or described in terms of such damage" ("Institute of Medicine (US) Committee on Advancing Pain Research, Care, and Education," 2011). Chronic pain is experienced by a staggering 43 percent of the US population alone, and pain experts suggest that "in many cases, chronic pain is a disease in its own right ... [and] requires direct, appropriate treatment rather than being sidelined while clinicians attempt to identify some underlying condition that may have caused it" ("Institute of Medicine (US) Committee on Advancing Pain Research, Care, and Education," 2011). Untreated pain can lead to a host of seemingly unrelated biological problems, as well as to psychological and social problems (Lee, 2016). Moreover, pain, stress, and anxiety are closely linked. Pain is commonly associated with stress responses, specifically with increased activity in the autonomic and endocrine systems (Fekete et al., 2022). Anxiety commonly accompanies pain, especially the anticipation of upcoming pain, creating a cyclical dynamic that then increases subsequent pain (Bernatzky et al., 2011).

Traditional treatments, as with those for anxiety and depression, are often pharmacological. Pain treatment often includes opioids, nonsteroidal anti-inflammatory agents, and epidural injections. Yet, these traditional treatments are less effective than we might hope, and sometimes cause more harm to the patient by decreasing their quality of life due to the side effects, by increasing the potential for addiction, or by introducing drug-associated complications (Bradt et al., 2016). Arts-based interventions have become increasingly popular in the last decade as complementary treatments for acute and chronic pain. Music interventions, specifically, have been commonly used and studied as a tool to reduce patients' pain and distress associated with a variety of medical issues.

Music interventions can either be listening-based or making-based. Listening interventions are also administered in various ways: either through more passive listening experiences in which patients listen to music that was administered or prescribed by a medical professional (termed *music medicine*, or MM), or through more active music listening with a music therapist, such that there is a carefully planned relationship between the patient and the therapist tailored to foster therapeutic outcomes (termed *music therapy*, or MT). Similarly, music-making interventions can be grouped as either MM, or as MT, depending on the administration (Dileo & Bradt, 2005; Lee, 2016). In a 2016 meta-analysis of nearly 100 studies, Jin Hyung Lee found that music interventions involving listening – regardless of how they are administered (i.e., through MT or MM) – reduce pain intensity, emotional distress from pain, and patient use of anesthetics. They also seem to beneficially impact heart rate, systolic and diastolic blood pressure, and respiration rate.

There is also significant individual variability in the effectiveness of these interventions. Overall, children may benefit more from music interventions than do adults and may benefit most from MT; music interventions seem to impact acute pain more than chronic pain; and the interventions appear to be most effective for people with higher pain intensity (Lee, 2016). Moreover, whether someone enjoys, is absorbed by, and likes the art that they are engaging with also seems to matter for pain-related outcomes (Howlin & Rooney, 2021; Howlin et al., 2022). In one set of studies, music that elicits pleasant emotions significantly reduced both pain intensity and unpleasantness of thermal pain applied to the skin compared to silence and to unpleasant music (Roy et al., 2008). Similarly, a different study showed that, when listening to preferred music, individuals had higher pain tolerances for ice-water hand immersions, relative to both no music and music that they did not like (Hekmat & Hertel, 1993).

Joke Bradt, a leading researcher in the domain of music and pain, suggests that more active MT approaches show promise for reducing and potentially eliminating pain. In recent years, they have developed and tested an 8- and a 12-week multidimensional vocal MT program targeting the biological, psychological, and social components of pain. The program involves toning (i.e., singing of elongated vowels), deep breathing, group singing, vocal improvisations, and discussions focusing on the emotions and thoughts evoked by the music experiences (Bradt et al., 2016; Low et al., 2020). The findings across both feasibility studies demonstrate that the vocal MT program is

> effective in building essential stepping stones for chronic pain management, namely developing: 1) a positive relationship with one's self; 2) enhanced self-efficacy; 3) motivation and empowerment to take charge of one's pain management; and 4) renewed social engagement. These components may lay important and necessary groundwork for patient engagement in subsequent interventions such as physical therapy and exercise. (Bradt et al., 2016, p. 13)

Both studies also demonstrate large reductions in anxiety and depression, and in physical pain intensity. Interviews with participating patients indicated that they experienced a host of meaningful benefits. They described enhanced physical functioning (e.g., increased activity levels; increased capacity to engage in chores), reduced pain (through music's soothing qualities, by redirecting attention), increased mindfulness (i.e., ability to be more present by creating a relaxed and clearer state of mind), feelings of empowerment to prioritize self-care, feelings of hope and motivation, an enhanced mind-body connection such that they now have a greater awareness of the impact of their emotional and cognitive state on their pain management, enhanced spirituality and connection to the world, increased capacity to manage their emotions, and more social connectedness as a result of the group music experience (Low et al., 2020).

Even given these robust results about music and MT's effectiveness, the mechanisms underlying music's role in pain mitigation are a rich area for further research. Pain mitigation may occur partly due to cognitive factors such as increased feelings of self-control and decreased feelings of helplessness and isolation. Music activates many brain structures and networks related to pain: Research points out that listening to music releases neuropeptides, such as oxytocin, and activates the opioid-rich midbrain nuclei that regulate pain and influence activity in the frontal and limbic brain structures involved in affective and cognitive modulation of pain and in the reduction of stress (Koelsch, 2014). Also, as we discuss in Chapter 5, music encourages us to move rhythmically and in connection with others. This can increase bodily awareness and presence. People with chronic pain often try to dissociate from their body to reduce their physical pain. Reconnecting with one's body to foster wellbeing is thus a critical treatment target. Moving with others, and making music together, also promotes social inclusion and social cohesion. This is also a critical target for chronic pain management, since those with pain often feel isolation and loneliness, disconnected from themselves and the world (Bradt et al., 2016).

Although more research has been done on how music can be used to manage pain than other art forms, there is also evidence to suggest that other arts interventions may also be useful (Fekete et al., 2022). Like music, visual artworks that people find beautiful and wonder-inducing can influence cortical areas that modulate activity in pain-related structures in the brainstem. The mechanisms for this are still unclear, but one suggestion is that attentional resources are allocated toward engaging and enjoyable art, distracting from the current experience of pain (Tommaso et al., 2008). Moreover, a core facet of pain modulation through MT is that it strengthens the sense of self and increases self-efficacy. Visual art similarly leads to changes in one's selfhood and emotion regulation, making it plausible as a pain-modulator.

A complementary consideration is that the arts may be a mechanism for patients to express their pain and to receive more careful and targeted treatment from healthcare providers as a result. As we know, pain is multifaceted and challenging to express, and the typical question of "how are you feeling?" or the pain intensity scales patients are given at hospitals are inadequate in many ways. In her essay exploring the history of pain narratives, Joanne Bourke (2012) writes that "[e]ven when suffering, people in pain are often highly creative in expressing their suffering—sometimes in words, other times in images and art, and still other times in gestures, ritual utterances, symbols, posture, and performance" (p. 2421).

The arts may be especially important for helping patients meaningfully communicate with their care providers so that their pain narratives are heard and understood. Language may not always be the most effective means of communication, and where it fails, the arts can be a powerful alternative. This may be especially true for children, who often lack the language skills to describe their pain, particularly as they are still developing tools to understand and manage their emotions. There is extensive evidence documenting the effectiveness of arts interventions in hospital settings for increasing children's (and adults') wellbeing in multifaceted ways, as we described earlier in this chapter. More targeted research can also identify how this might relate to improving pain narratives and connections among patients, healthcare providers, and other caregivers.

Parkinson's Disease

Earlier in this chapter, we described the role of arts interventions in treating aspects of our mental health. There are also conditions that may seem less obvious candidates to benefit from art therapy. For instance, a disease like Parkinson's (PD) in many ways seems to be more "physical" than anxiety and depression and less experiential than pain, and thereby less susceptible to treatment through art therapies. However, art therapies have become increasingly popular techniques in treating "physical" medical conditions. We focus here on PD because of the depth of literature on the role of arts-based interventions in its treatment, but there are other neurodegenerative diseases that may similarly benefit from integrative arts interventions (e.g., Alzheimer's, other dementias).

Parkinson's disease is a neurodegenerative disease affecting more than 10 million people worldwide. It is marked by a large reduction in the number of dopamine-producing neurons in the brain, and is associated with a host of motor symptoms, such as tremors, difficulty initiating movements, stiff limbs, gait and balance problems, and paucity of movement. There are also a variety of non-motor symptoms including, but not limited to, depression, anxiety, fatigue, apathy, hallucinations, and sleep disorders. Parkinson's disease is more likely to affect men than women, and is more likely to emerge with increasing age. The causes remain unknown (though there are a variety of environmental and genetic factors that contribute), and there is no cure (*Parkinson's Foundation*, n.d.). The most common treatments are pharmacological, including medications that act as dopamine replacement agents, that stimulate the production of dopamine, or that target the motor symptoms specifically. Unfortunately, these treatments are not always tolerated well by patients, and researchers have increasingly come to recommend more integrative approaches that are individually tailored and combine pharmacological interventions with physical activity, nutrition, sleep, social connection, and mind-body therapies (Kola & Subramanian, 2023).

Mind–body therapies that incorporate the arts, particularly if there are motor aspects of the intervention, may be especially well suited to treating PD. Dancing has gained interest as an intervention for PD because it can teach individuals to coordinate their movements to visual and auditory cues, while also engaging a host of non-motor functions. Physical exercise has also been consistently shown to improve PD symptoms (e.g., The Parkinson's Foundation recommends 150 minutes per week of at least moderate intensity exercise), and dancing is an excellent and engaging form of exercise. A recent metanalysis suggests that dancing is *the most effective* form of exercise for patients with PD, compared to 14 others, for fostering long-term changes in motor function (Zhang et al., 2023). There are now several certified dance programs for patients with PD, including NeuroTango, Dance for PD, and Dance Movement Therapy. Importantly, many studies have demonstrated that dancing programs such as these lead to positive motor and non-motor outcomes in patients with PD, including changes in neuromuscular control of gait and balance, improved motor velocity, decreased freezing, improved body awareness, increased body sensations, improved visuospatial and attentional skills, and improved psychological symptoms such as feeling more confident to participate in daily activities, increased participation in social activities, decreased depression, anxiety, and improved quality of life (Meulenberg et al., 2023; Sharp & Hewitt, 2014).

Despite this clinical promise, the neural substrates underlying the effectiveness of dance programs are still poorly understood and a ripe area for research (Koshimori & Thaut, 2018; Mahmoud et al., 2023). One important way to understand what dancing might do to the brains of those with PD is to examine what it does in those of healthy individuals.

> Dancing places various demands on the sensorimotor system, and studies in healthy older adults and young adults have revealed neuroplastic changes associated with dancing... Brain areas and circuits involved in movement initiation, planning, sequencing, and control, such as the premotor cortex, supplementary motor area, and cortico-striatal circuits including the basal ganglia (putamen and striatum), have been shown to benefit from dancing. However, these regions and functions often exhibit decreased activity and lower connectivity in patients with PD. (Meulenberg et al., 2023, p. 6)

Additionally, rhythm and music seem to modulate brain activity in the relevant dopaminergic and cerebellar pathways for PD patients (Koshimori & Thaut, 2018). This suggests that dancing is a way to encourage the systematic engagement of these sensorimotor brain areas, thereby improving functional connectivity in motor networks that could lead to short- and long-term effects (Brown et al., 2006). Accounting for individual variability and for auditory stimulus type is also key. For example, the severity of a person's PD symptoms, their beat perception capabilities, their familiarity and appreciation of the music that is used in the intervention, as well as their ability to synchronize their movements with music, may affect the success of the intervention (Hackney & Earhart, 2009).

Dance therapy is not the only form of art therapy that has become more popular for treating PD. Music therapies (without combined dancing but combined with exercises like walking) also seem to affect motor symptoms, improving gait, strides, and motor coordination (Kola & Subramanian, 2023). Visual art therapies have also been employed and seem to be especially useful for targeting visuospatial deficits in individuals with PD, including problems with contrast sensitivity, color discrimination, dark–light adaptation, and visual recognition (Cucca et al., 2021; Ettinger et al., 2023; Kola & Subramanian, 2023; Uc et al., 2005). Common across these therapeutic approaches is their targeting of the capacities to produce pleasure and reward, to engage dopamine-releasing neurons, to enhance the likelihood of getting into a creative flow state (discussed earlier in this chapter), and to increase social connectedness, thereby decreasing loneliness.

Prescribing the Arts

Integration of the arts into public health is in a period of renaissance. The WHO's landmark 2019 study recommended a host of policies and practices to ensure that arts and culture are publicly accessible, and that governments recognize and emphasize the health benefits of the arts. As such, there are several examples of promising policy developments at local, national, and international scales integrating the arts in a variety of ways into basic healthcare. Moreover, international commitments recognizing and pledging support for the arts and integration into health are rising. For example, National Arts Council Singapore's 2023–2027 Arts Plan is driven by the notion that "The arts belong to everyone. As audiences, participants, practitioners, patrons, or partners, we all contribute to the vibrancy and energy of the arts scene. In return, the arts touch and inspire us, root us in our identities, and help make our city iconic and distinctive" (*National Arts Council*, n.d.). Particular programs within their scope include bringing the arts to hospitals and nursing homes. Similarly, arts councils and agencies across various countries (e.g., USA, Wales, UK, Australia, Ethiopia) have made explicit commitments that include raising awareness and support for the benefits of the arts in health and policy settings (Dow et al., 2023).

A related emerging practice referred to as "social prescribing" positions community and cultural institutions directly as healthcare services. The practice can be broadly understood as

> using community-based services to address non-clinical and subclinical needs. In this model, patients can be referred by providers to resources ranging from housing and food assistance to job and skills training, volunteering, human-animal interaction, time in nature, and arts/culture activities such as dance classes, museum visits, musical performances, etc. (Golden et al., 2023, p. 2)

Social prescribing is driven by an understanding that communities themselves cultivate health through social connection and cultural identity. This practice is aimed at directly targeting the social determinants of health, including loneliness and social isolation, but also systemic issues like racism and ageism. An optimal social prescription is one that incorporates multiple spheres of social interaction so that it can target loneliness, social engagement, and collective identity formation, and is used in combination with other important factors like exercise, diet, and sleep habits (Kola & Subramanian, 2023).

"CultureRx," launched in 2020 by the Massachusetts state agency Mass Cultural Council to foster cultural life for state residents, was the first formal social prescription program in the US. This program directly connects healthcare providers with cultural partners so that they can prescribe specific community-based culture experiences to patients, and it provides cultural organizations with funding to provide free access to their services and to sustain the partnerships they make with healthcare providers. These arts and culture prescriptions are not viewed as a replacement for standard treatments, but as complements, to "foster connection(s), improve healthcare encounters, create moments of joy or beauty, and provide material for discussion with friends, family, and eventual therapists or counselors" (Golden et al., 2023, p. 15). Initial evaluations of this program suggest positive outcomes for both patients and providers. For patients, it reduces barriers to access. Providers report that their own wellbeing is bolstered, including their work satisfaction, as the program allows their relationship to patients to shift from being confined to telling people what they did wrong, to one in which they can provide meaningful resources beyond the clinic (Golden et al., 2023).

Despite the promise of these approaches and the uptake by governmental agencies, the scientific evidence of their effectiveness is only just beginning to be systematically examined and documented, and we should be cautious about drawing firm or sweeping conclusions or interpretations. The mechanisms by which these interventions work are complex and underspecified and remain an important area for future research (de Witte et al., 2021). Although there are scoping reviews, meta-analyses, and narrative reviews which inform much of the recent policy development, there are still limited numbers of experimental protocols and randomized clinical trials (RCTs), which offer the most robust and sound kind of evidence. Many of the RCTs that do exist have substantive risks of biases, including participants or researchers not being blinded to the assigned conditions (Kaasgaard et al., 2024). Moreover, as we have indicated throughout, more care may be required to distinguish different kinds of arts-based interventions, both with respect to their modalities and to the methodological and theoretical frameworks underwriting the approach.

The Arts as a Component of Objective Wellbeing

Theories of objective wellbeing often trace their roots to Aristotle's conception of *eudaimonia* as flourishing. On this view, and those who adopt similar approaches like contemporary scholars Martha Nussbaum's and Amartya Sen's capabilities approach (Nussbaum, 2011; Sen, 1999), flourishing is a matter of faring well as the kind of being that you are. The evaluation of faring well consists in assessing whether, and to what extent, a set of objective features of one's life and experience are present. When we say that these features are objective, we mean that they are identifiable or measurable independently of the subjective experience or judgment of the individual. For human beings, flourishing plausibly includes things like one's ability to act autonomously, to have meaningful relationships, to learn, to contribute to one's community, or to have a purpose in life; whether and to what extent these things are present in one's life is a matter of fact independent of anyone's experience of or judgment about them.

Demonstrating that the arts contribute to objective wellbeing would require showing that they contribute to our living good *human* lives. What this comes to will depend on the specific conception of human nature underlying a particular view. Nevertheless, the arguments we have provided across this book suggest an argument for art's contribution to flourishing: the arts and arts engagement contribute to our flourishing because they are a shared social practice through which we cultivate central cognitive abilities and capacities, and through which we develop a sense of self-identity and meaningful connections to other people. Insofar as we are social agents, and insofar as the cognitive capacities we have discussed (i.e., observation, emotional intelligence, open-minded engagement) are characteristic of human nature, then arts engagement contributes to our flourishing.

Following this line of argument, we would not say that "art" is itself a component of objective wellbeing ("art" would not appear in Figure 6.2 as an independent bubble). Instead, we would argue that the arts and arts engagement are an especially useful, valuable, or rich context in or through which we can develop and promote central capacities, the presence of which *is* a component of living a good life. For example, many people claim that autonomy is fundamentally important to a good human life. On this view, owning (in an important sense) one's ideas, being able to think for oneself, and having the freedom to live according to one's own sense of value and meaning, are characteristic of living humanly (or perhaps, humanely). Our suggestion is that arts engagement can cultivate central cognitive capacities that facilitate being autonomous. It can help us to understand ourselves and other people better. It can help us to identify our own beliefs and to revise them. It can help us to envision how we may want to live. And, it can help us to own and make our own all of these beliefs, by identifying them as *ours*.

This way of thinking about how the arts may contribute to objective wellbeing leaves room for those who say that one can develop these same capacities through other mechanisms (perhaps scientific study, engagement with nature, or other kinds of mechanical skill development are similarly rich fora for doing so). Thus, the arguments we have given here do not suggest that anyone who does not engage with any arts in their life is *necessarily* not living well. That would go too far. We can imagine several different kinds of social practices that have similar outcomes with respect to cognitive capacities. Attention to detail, effective coordination with other people (including those who are very different from you), and learning how to do some specific tasks or actions well are shared features of several social practices, ranging from political governance to teaching to coin collecting. At the same time, we have aimed to demonstrate that the arts are especially well suited to the use and development of skills and capacities that are of central importance to being human, namely: observation, emotional intelligence, and open-minded engagement. Moreover, the value of the arts with respect to our understanding of ourselves and others, our sense of who we are and what is meaningful, further demonstrates this suggestion that these skills are foundational for *human* flourishing.

Summary

That there is a meaningful and rich relationship between the arts and joy, pleasure, and happiness is uncontested. However, as with many questions we have explored, the exact nature of that relationship is multifaceted. Philosophers and psychologists approach the study of wellbeing in various ways, and the complexity of wellbeing itself makes empirical investigation of it difficult. Nevertheless, there is robust evidence for a profound connection between the arts and SWB. Moreover, the recent attention to the value of the arts for promoting the health of individuals and communities has brought welcome attention and resources to this important area of research. Finally, our argument throughout this book – that the arts shape how and what we know, and who we are – positions them as a vital support to our flourishing. As humans, we are social beings, and we are learning beings. By embracing our aesthetic selves, we can lead richer and flourishing lives by cultivating the cognitive skills of observation, emotional intelligence, and open-minded engagement.

Conclusion
Making the Arts Matter

We have argued that the arts can contribute in fundamental ways to how we know and who we are. We have surveyed and marshaled evidence that the arts make us feel a range of powerful emotions, elevate our moods, and help us to feel restored; that they open our minds, encourage us to interrogate our understandings of ourselves, of others, and of our communities; and that in doing so, they offer us unique ways to connect to each other. We have suggested that the arts change us and make us, through the skills they help us hone, through the understandings they offer, and through aiding us in healing our mental, physical, and social selves.

Perhaps the most important insight that emerges from our discussion is that when it comes to the arts, we should care less about things like taste, popularity, or status. We should not be afraid to like what we like. We should embrace the artworks and aesthetic practices that are important to us; the ones that we enjoy, the ones that connect us to who we are and to other people we care about. We should lean into enjoying and making what we like, what we find interesting, and what we find rewarding. We have also seen evidence that we should actually *do* these things. We should make time and space for engaging with art. We should make stuff (even if it is not very good or no one else will ever experience it). We should read, watch movies, and go to shows.

That being said, there are some habits or practices that also emerged across our discussion that can help enrich whatever it is that you choose to do, and can help you to push yourself to engage more fully with art. In this final chapter, rather than rehearsing the argument we have made, we reframe our discussion in a practical light in an effort to articulate more concretely the mechanisms by which we can deepen and enrich our engagement and connection to the arts. We do this by highlighting four key "habits of mind" to engage in during art-appreciating and art-making: slowing down, embracing uncertainty, self-reflecting, and engaging in shared meaning-making.

Slowing Down

In her book, *Slow Looking: The Art and Practice of Learning Through Observation*, Shari Tishman emphasizes that slow looking is a mode of learning through prolonged observation (Tishman, 2018). Although the term itself centers vision, as we discussed in Chapter 2, observation occurs through all senses. Slow looking is inherently the opposite of fast looking, which is how we most typically engage with the world due to our limited attentional resources. We scan the world quickly, make rapid judgments, and form first impressions (which matter more than we might think if we do not stop to interrogate them). We rely on shortcuts and biases to get things right just often enough, which means we tend to jump to conclusions quickly, to focus our attention either too narrowly or too broadly, and to spend too little time with things that seem to come easily to us. Vision *seems* easy; we feel like we can see everything quite rapidly, and yet we are highly biased in our initial judgments. Thus, a way to complement this cognitive style is to also engage in cognitive reflection that actively intervenes in one's (more or less automatic) fast-thinking strategies, either by slow looking or by encouraging oneself to keep an open mind. Slowing down gives us a chance for reflection, helps us be less susceptible to misinformation, and fosters curiosity.

What do we do when we slow-look? There is no right answer here, but Tishman describes four common strategies for slow looking that may serve as a guide:

1. *Categorizing* involves constraining and ordering your observations. If you decide to try out slow looking in the context of a painting, you might begin by focusing on what colors you see, on what types of lines, or on what shapes you see. These various categories will guide your exploration in distinct ways.
2. *Creating an open inventory* provides an explicit way to list out and structure all the things you observe of certain kinds. In practice, it might involve listing and describing all the different features, objects, and categories that you observe in a painting at any given moment.
3. *Attending to scale and scope* as a form of zooming in and out during observation. It involves examining our observations at various scales and distances: moving further away to bring a piece into broader perspective or moving closer to bring it into sharper focus.
4. *Juxtaposing* involves comparing observations to one another by highlighting their similarities and differences. We can compare the

colors of a painting at various scales or within various spaces in the composition. Although this is an approach that is more explicitly linked to observation and reception rather than to art-making, we can apply it more broadly.

There are, of course, other ways to slow-look, too, and other kinds of questions one can ask of oneself or of the world one is observing. But these are some ideas for how one might get started.

A key outcome of slow looking is the development of perceptual and cognitive skills that allow us to notice and discern complexity, both in ourselves and in the world. Tishman suggests that slow looking is particularly well-suited to fostering understanding of three types of complexity: the interplay of *parts and their interactions, shifts in perspective,* and *personal engagement.* Consider, for example, something as simple as a click-open pen. It may appear straightforward, but slow, careful inspection can reveal multiple parts and how they work together. That same object can be understood differently depending on your point of view. An engineer might see its mechanics, a designer its aesthetics and ergonomics, and a user may see its function. Finally, our own physical characteristics, psychological traits and states, and social and cultural positionality shape what we see, notice, and understand about the pen. Someone with arthritis, for example, may become more acutely aware of the difficulty of pushing down the click-open feature.

Reflecting on an object slowly might bring to the forefront not only information about the object or its maker, but also about yourself. Tishman writes that encouraging appreciators "to probe the complexity of their own visual engagement [helps] them uncover the biases and preconceptions they [bring] to the act of looking, and [exposes] them to works of art that might disrupt or disturb their tacit ideas about the neutrality of observation" (p. 150). Moreover, while increased attention and deepened engagement can be meaningful in their own right as a single interesting experience, they also provide potential for developing more sustained interest and curiosity.

The power of mindful attention and slow observation to deepen our experience and understanding of the arts is exemplified in Jennifer Roberts' essay "The power of patience" (Roberts, 2013). Roberts asks her art history students to spend three uninterrupted hours with one painting at a museum. What initially seems to be a tedious and overwhelming assignment becomes revelatory. Roberts (who, as an art historian, is an expert at viewing paintings) describes her own attempt at the exercise, viewing John Singleton Copley's *A Boy with a Flying Squirrel*, 1765:

> It took me nine minutes to notice that the shape of the boy's ear precisely echoes that of the ruff along the squirrel's belly – and that Copley was making some kind of connection between the animal and the human body and the sensory capacities of each. It was 21 minutes before I registered the fact that the fingers holding the chain exactly span the diameter of the water glass beneath them. It took a good 45 minutes before I realized that the seemingly random folds and wrinkles in the background curtain are actually perfect copies of the shapes of the boy's ear and eye, as if Copley had imagined those sensory organs distributing or imprinting themselves on the surface behind him.

Following the insights gained from this careful observation, Roberts emphasizes that "access is not synonymous with learning. What turns access into learning is time and strategic patience." It takes more than walking up to a painting, reading the caption, and viewing it for 20 seconds silently to engage with and "get into" an artwork. Quick glances or passive attention can give us the perceptual basics of color, shape, and sound, but keen observation is needed to glean meaningful relationships between the sensory properties and their social and historical contexts.

This value of slow looking is also exemplified in Ruth Ozeki's 2022 memoir, *The Timecode of a Face*, in which she painstakingly documents and reflects on three hours she spent observing her own face (Ozeki, 2022). Many of us look in the mirror every day, and yet, there is a lot we do not know about our own bodies. When you look at any single thing for a sustained period or time, the familiar becomes strange. It takes on new meanings and appearances. Ozeki describes becoming more attuned to how the small changes in her own face relate to her emotions and impressions, something she carries forward into her interactions with others. She began looking at others' faces more slowly. Ozeki writes,

> The observation experiment, like meditation, has had the effect of waking me up to things that I ordinarily would not notice or would have ignored. In the days and weeks and months that have followed, I find myself looking at people's faces more closely. There's a new subjectivity in my gaze when I look at others. Their faces mirror mine, and my face mirrors theirs, and this gives rise to a feeling of recursive kindliness and kinship that I haven't felt in quite this way before... So now, on the subway, while the other passengers are enthralled by their devices, I take the opportunity to observe them, unseen. What would it feel like to look like that woman? Who does she see in her face in the mirror? Do her jowls bother her, or is she more preoccupied by the lines on her forehead? Does she have a mirror face? (p. 34)

Our own recent research supports these insights, pointing to the flourishing benefits of slow looking in a museum. When visitors were asked to spend 10 minutes quietly engaging with an artwork on display in a small gallery, they reported being surprised at their ability to actually do it, as well as surprise at how valuable slowing down in that way actually was. They talked about hitting a wall within the first few minutes, during which they would typically move on to the next piece, but being "forced" to stay and sit with the discomfort of not knowing what else to examine helped them to accept the experience and find continued value. Slowing down helped them to understand the piece better, and led to increases in positive emotions, including feeling more reflective, inspired, creative, and empathetic. It also helped them feel more attentive both to themselves and to the natural world around them, promoting a state of mindfulness (Sherman et al., 2025).

None of this is to say that actually slowing down is easy. Contemporary culture is structured around speed and saturation, particularly when it comes to visual media. Social media platforms are deliberately designed to capture and fragment our attention, encouraging rapid attentional shifting between disconnected visual and multisensory media. The constant flickering of our attention undermines our capacity for sustained focus and makes practicing slow looking something we must set out to do. As with the subjects in Sherman et al.'s 2025 study, people may not believe they are "actually able to do it."

We would suggest that, to the contrary, we are able to do it. We practice similar skills in other parts of our lives that can be brought to bear here. Consider travel. When we visit a new city, with a different language and different customs, slowing down and engaging effortfully is required. We must pay close attention to our surroundings, perhaps becoming even more attuned to visual, gestural, and spatial cues. Depending on the country you are visiting, cars may drive on the "opposite" side of the road, so something as routine as crossing the street demands heightened awareness and recalibration of habits. In a new city, everyday activities become occasions for careful observation, dwelling in uncertainty, and slowly piecing together meaning. New-city-engagement, born of necessity but also of curiosity, mirrors the slow-looking mindset that we encourage for engaging with the arts.

Just as a new city is impossible to immediately comprehend, so too does art resist immediate legibility. Art speaks to us in a language that is more complicated than everyday speech, and one that is often abstract. If we assume that we can readily understand art, we "short-circuit" the encounter. Approaching art as we approach new places, however – with patience, humility, curiosity, and active attention – allows us to slowly begin to learn the syntax of art, to cohere fragments into patterns of meaning (Winterson, 1997). Slow looking is a mode of translation, an intentional effort to inhabit an artwork's visual and affective landscape on its own terms rather than imposing ourselves on it.

Embracing Uncertainty

Just as slowing down is hard but rewarding, so too is engaging with unfamiliar experiences. In unfamiliar contexts, confusion is inevitable. It is natural to want to disengage when we immediately feel we do not understand or even do not like something. Grappling with uncertainty can be uncomfortable and anxiety-provoking. Thinking again of landing in a new city, you might find yourself standing in a metro station surrounded by fast-moving crowds, struggling to decipher the signage or to understand the announcements. It can be overwhelming to not know where to go or even how to ask for help. In these moments, it can be tempting to turn back, to stick to the easiest to access tourist zones, or to just hail a taxi. But if we resist the urge to withdraw and can remain in the moment and allow ourselves to be a bit vulnerable, we often find that understanding emerges, and new discoveries, perhaps about the culture we are immersed in, or even about our own ability to figure something out, come to the fore. In these ways, unfamiliarity can be exciting and interesting.

The same is true of art: Confusion is not a dead end, but the beginning of new understandings. A painting may seem inscrutable or even deceptively simple. A performance might leave us speechless. Rather than seeking out immediate clarity, we can choose to stay a little longer with not-knowing. This can make uncertainty a generative, rather than anxiety-producing space. A space where we can ask questions, consider alternatives, or form associations. Especially notable and important here is that many art experts – critics, art historians, and the like – continue to feel this way about art. In *The Imaginary Museum*, Ben Eastham writes:

> [An artwork] rewards different interpretations as the world changes around it. I keep returning to [Beatriz González's Interior Decoration (1981)] not to experience the same reaction to its patterns and colors, but because I anticipate a different one. As such, it offers a yardstick against which to gauge how I, and the world of which I am a part, have shifted. The "meaning" of a painting, like the "meaning" of the world, emerges through your encounter with it . . . works of art are not fully knowable any more than people are fully knowable. (Eastham, 2020)

What makes art interesting is that you can return to it to make new discoveries and to deepen your understanding. The next time you see the same artwork, you could be in a different place in your life and, as a result, notice wholly different things (that were there all along), or make connections you would never have been able to make before. Or the artwork could be in a totally different location or in a different museum and, on the new viewing, reveal to you how much the context and surroundings influence your initial perceptions and interpretations. Acknowledging the unknown and the not-fully-knowable can be an empowering tool for inciting curiosity. It might lead you to consider new things, or it may increase your desire to find out more about something, or to open conversations about possibilities, and can also encourage space for independent thought.

Museum education often wrestles to find a balance between educating the visitor on the content they "should" learn about the pieces, and demonstrating the importance and validity of the observations, interpretations, and views that the visitors bring to their experiences with the artworks. We do not mean to suggest here that we should always prioritize our own observations and interpretations when we engage with artworks, especially in isolation from the sociocultural and historical contexts that inform and shape the work itself. The importance of expert analyses through museum captions or texts cannot be overstated, as art is rooted in sociocultural context and should be interpreted as such. But we also agree with many scholars who suggest that the arts always leave room for continued interpretation. In this way, embracing uncertainty is a productive strategy for deepening engagement because it can challenge the traditional divide between expert and visitor, encouraging active participation and dialogue, and allowing the visitor to gain confidence in their voice. Rather than privileging expert knowledge or definitive readings, uncertainty invites democratization of meaning-making. The shift makes the arts more accessible, more active, and more transformative. Staying active in observing and asking questions reminds us that our observations are relevant, that the connections we are making between our own experiences and what we see in the art matter, and that interpreting art is an open-ended process, rather than a fixed task that one gets "right or wrong."

Immersion and uncertainty tolerance are essential components in developing long-lasting and meaningful relationships with the arts, which we argue are fundamental to the process of learning. Our argument is built on the principle that genuine learning and connection occur when we commit to nurturing a sustained, evolving relationship with art. A single encounter with an artwork can indeed be powerful, especially when it is emotionally resonant, intellectually stimulating, and aesthetically pleasurable. Most critically, such an experience lays the groundwork for future experiences, which foster the development of a rich set of cognitive outcomes. Engaging in slow looking and embracing uncertainty are not merely about experiencing individual moments of insight, but about building a framework for ongoing learning that deepens one's connection with and understanding of oneself and the world.

Making Meaning (Personally and Collectively)

At their core, meaningful art experiences are about *making* meaning. Meaning, as we have suggested, is not passively handed to us through didactic captions or gleaned only through quick glances or listening to music "in the background." Rather, it emerges through observation and open-minded engagement. Making meaning is about making sense of both the external experience that we are interpreting and our internal landscape in relationship with the experience (e.g., the emotions felt, the memories surfaced, the wax and wane of attention).

As educators, we are keenly aware that true learning does not happen through exposure alone. Our students do not learn just by receiving information through lectures. They learn by actively engaging in the process: by testing out their ideas through experimentation, by exploring concepts with peers, and by making mistakes along the way. Reflection is a vital part of the learning process. In reflection, learners step back and explicitly consider *how* they are learning and why the things they learned and their learning process matter. Reflection can happen in any number of ways: introspecting, journaling, having peer-to-peer conversations, or engaging in a larger classroom dialogue. It is an opportunity to become conscious of one's own thinking and a chance to explicitly articulate our experiences. By naming our thoughts, questions, insights, and challenges, we concretize and externalize our mental states and make them available for further exploration and refinement. Reflection, thus, is at the heart of what it means for learning to be an active, inquiry-driven process.

The same applies to our learning from, with, or through art experiences. Reflecting on our art encounters enriches our learning about both the art and ourselves. While reflection can certainly happen privately through introspection or through things like writing and journaling, it can also be a social experience. This aligns with Paulo Freire's theory of dialogic action, which suggests that learning and curiosity are best fostered in an environment that requires the learner to participate in an interactive dialogue with others, thereby developing their critical consciousness (Freire, 2000; Mayo, 2013). As Eastham puts this point in the context of the arts: "In talking about art, we learn to talk about ourselves and the world in which we live." This has been taken up more widely in recent years; for example, the International Slow Art Day movement encourages visitors to discuss their experience after the fact with another visitor, as a way to bolster new perspectives, deepen understanding, and enhance memory of the experience.

People rarely go to museums alone. The majority of visitors go with a companion or in groups, and when going to museums they often have socially guided or learning-centered motivations (Hein, 2002). Concerts, dance floors, performances, book clubs, and the like are structured around shared engagement, and it is this shared experience that is often a motivating reason for our participation. We discussed this kind of affinity and its importance to the nature of arts engagement in Chapter 5. As Stephane Debenedetti (2003) explains with respect to the museum specifically: "Actively sharing the museum experience represents more than the simple co-presence of friends: it serves to form social bonds and transform the cultural into the social" (p. 56). Explicitly connecting to others, particularly through collective meaning-making even when you are seeking a solitary art experience, is one important way to enrich your experience, understanding, and wellbeing.

Recent empirical research supports these claims. A study at Manchester Art Gallery in the UK by Aleksandra Igdalova and colleagues explored how group dialogue impacts people's experience of art (Igdalova et al., 2025). Participants viewed paintings while engaging in a slow-looking exercise either alone, with others in silence, or in a guided group discussion. All groups reported positive experiences, but those who engaged in dialogue reported the most significant wellbeing impacts, including positive affect, social connectedness, and feelings of group closeness. These findings align well with other research on shared museum experiences, which shows that when people explore museums in pairs or groups, they feel more comfortable, report a greater sense of belonging, and tend to spend more time with the artworks. Individuals visiting on their own, in contrast, tend to spend more time reading labels than examining works (Packer & Ballantyne, 2005; Smith & Smith, 2001; Smith et al., 2017).

To be clear, we are not suggesting that solo arts experiences are a bad thing. However, evidence suggests that a group setting may sometimes enhance the experience by promoting slower looking and encouraging shared idea exchange. Indeed, our recent research at OxyArts, a campus-affiliated gallery, showed exactly this. A guided interview that we conducted with visitors after they engaged in slow-looking visual artwork was key to unlocking benefits related to personal growth, positive emotion, and understanding. Whereas the slow-looking process encouraged participants to observe, sit with uncertainty, and introspect, we found that the guided interview encouraged more active reflection in which participants worked to verbalize their understandings about the artwork, to draw connections between the themes they saw reflected in the artwork and their own life experiences, and to consider their preconceptions in the context of the art encounter (Sherman et al., 2025). An open question for future research is whether it is the act of verbalization itself that drives this deeper engagement, or whether similar benefits might arise from prompts to engage in private self-reflection or expressive writing. Regardless of the specific mechanism, what seems essential is the opportunity to slow down, reflect, and give voice – internally or externally – to the personal significance of the encounter.

The Arts Matter

We conclude with a reemphasis of the critical importance of the arts in our lives. The arts make us who we are, and they do so especially when we focus on and lean into the social practices and processes of art-making and art-appreciating. Our argument has woven together philosophical argument and empirical evidence to showcase ways in which the arts contribute to knowledge generation, identity formation, and wellbeing. The arts matter much more and for many more reasons than our society often gives them credit for. The arts are not just pastimes or leisure activities. They are not only for the elite. They do not include only (or even primarily!) the objects in museums classified as the "fine arts." They are for everyone to enjoy, to wonder at, and to learn about, with, and through. We will do better to recognize their value by including them more deeply and intentionally in our important social institutions, including education, healthcare, and community work.

References

Abbing, A., Baars, E. W., de Sonneville, L., Ponstein, A. S., & Swaab, H. (2019). The effectiveness of art therapy for anxiety in adult women: A randomized controlled trial. *Frontiers in Psychology, 10*. https://doi.org/10.3389/fpsyg.2019.01203

Abbing, A. C., Baars, E. W., Van Haastrecht, O., & Ponstein, A. S. (2019). Acceptance of anxiety through art therapy: A case report exploring how anthroposophic art therapy addresses emotion regulation and executive functioning. *Case Reports in Psychiatry, 2019*(1), 4875381. https://doi.org/10.1155/2019/4875381

Adajian, T. (2024). The definition of art. In E. N. Zalta & U. Nodelman (Eds.), *The Stanford Encyclopedia of Philosophy* (Fall 2024). Metaphysics Research Lab, Stanford University. https://plato.stanford.edu/archives/fall2024/entries/art-definition/

Akers, M., & Dupre, J. (Directors). (2012, July 5). *Marina Abramović: The artist is present*. Show of Force, AVRO Close Up, Dakota Group.

Alain, C., Zendel, B. R., Hutka, S., & Bidelman, G. M. (2014). Turning down the noise: The benefit of musical training on the aging auditory brain. *Hearing Research, 308*, 162–173. https://doi.org/10.1016/j.heares.2013.06.008

Aldao, A. (2013). The future of emotion regulation research: Capturing context. *Perspectives on Psychological Science: A Journal of the Association for Psychological Science, 8*(2), 155–172. https://doi.org/10.1177/1745691612459518

American Art Therapy Association I. Newsletter, XK. (2007). American Art Therapy Association.

Anelli, M., Abramović, M., Biesenbach, K., & Iles, C. (2012). *Portraits in the presence of Marina Abramović*. Distributed Art Pub Incorporated.

Antinori, A., Carter, O. L., & Smillie, L. D. (2017). Seeing it both ways: Openness to experience and binocular rivalry suppression. *Journal of Research in Personality, 68*, 15–22. https://doi.org/10.1016/j.jrp.2017.03.005

APA Dictionary of Psychology. (2018). Retrieved October 14, 2024, from https://dictionary.apa.org/

Arboleda, Y. (2010, May 28). *Bringing Marina flowers*. HuffPost. www.huffpost.com/entry/bringing-marina-flowers_b_592597

Aristotle. (1999). *Nicomachean ethics* (T. Irwin, Trans.; 2nd ed.). Hackett Publishing.

Asakura, K., Lundy, J., Black, D., & Tierney, C. (2020). Art as a transformative practice: A participatory action research project with trans* youth. *Qualitative Social Work, 19*(5–6), 1061–1077. https://doi.org/10.1177/1473325019881226

Atkinson, A. P., Dittrich, W. H., Gemmell, A. J., & Young, A. W. (2004). Emotion perception from dynamic and static body expressions in point-light and full-light displays. *Perception, 33*(6), 717–746. https://doi.org/10.1068/p5096

Baehr, J. (2011). The structure of open-mindedness. *Canadian Journal of Philosophy, 41*(2), 191–213.

Baird, A., & Samson, S. (2015). Music and dementia. In Eckart Altenmüller, Stanley Finger, & François Boller (Eds.), *Progress in Brain Research* (Vol. 217, pp. 207–235). Elsevier. https://doi.org/10.1016/bs.pbr.2014.11.028

Balteş, F. R., & Miu, A. C. (2014). Emotions during live music performance: Links with individual differences in empathy, visual imagery, and mood. *Psychomusicology: Music, Mind, and Brain, 24*(1), 58–65. https://doi.org/10.1037/pmu0000030

Banse, R., & Scherer, K. R. (1996). Acoustic profiles in vocal emotion expression. *Journal of Personality and Social Psychology, 70*(3), 614–636. https://doi.org/10.1037/0022-3514.70.3.614

Bänziger, T., Grandjean, D., & Scherer, K. R. (2009). Emotion recognition from expressions in face, voice, and body: The Multimodal Emotion Recognition Test (MERT). *Emotion, 9*(5), 691–704. https://doi.org/10.1037/a0017088

Bardes, C. L., Gillers, D., & Herman, A. E. (2001). Learning to look: Developing clinical observational skills at an art museum. *Medical Education, 35*(12), 1157–1161. https://doi.org/10.1046/j.1365-2923.2001.01088.x

Barford, K. A., & Smillie, L. D. (2016). Openness and other big five traits in relation to dispositional mixed emotions. *Personality and Individual Differences, 102*, 118–122. https://doi.org/10.1016/j.paid.2016.07.002

Barrett, L. F., Gross, J., Christensen, T. C., & Benvenuto, M. (2001). Knowing what you're feeling and knowing what to do about it: Mapping the relation between emotion differentiation and emotion regulation. *Cognition and Emotion, 15*(6), 713–724. https://doi.org/10.1080/02699930143000239

Barrett, N. F., & Schulkin, J. (2017). A neurodynamic perspective on musical enjoyment: The role of emotional granularity. *Frontiers in Psychology, 8*. https://doi.org/10.3389/fpsyg.2017.02187

Bayles, D., & Orland, T. (2010). *Art & fear: Observations on the perils (and rewards) of artmaking*. Image Continuum Press.

Beaty, R. E., Kenett, Y. N., Christensen, A. P., Rosenberg, M. D., Benedek, M., Chen, Q., Fink, A., Qiu, J., Kwapil, T. R., Kane, M. J., & Silvia, P. J.

(2018). Robust prediction of individual creative ability from brain functional connectivity. *Proceedings of the National Academy of Sciences, 115*(5), 1087–1092. https://doi.org/10.1073/pnas.1713532115

Beaumont, S. L. (2013). Art therapy for complicated grief: A focus on meaning-making approaches. *Canadian Art Therapy Association Journal, 26*(2), 1–7. https://doi.org/10.1080/08322473.2013.11415582

Benear, S. L., Sunday, M. A., Davidson, R., Palmeri, T. J., & Gauthier, I. (2024). Can art change the way we see? *Psychology of Aesthetics, Creativity, and the Arts, 18*(5), 882–893. https://doi.org/10.1037/aca0000288

Bentwich, M. E., & Gilbey, P. (2017). More than visual literacy: Art and the enhancement of tolerance for ambiguity and empathy. *BMC Medical Education, 17*(1), 200. https://doi.org/10.1186/s12909-017-1028-7

Bergman Nutley, S., Darki, F., & Klingberg, T. (2014). Music practice is associated with development of working memory during childhood and adolescence. *Frontiers in Human Neuroscience, 7*. https://doi.org/10.3389/fnhum.2013.00926

Bernatzky, G., Presch, M., Anderson, M., & Panksepp, J. (2011). Emotional foundations of music as a non-pharmacological pain management tool in modern medicine. *Neuroscience and Biobehavioral Reviews, 35*(9), 1989–1999. https://doi.org/10.1016/j.neubiorev.2011.06.005

Bertrand, R. (2013). *The problems of philosophy*. Martino Fine Books.

Besser-Jones, L. (2024). *The art of the interesting: What we miss in our pursuit of the good life and how to cultivate it* (1st ed.). Balance.

Besser, L. L., & Oishi, S. (2020). The psychologically rich life. *Philosophical Psychology, 33*(8), 1053–1071. https://doi.org/10.1080/09515089.2020.1778662

Blessi, G. T., Grossi, E., Sacco, P. L., Pieretti, G., & Ferilli, G. (2014). Cultural participation, relational goods and individual subjective well-being: Some empirical evidence. *Review of Economics. 4*(3), 33–46. https://doi.org/10.13140/2.1.3584.1925

Boothby, E. J., Clark, M. S., & Bargh, J. A. (2014). Shared experiences are amplified. *Psychological Science, 25*(12), 2209–2216. https://doi.org/10.1177/0956797614551162

Bourke, J. (2012). Languages of pain. *The Lancet, 379*(9835), 2420–2421. https://doi.org/10.1016/S0140-6736(12)61055-1

Bradt, J., Norris, M., Shim, M., Gracely, E. J., & Gerrity, P. (2016). Vocal music therapy for chronic pain management in inner-city African Americans: A mixed methods feasibility study. *Journal of Music Therapy, 53*(2), 178–206. https://doi.org/10.1093/jmt/thw004

Brajša-Žganec, A., Merkaš, M., & Šverko, I. (2011). Quality of life and leisure activities: How do leisure activities contribute to subjective well-being? *Social Indicators Research, 102*(1), 81–91. https://doi.org/10.1007/s11205-010-9724-2

Brattico, E., Alluri, V., Bogert, B., Jacobsen, T., Vartiainen, N., Nieminen, S., & Tervaniemi, M. (2011). A functional MRI study of happy and sad emotions in music with and without lyrics. *Frontiers in Psychology*, *2*, 308. https://doi.org/10.3389/fpsyg.2011.00308

Brokerhof, I. M., Bal, P. M., Jansen, P. G. W., & Solinger, O. N. (2018). Fictional narratives and identity change: Three pathways through which stories influence the Dialogical Self. In M. M. Puchalska-Wasy, P. K. Oleś, & H. J. M. Hermans (Eds.), *Dialogical Self* (pp. 29–57). Towarzystwo Naukowe Katolickiego Uniwersytetu Lubelskiego Jana Pawła II.

Brown, S., Martinez, M. J., & Parsons, L. M. (2006). The neural basis of human dance. *Cerebral Cortex*, *16*(8), 1157–1167. https://doi.org/10.1093/cercor/bhj057

Bryan-Wilson, J., & Heffernan, M. B. (2020, June 30). Facing social practice: Mary Beth Heffernan in conversation with Julia Bryan-Wilson. *Art Journal Open*. http://artjournal.collegeart.org/?p=13808

Bryson, A., & MacKerron, G. (2017). Are you happy while you work? *The Economic Journal*, *127*(599), 106–125. https://doi.org/10.1111/ecoj.12269

Budner, S. (1962). Intolerance of ambiguity as a personality variable. *Journal of Personality*, *30*(1), 29–50. https://doi.org/10.1111/j.1467-6494.1962.tb02303.x

Burkhart, B. (2019). *Indigenizing philosophy through the land: A trickster methodology for decolonizing environmental ethics and indigenous futures* (1st ed.). Michigan State University Press.

Calvo-Merino, B., Glaser, D. E., Grèzes, J., Passingham, R. E., & Haggard, P. (2005). Action observation and acquired motor skills: An fMRI study with expert dancers. *Cerebral Cortex*, *15*(8), 1243–1249. https://doi.org/10.1093/cercor/bhi007

Calvo-Merino, B., Grèzes, J., Glaser, D. E., Passingham, R. E., & Haggard, P. (2006). Seeing or doing? Influence of visual and motor familiarity in action observation. *Current Biology*, *16*(19), 1905–1910. https://doi.org/10.1016/j.cub.2006.07.065

Cameron, L., Rutland, A., Brown, R., & Douch, R. (2006). Changing children's intergroup attitudes toward refugees: Testing different models of extended contact. *Child Development*, *77*(5), 1208–1219. https://doi.org/10.1111/j.1467-8624.2006.00929.x

Carel, H., & Kidd, I. J. (2020). Expanding transformative experience. *European Journal of Philosophy*, *28*(1), 199–213. https://doi.org/10.1111/ejop.12480

Carroll, N. (2002). The wheel of virtue: Art, literature, and moral knowledge. *The Journal of Aesthetics and Art Criticism*, *60*(1), 3–26.

(2012). *Art in three dimensions*. Oxford University Press.

Carson, S. H., Peterson, J. B., & Higgins, D. M. (2003). Decreased latent inhibition is associated with increased creative achievement in high-functioning individuals. *Journal of Personality and Social Psychology*, *85*(3), 499–506. https://doi.org/10.1037/0022-3514.85.3.499

Caspari, S., Nåden, D., & Eriksson, K. (2007). Why not ask the patient? An evaluation of the aesthetic surroundings in hospitals by patients.

Quality Management in Health Care, 16(3), 280–292. https://doi.org/10.1097/01.QMH.0000281064.60849.a6

Caulfield, M., Andolsek, K., Grbic, D., & Roskovensky, L. (2014). Ambiguity tolerance of students matriculating to U.S. medical schools. *Academic Medicine, 89*(11), 1526. https://doi.org/10.1097/ACM.0000000000000485

Chabris, C. F., & Simons, D. (2010). *The invisible gorilla: And other ways our intuitions deceive us* (1. paperback ed.). Broadway Paperbacks.

Chamberlain, R., Drake, J. E., Kozbelt, A., Hickman, R., Siev, J., & Wagemans, J. (2019). Artists as experts in visual cognition: An update. *Psychology of Aesthetics, Creativity, and the Arts, 13*(1), 58–73. https://doi.org/10.1037/aca0000156

Chamberlain, R., Swinnen, L., Heeren, S., & Wagemans, J. (2018). Perceptual flexibility is coupled with reduced executive inhibition in students of the visual arts. *British Journal of Psychology, 109(2),* 244–258. https://doi.org/10.1111/bjop.12253

Chamberlain, R., & Wagemans, J. (2015). Visual arts training is linked to flexible attention to local and global levels of visual stimuli. *Acta Psychologica, 161,* 185–197. https://doi.org/10.1016/j.actpsy.2015.08.012

Chamorro-Premuzic, T., Reimers, S., Hsu, A., & Ahmetoglu, G. (2009). Who art thou? Personality predictors of artistic preferences in a large UK sample: The importance of openness. *British Journal of Psychology, 100*(3), 501–516. https://doi.org/10.1348/000712608X366867

Chan, H. W., Ignacio, A., Rebello, C., & Cupchik, G. C. (2022). The therapeutic value of creative art-making during the Covid-19 pandemic. *Journal of Gifted Education and Creativity, 9*(1): 93–113.

Chappell, S. G. (2019). Introducing epiphanies. *Zeitschrift Für Ethik Und Moralphilosophie, 2*(1), 95–121. https://doi.org/10.1007/s42048-019-00029-4

Charon, R. (2001). Narrative medicine: A model for empathy, reflection, profession, and trust. *JAMA, 286*(15), 1897–1902. https://doi.org/10.1001/jama.286.15.1897

Chatterjee, A., & Vartanian, O. (2014). Neuroaesthetics. *Trends in Cognitive Sciences, 18*(7), 370–375. https://doi.org/10.1016/j.tics.2014.03.003

Chen, P.-J., Huang, C.-D., & Yeh, S.-J. (2017). Impact of a narrative medicine programme on healthcare providers' empathy scores over time. *BMC Medical Education, 17*(1), 108. https://doi.org/10.1186/s12909-017-0952-x

Chirico, A., Pizzolante, M., Kitson, A., Gianotti, E., Riecke, B. E., & Gaggioli, A. (2022). Defining transformative experiences: A conceptual analysis. *Frontiers in Psychology, 13*,790300. https://doi.org/10.3389/fpsyg.2022.790300

Chirumbolo, A., Livi, S., Mannetti, L., Pierro, A., & Kruglanski, A. W. (2004). Effects of need for closure on creativity in small group interactions. *European Journal of Personality, 18*(4), 265–278. https://doi.org/10.1002/per.518

Chirumbolo, A., Mannetti, L., Pierro, A., Areni, A., & Kruglanski, A. W. (2005). Motivated closed-mindedness and creativity in small groups. *Small Group Research, 36*(1), 59–82. https://doi.org/10.1177/1046496404268535

Chisolm, M. S., Kelly-Hedrick, M., & Wright, S. M. (2021). How visual arts–based education can promote clinical excellence. *Academic Medicine*, *96*(8), 1100. https://doi.org/10.1097/ACM.0000000000003862

Christensen, A. P., Cotter, K. N., & Silvia, P. J. (2019). Reopening openness to experience: A network analysis of four openness to experience inventories. *Journal of Personality Assessment*, *101*(6), 574–588. https://doi.org/10.1080/00223891.2018.1467428

Christensen, A. P., Kenett, Y. N., Cotter, K. N., Beaty, R. E., & Silvia, P. J. (2018). Remotely close associations: Openness to experience and semantic memory structure. *European Journal of Personality*, *32*(4), 480–492. https://doi.org/10.1002/per.2157

Christensen, J. F., Gomila, A., Gaigg, S. B., Sivarajah, N., & Calvo-Merino, B. (2016). Dance expertise modulates behavioral and psychophysiological responses to affective body movement. *Journal of Experimental Psychology: Human Perception and Performance*, *42*(8), 1139–1147. https://doi.org/10.1037/xhp0000176

Chung, B., Jones, L., Jones, A., Corbett, C. E., Booker, T., Wells, K. B., & Collins, B. (2009). Using community arts events to enhance collective efficacy and community engagement to address depression in an African American community. *American Journal of Public Health*, *99*(2), 237–244. https://doi.org/10.2105/AJPH.2008.141408

Cirelli, L. K., Wan, S. J., Spinelli, C., & Trainor, L. J. (2017). Effects of interpersonal movement synchrony on infant helping behaviors. *Music Perception*, *34*(3), 319–326. https://doi.org/10.1525/mp.2017.34.3.319

Clennon, O. D., Kagan, C., Lawthom, R., & Swindells, R. (2016). Participation in community arts: Lessons from the inner-city. *International Journal of Inclusive Education*, *20*(3), 331–346. https://doi.org/10.1080/13603116.2015.1047660

Clow, A., & Fredhoi, C. (2006). Normalisation of salivary cortisol levels and self-report stress by a brief lunchtime visit to an art gallery by London City workers. *Journal of Holistic Healthcare*, *3*(2), Article 2.

Cohen, T. (1993). High and low thinking about high and low art. *The Journal of Aesthetics and Art Criticism*, *51*(2), 151–156. https://doi.org/10.2307/431380

Collins, A. L., Sarkisian, N., & Winner, E. (2009). Flow and happiness in later life: An investigation into the role of daily and weekly flow experiences. *Journal of Happiness Studies*, *10*(6), 703–719. https://doi.org/10.1007/s10902-008-9116-3

Connelly, B. S., Ones, D. S., Davies, S. E., & Birkland, A. (2014). Opening up openness: A theoretical sort following critical incidents methodology and a meta-analytic investigation of the trait family measures. *Journal of Personality Assessment*, *96*(1), 17–28. https://doi.org/10.1080/00223891.2013.809355

Constitution of the World Health Organization. (n.d.). Retrieved July 30, 2025, from www.who.int/about/governance/constitution

Conway, M. A. (1990). *Autobiographical memory: An introduction* (pp. xviii, 200). Open University Press.

Cooper, D., Yap, K., & Batalha, L. (2018). Mindfulness-based interventions and their effects on emotional clarity: A systematic review and meta-analysis. *Journal of Affective Disorders*, *235*, 265–276. https://doi.org/10.1016/j.jad.2018.04.018

Cooper, J. M. (Ed.). (1997). *Plato: Complete works*. Hackett Publishing.

Costa-Giomi, E. (2004). Effects of three years of piano instruction on children's academic achievement, school performance and self-esteem. *Psychology of Music*, *32*(2), 139–152. https://doi.org/10.1177/0305735604041491

Cramer, V., Torgersen, S., & Kringlen, E. (2005). Quality of life and anxiety disorders: A population study. *The Journal of Nervous and Mental Disease*, *193*(3), 196–202. https://doi.org/10.1097/01.nmd.0000154836.22687.13

Crane, T., Buultjens, M., & Fenner, P. (2021). Art-based interventions during pregnancy to support women's wellbeing: An integrative review. *Women and Birth: Journal of the Australian College of Midwives*, *34*(4), 325–334. https://doi.org/10.1016/j.wombi.2020.08.009

Cross, I. (2014). Music and communication in music psychology. *Psychology of Music*, *42*(6), 809–819. https://doi.org/10.1177/0305735614543968

Csikszentmihalyi, M. (1982). Toward a psychology of optimal experience. In L. Wheeler (Ed.), *Review of personality and social psychology: Volume 2* (pp. 13–36). Sage.

(1996). *Creativity: Flow and the psychology of discovery and invention*. HarperCollins Publishers.

Cucca, A., Di Rocco, A., Acosta, I., Beheshti, M., Berberian, M., Bertisch, H. C., Droby, A., Ettinger, T., Hudson, T. E., Inglese, M., Jung, Y. J., Mania, D. F., Quartarone, A., Rizzo, J.-R., Sharma, K., Feigin, A., Biagioni, M. C., & Ghilardi, M. F. (2021). Art therapy for Parkinson's disease. *Parkinsonism & Related Disorders*, *84*, 148–154. https://doi.org/10.1016/j.parkreldis.2021.01.013

Cupchik, G. C., Vartanian, O., Crawley, A., & Mikulis, D. J. (2009). Viewing artworks: Contributions of cognitive control and perceptual facilitation to aesthetic experience. *Brain and Cognition*, *70*(1), 84–91. https://doi.org/10.1016/j.bandc.2009.01.003

Currie, G. (2020). *Imagining and knowing: The shape of fiction*. Oxford University Press. https://doi.org/10.1093/oso/9780199656615.001.0001

D'Cunha, N. M., McKune, A. J., Isbel, S., Kellett, J., Georgousopoulou, E. N., & Naumovski, N. (2019). Psychophysiological responses in people living with dementia after an art gallery intervention: An exploratory study. *Journal of Alzheimer's Disease: JAD*, *72*(2), 549–562. https://doi.org/10.3233/JAD-190784

Dance from the State of Veracruz. (n.d.). Retrieved October 14, 2024, from https://mexicandancecompany.org/mexican-dance/veracruz.html

Danvers, A. F., & Shiota, M. N. (2017). Going off script: Effects of awe on memory for script-typical and -irrelevant narrative detail. *Emotion*, *17*(6), 938–952. https://doi.org/10.1037/emo0000277

De Cruz, H. (2024). *Wonderstruck: How wonder and awe shape the way we think*. Princeton University Press. https://doi.org/10.2307/jj.7249506

de Manzano, O., Theorell, T., Harmat, L., & Ullén, F. (2010). The psychophysiology of flow during piano playing. *Emotion (Washington, D.C.)*, *10*(3), 301–311. https://doi.org/10.1037/a0018432

de Witte, M., Orkibi, H., Zarate, R., Karkou, V., Sajnani, N., Malhotra, B., Ho, R. T. H., Kaimal, G., Baker, F. A., & Koch, S. C. (2021). From therapeutic factors to mechanisms of change in the creative arts therapies: A scoping review. *Frontiers in Psychology*, *12*. https://doi.org/10.3389/fpsyg.2021.678397

Debenedetti, S. (2003). Investigating the role of companions in the art museum experience. *International Journal of Arts Management*, *5*(3), 52–63.

Dellacherie, D., Roy, M., Hugueville, L., Peretz, I., & Samson, S. (2011). The effect of musical experience on emotional self-reports and psychophysiological responses to dissonance. *Psychophysiology*, *48*(3), 337–349. https://doi.org/10.1111/j.1469-8986.2010.01075.x

DeYoung, C. G., Grazioplene, R. G., & Peterson, J. B. (2012). From madness to genius: The Openness/Intellect trait domain as a paradoxical simplex. *Journal of Research in Personality*, *46*(1), 63–78. https://doi.org/10.1016/j.jrp.2011.12.003

DeYoung, C. G., Quilty, L. C., & Peterson, J. B. (2007). Between facets and domains: 10 aspects of the Big Five. *Journal of Personality and Social Psychology*, *93*(5), 880–896. https://doi.org/10.1037/0022-3514.93.5.880

Di Bernardo, G. A., Vezzali, L., Stathi, S., Cadamuro, A., & Cortesi, L. (2017). Vicarious, extended and imagined intergroup contact: A review of interventions based on indirect contact strategies applied in educational settings. *TPM-Testing, Psychometrics, Methodology in Applied Psychology*, *24*(1), 3–211.

Dileo, C., & Bradt, J. (2005). *Medical music therapy: A meta-analysis & agenda for future research*. Jeffrey Books.

Dissanayake, E. (1990). *What is art for?* University of Washington Press.

Djikic, M., Oatley, K., & Moldoveanu, M. C. (2013). Opening the closed mind: The effect of exposure to literature on the need for closure. *Creativity Research Journal*, *25*(2), 149–154. https://doi.org/10.1080/10400419.2013.783735

Djikic, M., Oatley, K., Zoeterman, S., & Peterson, J. B. (2009). On being moved by art: How reading fiction transforms the self. *Creativity Research Journal*, *21*(1), 24–29. https://doi.org/10.1080/10400410802633392

Dodell-Feder, D., & Tamir, D. I. (2018). Fiction reading has a small positive impact on social cognition: A meta-analysis. *Journal of Experimental Psychology: General*, *147*(11), 1713–1727. https://doi.org/10.1037/xge0000395

Dollinger, S. J., Urban, K. K., & James, T. A. (2004). Creativity and openness: Further validation of two creative product measures. *Creativity Research Journal*, *16*(1), 35–47. https://doi.org/10.1207/s15326934crj1601_4

Dow, R., Warran, K., Letrondo, P., & Fancourt, D. (2023). The arts in public health policy: Progress and opportunities. *The Lancet Public Health*, *8*(2), e155–e160. https://doi.org/10.1016/S2468-2667(22)00313-9
Drake, J. E., Simmons, S., Rouser, S., Poloes, I., & Winner, E. (2021). Artists excel on image activation but not image manipulation tasks. *Empirical Studies of the Arts*, *39*(1), 3–16. https://doi.org/10.1177/0276237419868941
Eastham, B. (2020). *The imaginary museum: A personal tour of contemporary art featuring ghosts, nudity and disagreements*. TLS Books.
Ebert, M., Hoffmann, J. D., Ivcevic, Z., Phan, C., & Brackett, M. A. (2015). Teaching emotion and creativity skills through art: A workshop for children. *The International Journal of Creativity and Problem Solving*, *25*(2), 23–36.
Edgerton, S. Y. (2009). *The Mirror, the window, and the telescope: How Renaissance linear perspective changed our vision of the universe*. Cornell University Press.
Elgin, C. Z. (2002). Art in the advancement of understanding. *American Philosophical Quarterly*, *39*(1), 1–12.
Endres, M. L., Camp, R., & Milner, M. (2015). Is ambiguity tolerance malleable? Experimental evidence with potential implications for future research. *Frontiers in Psychology*, *6*, 619. https://doi.org/10.3389/fpsyg.2015.00619
Ettinger, T., Berberian, M., Acosta, I., Cucca, A., Feigin, A., Genovese, D., Pollen, T., Rieders, J., Kilachand, R., Gomez, C., Kaimal, G., Biagioni, M., Di Rocco, A., Ghilardi, F. M., & Rizzo, J.-R. (2023). Art therapy as a comprehensive complementary treatment for Parkinson's disease. *Frontiers in Human Neuroscience*, *17*, 1–14. https://doi.org/10.3389/fnhum.2023.1110531
Eyal, T., Steffel, M., & Epley, N. (2018). Perspective mistaking: Accurately understanding the mind of another requires getting perspective, not taking perspective. *Journal of Personality and Social Psychology*, *114*(4), 547–571. https://doi.org/10.1037/pspa0000115
Fairey, T. (2018). Participatory arts and peacebuilding: Embodying and challenging reconciliation. In I. Sertić (Ed.), *Participatory Arts for Invisible Communities* (pp. 204–214). Omnimedia.
Falk, J. H., & Dierking, L. D. (2013). *The museum experience revisited*. Routledge.
Fancourt, D., & Finn, S. (2019). *What is the evidence on the role of the arts in improving health and well-being? A scoping review*. WHO Regional Office for Europe. www.ncbi.nlm.nih.gov/books/NBK553773/
Fancourt, D., & Steptoe, A. (2019). The art of life and death: 14 year follow-up analyses of associations between arts engagement and mortality in the English Longitudinal Study of Ageing. *BMJ*, *367*, l6377. https://doi.org/10.1136/bmj.l6377
Fayn, K., Silvia, P. J., Erbas, Y., Tiliopoulos, N., & Kuppens, P. (2018). Nuanced aesthetic emotions: Emotion differentiation is related to knowledge of the arts and curiosity. *Cognition and Emotion*, *32*(3), 593–599. https://doi.org/10.1080/02699931.2017.1322554
Feist, G. J. (1998). A meta-analysis of personality in scientific and artistic creativity. *Personality and Social Psychology Review*, *2*(4), 290–309. https://doi.org/10.1207/s15327957pspr0204_5

Fekete, A., Maidhof, R. M., Specker, E., Nater, U. M., & Leder, H. (2022). Does art reduce pain and stress? A registered report protocol of investigating autonomic and endocrine markers of music, visual art, and multimodal aesthetic experience. *PLOS One*, *17*(4), e0266545. https://doi.org/10.1371/journal.pone.0266545

Fincham, D. (2014). How law defines art. *John Marshall Review of Intellectual Property Law*, *14*, 314–325.

Fingerhut, J., Gomez-Lavin, J., Winklmayr, C., & Prinz, J. J. (2021). The aesthetic self. The importance of aesthetic taste in music and art for our perceived identity. *Frontiers in Psychology*, *11*, 577703. https://doi.org/10.3389/fpsyg.2020.577703

Fleming, R., & Collins, F. S. (2024). *Music and mind: Harnessing the arts for health and wellness*. Penguin Publishing Group.

Folan, K. (2017). The painting that changed my life. *Literary Hub*. https://lithub.com/the-painting-that-changed-my-life/

Freedberg, D., & Gallese, V. (2007). Motion, emotion and empathy in esthetic experience. *Trends in Cognitive Sciences*, *11*(5), 197–203. https://doi.org/10.1016/j.tics.2007.02.003

Freire, P. (2000). *Pedagogy of the oppressed* (30th anniversary ed.). Continuum.

Friscia, S. (2019). Inside the history and techniques of folklórico. *Dance Spirit*. https://dancespirit.com/baile-folklorico-world-dance/

Fuchs, G. L., Kumar ,V. K., & Porter, J. (2007). Emotional creativity, alexithymia, and styles of creativity. *Creativity Research Journal*, *19*(2–3), 233–245. https://doi.org/10.1080/10400410701397313

Furnham, A., & Walker, J. (2001). Personality and judgements of abstract, pop art, and representational paintings. *European Journal of Personality*, *15*(1), 57–72. https://doi.org/10.1002/per.340

Gabora, L. (2010). Revenge of the "neurds": Characterizing creative thought in terms of the structure and dynamics of memory. *Creativity Research Journal*, *22*(1), 1–13. https://doi.org/10.1080/10400410903579494

Gaiha, S. M., Salisbury, T. T., Usmani, S., Koschorke, M., Raman, U., & Petticrew, M. (2021). Effectiveness of arts interventions to reduce mental-health-related stigma among youth: A systematic review and meta-analysis. *BMC Psychiatry*, *21*(1), 364. https://doi.org/10.1186/s12888-021-03350-8

Garcia, X. (2017, March 17). Beneath the fold: The many uses of tessellation and Miura folds. *Science Friday*. www.sciencefriday.com/educational-resources/tessellation-and-miura-folds/

Garfield, J. L., & Priest, G. (2020). Skill and virtuosity in Buddhist and Daoist philosophy. In Ellen Fridland & Carlotta Pavese (Eds.), *The Routledge handbook of philosophy of skill and expertise*. Routledge.

George, E. M., & Coch, D. (2011). Music training and working memory: An ERP study. *Neuropsychologia*, *49*(5), 1083–1094. https://doi.org/10.1016/j.neuropsychologia.2011.02.001

Gernot, G., Pelowski, M., & Leder, H. (2018). Empathy, Einfühlung, and aesthetic experience: The effect of emotion contagion on appreciation of representational and abstract art using fEMG and SCR. *Cognitive Processing, 19*(2), 147–165. https://doi.org/10.1007/s10339

Gobet, F., & Simon, H. A. (1996). Templates in chess memory: A mechanism for recalling several boards. *Cognitive Psychology, 31*(1), 1–40. https://doi.org/10.1006/cogp.1996.0011

Goldsmith, L. T., Hetland, L., Hoyle, C., & Winner, E. (2016). Visual-spatial thinking in geometry and the visual arts. *Psychology of Aesthetics, Creativity, and the Arts, 10*(1), 56–71. https://doi.org/10.1037/aca0000027

Golden, T. L., Maier Lokuta, A., Mohanty, A., Tiedemann, A., Ng, T. W. C., Mendu, M., Morgan, N., Kuge, M. N., & Brinza, T. (2023). Social prescription in the US: A pilot evaluation of Mass Cultural Council's "CultureRx." *Frontiers in Public Health, 10*. https://doi.org/10.3389/fpubh.2022.1016136

Goldstein, T. (2009). The pleasure of unadulterated sadness: Experiencing sorrow in fiction, nonfiction, and "in person." *Psychology of Aesthetics, Creativity, and the Arts, 3*, 232–237. https://doi.org/10.1037/a0015343

Goldstein, T. R. (2024). *Why theatre education matters: Understanding its cognitive, social, and emotional benefits*. Teachers College Press.

Goldstein, T. R., & Lerner, M. D. (2018). Dramatic pretend play games uniquely improve emotional control in young children. *Developmental Science, 21*(4), e12603. https://doi.org/10.1111/desc.12603

Goldstein, T. R., Tamir, M., & Winner, E. (2013). Expressive suppression and acting classes. *Psychology of Aesthetics, Creativity, and the Arts, 7*(2), 191–196. https://doi.org/10.1037/a0030209

Goldstein, T. R., & Winner, E. (2012). Enhancing empathy and theory of mind. *Journal of Cognition and Development, 13*(1), 19–37. https://doi.org/10.1080/15248372.2011.573514

Goldstein, T. R., Wu, K., & Winner, E. (2009). Actors are skilled in theory of mind but not empathy. *Imagination, Cognition and Personality, 29*(2), 115–133. https://doi.org/10.2190/IC.29.2.c

Good, A., & Russo, F. (2016). Singing promotes cooperation in a diverse group of children. *Social Psychology, 47*, 340–344. https://doi.org/10.1027/1864-9335/a000282

Gowda, D., Dubroff, R., Willieme, A., Swan-Sein, A., & Capello, C. (2018). Art as sanctuary: A four-year mixed-methods evaluation of a visual art course addressing uncertainty through reflection. *Academic Medicine, 93*(11S), S8. https://doi.org/10.1097/ACM.0000000000002379

Grant, M., Salsman, N. L., & Berking, M. (2018). The assessment of successful emotion regulation skills use: Development and validation of an English version of the Emotion Regulation Skills Questionnaire. *PLOS One, 13*(10), e0205095. https://doi.org/10.1371/journal.pone.0205095

Gratz, K. L., & Roemer, L. (2004). Multidimensional assessment of emotion regulation and dysregulation: Development, factor structure, and initial validation of the difficulties in emotion regulation scale. *Journal of Psychopathology and Behavioral Assessment, 26*(1), 41–54. https://doi.org/10.1023/B:JOBA.0000007455.08539.94

Green, D., Karafa, K., & Wilson, S. (2021). Art therapy with grieving children: Effect on affect in the dual-process model. *Art Therapy, 38*(4), 211–215. https://doi.org/10.1080/07421656.2020.1823197

Green, M. C., & Appel, M. (2024). Chapter One – Narrative transportation: How stories shape how we see ourselves and the world. In B. Gawronski (Ed.), *Advances in Experimental Social Psychology* (Vol. 70, pp. 1–82). Academic Press. https://doi.org/10.1016/bs.aesp.2024.03.002

Griskevicius, V., Shiota, M. N., & Neufeld, S. L. (2010). Influence of different positive emotions on persuasion processing: A functional evolutionary approach. *Emotion, 10*(2), 190–206. https://doi.org/10.1037/a0018421

Gross, J. J. (1998). The emerging field of emotion regulation: An integrative review. *Review of General Psychology, 2*(3), 271–299. https://doi.org/10.1037/1089-2680.2.3.271

(2015). Emotion regulation: Current status and future prospects. *Psychological Inquiry, 26*(1), 1–26. https://doi.org/10.1080/1047840X.2014.940781

Gross, J. J., & John, O. P. (2003). Individual differences in two emotion regulation processes: Implications for affect, relationships, and well-being. *Journal of Personality and Social Psychology, 85*(2), 348–362. https://doi.org/10.1037/0022-3514.85.2.348

Grossi, E., Tavano Blessi, G., & Sacco, P. L. (2019). Magic moments: Determinants of stress relief and subjective wellbeing from visiting a cultural heritage site. *Culture, Medicine, and Psychiatry, 43*(1), 4–24. https://doi.org/10.1007/s11013-018-9593-8

Guendelman, S., Medeiros, S., & Rampes, H. (2017). Mindfulness and emotion regulation: Insights from neurobiological, psychological, and clinical studies. *Frontiers in Psychology, 8*, 220. https://doi.org/10.3389/fpsyg.2017.00220

Gurwin, J., Revere, K. E., Niepold, S., Bassett, B., Mitchell, R., Davidson, S., DeLisser, H., & Binenbaum, G. (2018). A randomized controlled study of art observation training to improve medical student ophthalmology skills. *Ophthalmology, 125*(1), 8–14. https://doi.org/10.1016/j.ophtha.2017.06.031

Hackney, M. E., & Earhart, G. M. (2009). Short duration, intensive tango dancing for Parkinson disease: An uncontrolled pilot study. *Complementary Therapies in Medicine, 17*(4), 203–207. https://doi.org/10.1016/j.ctim.2008.10.005

Haeyen, S., & Heijman, J. (2020). Compassion focused art therapy for people diagnosed with a cluster B/C personality disorder: An intervention mapping study. *The Arts in Psychotherapy, 69*, 101663. https://doi.org/10.1016/j.aip.2020.101663

Hamann, S. (2001). Cognitive and neural mechanisms of emotional memory. *Trends in Cognitive Sciences, 5*(9), 394–400. https://doi.org/10.1016/s1364-6613(00)01707-1

Hanich, J., Wagner, V., Shah, M., Jacobsen, T., & Menninghaus, W. (2014). Why we like to watch sad films. The pleasure of being moved in aesthetic experiences. *Psychology of Aesthetics, Creativity, and the Arts, 8*(2), 130–143. https://doi.org/10.1037/a0035690

Hannon, E. E., & Trainor, L. J. (2007). Music acquisition: Effects of enculturation and formal training on development. *Trends in Cognitive Sciences*, *11*(11), 466–472. https://doi.org/10.1016/j.tics.2007.08.008

Hardy, C. (2017). Empathizing with patients: The role of interaction and narratives in providing better patient care. *Medicine, Health Care and Philosophy*, *20*(2), 237–248. https://doi.org/10.1007/s11019-016-9746-x

Harlap, Y. (2006). *Toward training: The meanings and practices of social change work in the arts*. Judith Marcuse Projects.

Harris, P. B., McBride, G., Ross, C., & Curtis, L. (2002). A place to heal: Environmental sources of satisfaction among hospital patients. *Journal of Applied Social Psychology*, *32*(6), 1276–1299. https://doi.org/10.1111/j.1559-1816.2002.tb01436.x

Harvey, M. L., & Miles, D. (2009). *And then they came for me*: The effectiveness of a theatrical performance and study guide on middle-school students' Holocaust knowledge and empathic concern. *Youth Theatre Journal*, *23*(2), 91–102. https://doi.org/10.1080/08929090903281402

Heide, F. J., Porter, N., & Saito, P. K. (2012). Do you hear the people sing? Musical theatre and attitude change. *Psychology of Aesthetics, Creativity, and the Arts*, *6*(3), 224–230. https://doi.org/10.1037/a0027574

Hein, G. E. (2002). *Learning in the museum*. Routledge. https://doi.org/10.4324/9780203028322

Heinich, N. (1996). It's a bird: Brancusi vs USA: When law defines art. *Droit et Societe*, *34*, 649.

Hekmat, H. M., & Hertel, J. B. (1993). Pain attenuating effects of preferred versus non-preferred music interventions. *Psychology of Music*, *21*(2), 163–173. https://doi.org/10.1177/030573569302100205

Henderson, C., Evans-Lacko, S , & Thornicroft, G (2013). Mental illness stigma, help seeking, and public health programs. *American Journal of Public Health*, *103*(5), 777–780. https://doi.org/10.2105/AJPH.2012.301056

Herron, A., & Jamieson, A. (2020). Grandfathers at Melbourne museum: Shining a spotlight on overlooked museum visitors. *Visitor Studies*, *23*(2), 101–119. https://doi.org/10.1080/10645578.2020.1772616

Hikiji, R. (2005). *A música e o risco. [Music and social risk]*. EDUSP.

Hill-Jarrett, T. G. (2023). The Black radical imagination: A space of hope and possible futures. *Frontiers in Neurology*, *14*, 1241922. https://doi.org/10.3389/fneur.2023.1241922

Hill-Jarrett, T. G., Jackson, A. J., Amuiri, A., & Aguirre, G. A. (2025). Radical imagination: An Afrofuturism and creative aging program for Black women's brain health and wellness. *International Journal of Environmental Research and Public Health*, *22*(6), 875. https://doi.org/10.3390/ijerph22060875

Hitsuwari, J., & Nomura, M. (2023). Ambiguity tolerance can improve through poetry appreciation and creation. *The Journal of Creative Behavior*, *57*(2), 178–185. https://doi.org/10.1002/jocb.574

Hoffmann, J. D., Ivcevic, Z., & Maliakkal, N. (2021). Emotions, creativity, and the arts: Evaluating a course for children. *Empirical Studies of the Arts*, *39*(2), 123–148. https://doi.org/10.1177/0276237420907864

Home | National Arts Council. (n.d.). Retrieved October 14, 2024, from www.nac.gov.sg/

How Art Changed Me | Randy | Season 1 | Episode 3 | PBS. (2024, October 14). [Video recording]. www.pbs.org/video/randy-kjgyfn/

Howlin, C., & Rooney, B. (2021). Cognitive agency in music interventions: Increased perceived control of music predicts increased pain tolerance. *European Journal of Pain (London, England)*, *25*(8), 1712–1722. https://doi.org/10.1002/ejp.1780

Howlin, C., Stapleton, A., & Rooney, B. (2022). Tune out pain: Agency and active engagement predict decreases in pain intensity after music listening. *PLOS One*, *17*(8), e0271329. https://doi.org/10.1371/journal.pone.0271329

Hughes, J., & Wilson, K. (2004). Playing a part: The impact of youth theatre on young people's personal and social development. *Research in Drama Education: The Journal of Applied Theatre and Performance*, *9*(1), 57–72. https://doi.org/10.1080/1356978042000185911

Hur, Y.-J., Gerger, G., Leder, H., & McManus, I. C. (2020). Facing the sublime: Physiological correlates of the relationship between fear and the sublime. *Psychology of Aesthetics, Creativity, and the Arts*, *14*(3), 253–263. https://doi.org/10.1037/aca0000204

Ickes, W. (2001). Measuring empathic accuracy. In J. A. Hall & F. J. Bernieri (Eds.), *Interpersonal sensitivity: Theory and measurement* (pp. 219–241). Lawrence Erlbaum Associates.

Igdalova, A., Nawaz, S., & Chamberlain, R. (2025). A view worth talking about: The influence of social interaction on aesthetic experience and well-being outcomes in the gallery. *Psychology of Aesthetics, Creativity, and the Arts*. https://doi.org/10.1037/aca0000733 (advance online publication).

Institute of Medicine (US) Committee on Advancing Pain Research, Care, and Education. (2011). *Relieving pain in America: A blueprint for transforming prevention, care, education, and research*. National Academies Press. www.ncbi.nlm.nih.gov/books/NBK92525/

Irwin, L., Rhodes, P., & Boydell, K. (2022). Evaluation of a gallery-based arts engagement program for depression. *Australian Psychologist*, *57*(3), 186–196. https://doi.org/10.1080/00050067.2022.2061329

Ivcevic, Z., & Nusbaum, E. C. (2017). From having an idea to doing something with it: Self-regulation for creativity. In M. Karwowski & J. C. Kaufman (Eds.), *The Creative Self* (pp. 343–365). Academic Press. https://doi.org/10.1016/B978-0-12-809790-8.00020-0

Izountouemoi, A., & Esteves, F. (2023). Does dance expertise enhance sensitivity? A comparative study. *Empirical Studies of the Arts*, *43*(2), 02762374231206720. https://doi.org/10.1177/02762374231206720

Jackson, F. (1986). What Mary didn't know. *The Journal of Philosophy, 83*(5), 291–295. https://doi.org/10.2307/2026143

Jakobsson Støre, S., & Jakobsson, N. (2022). The effect of mandala coloring on state anxiety: A systematic review and meta-analysis. *Art Therapy, 39*(4), 173–181. https://doi.org/10.1080/07421656.2021.2003144

James Turrell | Artist | Royal Academy of Arts. (n.d.). Retrieved October 15, 2024, from www.royalacademy.org.uk/art-artists/name/james-turrell-hon-ra

Japee, S., Jordan, J., Licht, J., Lokey, S., Chen, G., Snow, J., Jabs, E. W., Webb, B. D., Engle, E. C., Manoli, I., Baker, C., & Ungerleider, L. G. (2023). Inability to move one's face dampens facial expression perception. *Cortex, 169*, 35–49. https://doi.org/10.1016/j.cortex.2023.08.014

Jasani, S. K., & Saks, N. S. (2013). Utilizing visual art to enhance the clinical observation skills of medical students. *Medical Teacher, 35*(7), e1327–e1331. https://doi.org/10.3109/0142159X.2013.770131

Jeffers, K. S., Mango, J. D., Tang, L., Saks, E. R., Wells, K. B., & Chung, B. (2022). Impact of opera on mental health stigma: Pilot of provider/community workshop. *Community Mental Health Journal, 58*(5), 992–999. https://doi.org/10.1007/s10597

Juslin, P. N. (2016). *Emotional reactions to music* (S. Hallam, I. Cross, & M. Thaut, Eds.). Oxford University Press. https://doi.org/10.1093/oxfordhb/9780198722946.013.17

Juslin, P. N., & Laukka, P. (2003). Communication of emotions in vocal expression and music performance: Different channels, same code? *Psychological Bulletin, 129*(5), 770–814. https://doi.org/10.1037/0033-2909.129.5.770

Juslin, P., & Västfjäll, D. (2008). All emotions are not created equal: Reaching beyond the traditional disputes. *The Behavioral and Brain Sciences, 31*, 600–621. https://doi.org/10.1017/S0140525X08005554

Kaasgaard, M., Grebosz-Haring, K., Davies, C., Musgrave, G., Shriraam, J., McCrary, J. M., & Clift, S. (2024). Is it premature to formulate recommendations for policy and practice, based on culture and health research? A robust critique of the CultureForHealth (2022) report. *Frontiers in Public Health, 12*, 1414070. https://doi.org/10.3389/fpubh.2024.1414070

Kabat-Zinn, J. (1994). *Mindfulness meditation for everyday life*. Piatkus.

Kai-Kee, E., Latina, L., & Sadoyan, L. (2020). *Activity-based teaching in the art museum: Movement, embodiment, emotion*. J. Paul Getty Museum.

Kane, M. J., Conway, A. R. A., Miura, T. K., & Colflesh, G. J. H. (2007). Working memory, attention control, and the N-back task: A question of construct validity. *Journal of Experimental Psychology. Learning, Memory, and Cognition, 33*(3), 615–622. https://doi.org/10.1037/0278-7393.33.3.615

Kantor-Martynuska, J., & Bigand, E. (2013). Individual differences in granularity of the affective responses to music. *Polish Psychological Bulletin, 44*(4), 399–408. https://doi.org/10.2478/ppb-2013-0043

Kantor-Martynuska, J., & Horabik, J. (2015). Granularity of emotional responses to music: The effect of musical expertise. *Psychology of Aesthetics, Creativity, and the Arts, 9*(3), 235–247. https://doi.org/10.1037/a0039107

Kaplan, S. (1995). The restorative benefits of nature: Toward an integrative framework. *Journal of Environmental Psychology*, *15*(3), 169–182. https://doi.org/10.1016/0272-4944(95)90001-2

Katz, J. T., & Khoshbin, S. (2014). Can visual arts training improve physician performance? *Transactions of the American Clinical and Climatological Association*, *125*, 331–341; discussion 341–342.

Kaufman, S. B. (2013). Opening up openness to experience: A four-factor model and relations to creative achievement in the arts and sciences. *The Journal of Creative Behavior*, *47*(4), 233–255. https://doi.org/10.1002/jocb.33

Kaufman, S. B., Quilty, L. C., Grazioplene, R. G., Hirsh, J. B., Gray, J. R., Peterson, J. B., & DeYoung, C. G. (2016). Openness to experience and intellect differentially predict creative achievement in the arts and sciences. *Journal of Personality*, *84*(2), 248–258. https://doi.org/10.1111/jopy.12156

Keen, S. (2006). A theory of narrative empathy. *Narrative*, *14*(3), 207–236. https://doi.org/10.1353/nar.2006.0015

Kelemen, L. J., & Shamri-Zeevi, L. (2022). Art therapy open studio and teen identity development: Helping adolescents recover from mental health conditions. *Children (Basel, Switzerland)*, *9*(7), 1029. https://doi.org/10.3390/children9071029

Kemp, R. (2012). *Embodied acting: What neuroscience tells us about performance*. Routledge. https://doi.org/10.4324/9780203126110

Kessler, R. C., Chiu, W. T., Demler, O., Merikangas, K. R., & Walters, E. E. (2005). Prevalence, severity, and comorbidity of 12-month DSM-IV disorders in the National Comorbidity Survey Replication. *Archives of General Psychiatry*, *62*(6), 617–627. https://doi.org/10.1001/archpsyc.62.6.617

Kidd, D. C., & Castano, E. (2013). Reading literary fiction improves theory of mind. *Science*, *342*(6156), 377–380. https://doi.org/10.1126/science.1239918

Kirschner, S., & Tomasello, M. (2010). Joint music making promotes prosocial behavior in 4-year-old children. *Evolution and Human Behavior*, *31*(5), 354–364. https://doi.org/10.1016/j.evolhumbehav.2010.04.004

Klugman, C. M., Peel, J., & Beckmann-Mendez, D. (2011). Art rounds: Teaching interprofessional students visual thinking strategies at one school. *Academic Medicine*, *86*(10), 1266. https://doi.org/10.1097/ACM.0b013e31822c1427

Koebner, I. J., Fishman, S. M., Paterniti, D., Sommer, D., Witt, C. M., Ward, D., & Joseph, J. G. (2019). The art of analgesia: A pilot study of art museum tours to decrease pain and social disconnection among individuals with chronic pain. *Pain Medicine*, *20*(4), 681–691. https://doi.org/10.1093/pm/pny148

Koelsch, S. (2014). Brain correlates of music-evoked emotions. *Nature Reviews Neuroscience*, *15*(3), 170–180. https://doi.org/10.1038/nrn3666

Koivisto, M., & Pallaris, C. (2024). Cognitive flexibility moderates the relationship between openness-to-experience and perceptual reversals of Necker cube. *Consciousness and Cognition*, *122*, 103698. https://doi.org/10.1016/j.concog.2024.103698

Kola, S., & Subramanian, I. (2023). Updates in Parkinson's Disease integrative therapies: An evidence-based review. *Current Neurology and Neuroscience Reports*, *23*(11), 717–726. https://doi.org/10.1007/s11910-023-01312-z

Koshimori, Y., & Thaut, M. H. (2018). Future perspectives on neural mechanisms underlying rhythm and music based neurorehabilitation in Parkinson's Disease. *Ageing Research Reviews*, *47*, 133–139. https://doi.org/10.1016/j.arr.2018.07.001

Kou, X., Konrath, S., & Goldstein, T. R. (2020). The relationship among different types of arts engagement, empathy, and prosocial behavior. *Psychology of Aesthetics, Creativity, and the Arts*, *14*(4), 481–492. https://doi.org/10.1037/aca0000269

Koutstaal, W., Brown, L., Lu, K., & Posson, K. (2025). Beyond openness: A variety of creative experiences increases flexibility and originality of visuospatial divergent thinking. *Creativity Research Journal*, *37*(3), 321–341. https://doi.org/10.1080/10400419.2023.2300575

Kraus, N., & Chandrasekaran, B. (2010). Music training for the development of auditory skills. *Nature Reviews Neuroscience*, *11*(8), 599–605. https://doi.org/10.1038/nrn2882

Kruglanski, A. W., & Webster, D. M. (1996). Motivated closing of the mind: "Seizing" and "freezing." *Psychological Review*, *103*(2), 263–283. https://doi.org/10.1037/0033-295X.103.2.263

Kuhn, T. S. (2009). *The structure of scientific revolutions*. University of Chicago Press.

Kuiken, D., Miall, D. S., & Sikora, S. (2004). Forms of self-implication in literary reading. *Poetics Today*, *25*(2), 171–203. https://doi.org/10.1215/03335372-25-2-171

Kwong, J. M. C. (2019). Cultivating open-mindedness. *Educational Theory*, *69*(4), 507–515. https://doi.org/10.1111/edth.12382

Lam, A. H. Y., Ho, L. M. K., Lam, S. K. K., Chan, C. K. Y., Chan, M. M. K., Pun, M. W. M., & Wang, K. M. P. (2024). Effectiveness and experiences of integrating Mindfulness into Peer-assisted Learning (PAL) in clinical education for nursing students: A mixed method study. *Nurse Education Today*, *132*, 106039. https://doi.org/10.1016/j.nedt.2023.106039

Larsen, L. T. (2022). Not merely the absence of disease: A genealogy of the WHO's positive health definition. *History of the Human Sciences*, *35*(1), 111–131. https://doi.org/10.1177/0952695121995355

Lauriola, M., Foschi, R., Mosca, O., & Weller, J. (2016). Attitude toward ambiguity: Empirically robust factors in self-report personality scales. *Assessment*, *23*(3), 353–373. https://doi.org/10.1177/1073191115577188

Lazarus, R. S. (1991). *Emotion and adaptation*. Oxford University Press.

Leder, H., Gerger, G., Brieber, D., & Schwarz, N. (2014). What makes an art expert? Emotion and evaluation in art appreciation. *Cognition & Emotion*, *28*(6), 1137–1147. https://doi.org/10.1080/02699931.2013.870132

Lee, J. H. (2016). The effects of music on pain: A meta-analysis. *Journal of Music Therapy*, *53*(4), 430–477. https://doi.org/10.1093/jmt/thw012

Lennartsson, A.-K., Horwitz, Eva Bojner, Theorell, Töres, & Ullén, F. (2017). Creative artistic achievement is related to lower levels of alexithymia. *Creativity Research Journal, 29*(1), 29–36. https://doi.org/10.1080/10400419.2017.1263507

Leroux, K., & Bernadska, A. (2014). Impact of the arts on individual contributions to US civil society. *Journal of Civil Society, 10*(2), 144–164. https://doi.org/10.1080/17448689.2014.912479

Lima, C. F., & Castro, S. L. (2011). Emotion recognition in music changes across the adult life span. *Cognition and Emotion, 25*(4), 585–598. https://doi.org/10.1080/02699931.2010.502449

Lin, E. (2022a). Well-being, part 1: The concept of well-being. *Philosophy Compass, 17*(2), e12812. https://doi.org/10.1111/phc3.12812

(2022b). Well-being, part 2: Theories of well-being. *Philosophy Compass, 17*(2), e12813. https://doi.org/10.1111/phc3.12813

Livingston, P. (2024). History of the ontology of art. In E. N. Zalta & U. Nodelman (Eds.), *The Stanford Encyclopedia of Philosophy* (Summer 2024). Metaphysics Research Lab, Stanford University. https://plato.stanford.edu/archives/sum2024/entries/art-ontology-history/

Lombardo, C., & Novak, P. (2024). Making with place: Community artists theorizing change. *LEARNing Landscapes, 17*(1), 143–164. https://doi.org/10.36510/learnland.v17i1.1125

Lopes, D. M. (2008). Nobody needs a theory of art. *The Journal of Philosophy, 105*(3), 109–127.

(2018). *Being for beauty: Aesthetic agency and value*. OUP Oxford. https://doi.org/10.1093/oso/9780198827214.001.0001

Low, M. Y., Lacson, C., Zhang, F., Kesslick, A., & Bradt, J. (2020). Vocal music therapy for chronic pain: A mixed methods feasibility study. *The Journal of Alternative and Complementary Medicine, 26*(2), 113–122. https://doi.org/10.1089/acm.2019.0249

Luke, J. J. (2021). "The bloody hell and holy cow moment:" Feeling awe in the art museum. *Curator: The Museum Journal, 64*(1), 41–55. https://doi.org/10.1111/cura.12397

Lutz, A., Slagter, H. A., Dunne, J. D., & Davidson, R. J. (2008). Attention regulation and monitoring in meditation. *Trends in Cognitive Sciences, 12*(4), 163–169. https://doi.org/10.1016/j.tics.2008.01.005

Lyusin, D., & Ovsyannikova, V. (2016). Measuring two aspects of emotion recognition ability: Accuracy vs. sensitivity. *Learning and Individual Differences, 52*, 129–136. https://doi.org/10.1016/j.lindif.2015.04.010

MacIntyre, A. (1984). *After virtue: A study in moral theory, second edition.* University of Notre Dame Press.

Magon, R., & Cupchik, G. (2023). Examining the role of aesthetic experiences in self-realization and self-transcendence: A thematic analysis. *Creativity. Theories – Research – Applications, 10*(1–2), 68–94. https://doi.org/10.2478/ctra-2023-0006

Mahmoud, H. M., Al-Turkistani, Z. I., Alayat, M. S., Abd El-Kafy, E. M., & El Fiky, A. A. R. (2023). Effect of dancing on freezing of gait in patients with

Parkinson's disease: A systematic review and meta-analysis. *NeuroRehabilitation*, *53*(3), 269–284. https://doi.org/10.3233/NRE-230114

Maierna, M. S., & Camodeca, M. (2021). Theatrical activities in primary school: Effects on children's emotion regulation and bullying. *International Journal of Bullying Prevention*, *3*(1), 13–23. https://doi.org/10.1007/s42380-019-00057-z

Mann, J. (2015). Towards a politics of whimsy: Yarn bombing the city. *Area*, *47*(1), 65–72.

Mar, R. A., & Oatley, K. (2008). The function of fiction is the abstraction and simulation of social experience. *Perspectives on Psychological Science*, *3*(3), 173–192. https://doi.org/10.1111/j.1745-6924.2008.00073.x

Mar, R. A., & Rain, M. (2015). Narrative fiction and expository nonfiction differentially predict verbal ability. *Scientific Studies of Reading*, *19*(6), 419–433. https://doi.org/10.1080/10888438.2015.1069296

Mar, R. A., Tackett, J. L., & Moore, C. (2010). Exposure to media and theory-of-mind development in preschoolers. *Cognitive Development*, *25*(1), 69–78. https://doi.org/10.1016/j.cogdev.2009.11.002

Marina Abramović: The Artist Is Present | MoMA. (2010). The Museum of Modern Art. Retrieved October 14, 2024, from www.moma.org/calendar/exhibitions/964

Martins, M., Pinheiro, A. P., & Lima, C. F. (2021). Does music training improve emotion recognition abilities? A critical review. *Emotion Review*, *13*(3), 199–210. https://doi.org/10.1177/17540739211022035

Mastandrea, S., Fagioli, S., & Biasi, V. (2019). Art and psychological well-being: Linking the brain to the aesthetic emotion. *Frontiers in Psychology*, *10*, 739. https://doi.org/10.3389/fpsyg.2019.00739

Mayer, J. D., & Salovey, P. (1997). What is emotional intelligence? In Peter Salovey & David Sluyter (Eds.), *Emotional development and emotional intelligence: Educational implications* (pp. 3–34). Basic Books.

Mayer, J. D., Salovey, P., & Caruso, D. (2000). Models of emotional intelligence. In Robert J. Sternberg (Ed.), *Handbook of intelligence* (pp. 396–420). Cambridge University Press. https://doi.org/10.1017/CBO9780511807947.019

Mayer, J. D., Salovey, P., Caruso, D. R., & Sitarenios, G. (2003). Measuring emotional intelligence with the MSCEIT V2.0. *Emotion*, *3*(1), 97–105. https://doi.org/10.1037/1528-3542.3.1.97

Mayo, P. (2013). Museums as sites of critical pedagogical practice. *Review of Education, Pedagogy, and Cultural Studies*, *35*(2), 144–153. https://doi.org/10.1080/10714413.2013.778661

Mayseless, O., & Kruglanski, A. W. (1987). What makes you so sure? Effects of epistemic motivations on judgmental confidence. *Organizational Behavior and Human Decision Processes*, *39*(2), 162–183. https://doi.org/10.1016/0749-5978(87)90036-7

McCaffrey, T., Cheung, P. S., Barry, M., Punch, P., & Dore, L. (2020). The role and outcomes of music listening for women in childbirth:

An integrative review. *Midwifery*, *83*, 102627. https://doi.org/10.1016/j.midw.2020.102627

McCammon, L. A., Saldaña, J., Hines, A., & Omasta, M. (2012). Lifelong impact: Adult perceptions of their high school speech and/or theatre participation. *Youth Theatre Journal*, *26*(1), 2–25. https://doi.org/10.1080/08929092.2012.678223

McDonald, M. G. (2008). The nature of epiphanic experience. *Journal of Humanistic Psychology*, *48*(1), 89–115. https://doi.org/10.1177/0022167807311878

McPhetres, J. (2019). Oh, the things you don't know: Awe promotes awareness of knowledge gaps and science interest. *Cognition and Emotion*, *33*(8), 1599–1615. https://doi.org/10.1080/02699931.2019.1585331

McRae, K., & Gross, J. J. (2020). Emotion regulation. *Emotion*, *20*(1), 1–9. https://doi.org/10.1037/emo0000703

Medina, D., & Barraza, P. (2019). Efficiency of attentional networks in musicians and non-musicians. *Heliyon*, *5*(3). https://doi.org/10.1016/j.heliyon.2019.e01315

Meinz, E. J., Hambrick, D. Z., Hawkins, C. B., Gillings, A. K., Meyer, B. E., & Schneider, J. L. (2012). Roles of domain knowledge and working memory capacity in components of skill in Texas Hold'Em poker. *Journal of Applied Research in Memory and Cognition*, *1*(1), 34–40. https://doi.org/10.1016/j.jarmac.2011.11.001

Melby-Lervåg, M., Redick, T. S., & Hulme, C. (2016). Working memory training does not improve performance on measures of intelligence or other measures of "far transfer." *Perspectives on Psychological Science*, *11*(4), 512–534. https://doi.org/10.1177/1745691616635612

Menninghaus, W., Wagner, V., Wassiliwizky, E., Schindler, I., Hanich, J., Jacobsen, T., & Koelsch, S. (2019). What are aesthetic emotions? *Psychological Review*, *126*(2), 171–195. https://doi.org/10.1037/rev0000135

Meulenberg, C. J. W., Rehfeld, K., Jovanović, S., & Marusic, U. (2023). Unleashing the potential of dance: A neuroplasticity-based approach bridging from older adults to Parkinson's disease patients. *Frontiers in Aging Neuroscience*, *15*, 1188855. https://doi.org/10.3389/fnagi.2023.1188855

Mikalonytė, E. S., Stevanov, J., Doran, R. P., Symons, K. A., & Schnall, S. (2026). Transformed by beauty: Aesthetic appreciation increases abstract thinking and self-transcendent emotions in an art museum. *Empirical Studies of the Arts*, *44*(1), 171–194. https://doi.org/10.1177/02762374251337699

Miksza, P. (2010). Investigating relationships between participation in high school music ensembles and extra-musical outcomes: An analysis of the education longitudinal study of 2002 using a bioecological development model. *Bulletin of the Council for Research in Music Education*, *186*, 7–25.

Miller, W. R., & Baca, J. C. (2001). *Quantum change: When epiphanies and sudden insights transform ordinary lives*. The Guilford Press.

Moral-Bofill, L., López de la Llave, A., Pérez-Llantada, M. C., & Holgado-Tello, F. P. (2022). Development of flow state self-regulation skills and coping with musical performance anxiety: Design and evaluation of an electronically implemented psychological program. *Frontiers in Psychology, 13*, 899621. https://doi.org/10.3389/fpsyg.2022.899621

Moreno, S. (2009). Can music influence language and cognition? *Contemporary Music Review, 28*(3), 329–345. https://doi.org/10.1080/07494460903404410

Morris, J. (2019). Exploring the affordances of digital storytelling in a media-arts restorative justice program. *Visual Communication, 18*(2), 205–230. https://doi.org/10.1177/1470357217752749

Mouriki-Zervou, A. (2011). The cognitive dimension of art: Aesthetic and educational value. *The International Journal of Learning: Annual Review, 18*(1), 1–12. https://doi.org/10.18848/1447-9494/CGP/v18i01/47413

Mualem, O., & Lavidor, M. (2015). Music education intervention improves vocal emotion recognition. *International Journal of Music Education, 33*(4), 413–425. https://doi.org/10.1177/0255761415584292

Mumper, M. L., & Gerrig, R. J. (2017). Leisure reading and social cognition: A meta-analysis. *Psychology of Aesthetics, Creativity, and the Arts, 11*(1), 109–120. https://doi.org/10.1037/aca0000089

Murdoch, I. (1999). *Existentialists and mystics: Writings on philosophy and literature*. Penguin Books.

Nagel, J. (2013). Knowledge as a mental state. In T. S. Gendler & J. Hawthorne (Eds.), *Oxford Studies in Epistemology Volume 4* (pp. 273–308). Oxford University Press.

Neimeyer, R. A., & Thompson, B. E. (2014). Meaning making and the art of grief therapy. In B. E. Thompson & R. A. Neimeyer (Eds.), *Grief and the Expressive Arts: Practices for Crafting Meaning*. Routledge.

Nelson, K., Lukawiecki, J., Waitschies, K., Jackson, E., & Zivot, C. (2024). Exploring the impacts of an art and narrative therapy program on participants' grief and bereavement Experiences. *OMEGA – Journal of Death and Dying*, 90(2): 726–745. https://doi.org/10.1177/00302228221111726

Nettle, D. (2006). Psychological profiles of professional actors. *Personality and Individual Differences, 40*(2), 375–383. https://doi.org/10.1016/j.paid.2005.07.008

Nijstad, B. A., De Dreu, C. K. W., Rietzschel, E. F., & Baas, M. (2010). The dual pathway to creativity model: Creative ideation as a function of flexibility and persistence. *European Review of Social Psychology, 21*(1), 34–77. https://doi.org/10.1080/10463281003765323

North, A. C., Hargreaves, D. J., & Hargreaves, J. J. (2004). Uses of music in everyday life. *Music Perception, 22*(1), 41–77. https://doi.org/10.1525/mp.2004.22.1.41

Nowicki, S., & Duke, M. P. (1994). Individual differences in the nonverbal communication of affect: The diagnostic analysis of nonverbal accuracy scale. *Journal of Nonverbal Behavior, 18*(1), 9–35. https://doi.org/10.1007/BF02169077

Nusbaum, E. C., & Silvia, P. J. (2011). Are intelligence and creativity really so different? Fluid intelligence, executive processes, and strategy use in divergent thinking. *Intelligence*, *39*(1), 36–45. https://doi.org/10.1016/j.intell.2010.11.002

Nussbaum, M. (1985). "Finely aware and richly responsible": Moral attention and the moral task of literature. *The Journal of Philosophy*, *82*(10), 516–529. https://doi.org/10.2307/2026358

Nussbaum, M. C. (2011). *Creating capabilities: The human development approach*. Belknap Press, An Imprint of Harvard University Press.

Oleynick, V. C., DeYoung, C. G., Hyde, E., Kaufman, S. B., Beaty, R. E., & Silvia, P. J. (2017). Openness/intellect: The core of the creative personality. In Gregory J. Feist, Roni Reiter-Palmon, & James C. Kaufman (Eds.), *The Cambridge handbook of creativity and personality research* (pp. 9–27). Cambridge University Press. https://doi.org/10.1017/9781316228036.002

Oliver, M. B., Hartmann, T., & Woolley, J. K. (2012). Elevation in response to entertainment portrayals of moral virtue. *Human Communication Research*, *38*(3), 360–378. https://doi.org/10.1111/j.1468-2958.2012.01427.x

Ostrofsky, J., & Shobe, E. (2015). The relationship between need for cognitive closure and the appreciation, understanding, and viewing times of realistic and nonrealistic figurative paintings. *Empirical Studies of the Arts*, *33*(1), 106–113. https://doi.org/10.1177/0276237415570016

Ozeki, R. (2022). *Timecode of a face*. Canongate Books.

Packer, J. (2008). Beyond learning: Exploring visitors' perceptions of the value and benefits of museum experiences. *Curator: The Museum Journal*, *51*(1), 33–54. https://doi.org/10.1111/j.2151-6952.2008.tb00293.x

Packer, J., & Ballantyne, R. (2005). Solitary vs. shared: Exploring the social dimension of museum learning. *Curator: The Museum Journal*, *48*(2), 177–192. https://doi.org/10.1111/j.2151-6952.2005.tb00165.x

Panero, M. E., Weisberg, D. S., Black, J., Goldstein, T. R., Barnes, J. L., Brownell, H., & Winner, E. (2016). Does reading a single passage of literary fiction really improve theory of mind? An attempt at replication. *Journal of Personality and Social Psychology*, *111*(5), e46–e54. https://doi.org/10.1037/pspa0000064

Paquette, S., & Mignault Goulet, G. (2014). Lifetime benefits of musical training. *Frontiers in Neuroscience*, *8*, 17667–17674. https://doi.org/10.3389/fnins.2014.00089

Park, S., Wiliams, L., & Chamberlain, R. (2022). Global saccadic eye movements characterise artists' visual attention while drawing. *Empirical Studies of the Arts*, *40*(2), 228–244. https://doi.org/10.1177/02762374211001811

Parsons, C. E., Young, K. S., Jegindø, E.-M. E., Vuust, P., Stein, A., & Kringelbach, M. L. (2014). Music training and empathy positively impact adults' sensitivity to infant distress. *Frontiers in Psychology*, *5*, 1440. https://doi.org/10.3389/fpsyg.2014.01440

Paul, L. A. (2016). *Transformative experience*. University Press.

Pavese, C. (2022). Knowledge how. In E. N. Zalta & U. Nodelman (Eds.), *The Stanford Encyclopedia of Philosophy* (Fall 2022). Metaphysics Research Lab,

Stanford University. https://plato.stanford.edu/archives/fall2022/entries/knowledge-how/

Pearson, M., Gaines, K., Pati, D., Colwell, M., Motheral, L., & Adams, N. G. (2019). The physiological impact of window murals on pediatric patients. *HERD*, *12*(2), 116–129. https://doi.org/10.1177/1937586718800483

Pellico, L. H., Friedlaender, L., & Fennie, K. P. (2009). Looking is not seeing: Using art to improve observational skills. *The Journal of Nursing Education*, *48*(11), 648–653. https://doi.org/10.3928/01484834-20090828-02

Pelowski, M. J. (2015). Tears and transformation: Feeling like crying as an indicator of insightful or "aesthetic" experience with art. *Frontiers in Psychology*, *6*, 1006. https://doi.org/10.3389/fpsyg.2015.01006

Pelowski, M., Cotter, K. N., Specker, E., Fingerhut, J., Trupp, M. D., & Speidel, K. (2024). How lasting is the impact of art?: An exploratory study of the incidence and duration of art exhibition-induced prosocial attitude change using a 2-week daily diary method. *Psychology of Aesthetics, Creativity, and the Arts*. https://doi.org/10.1037/aca0000670

Pennebaker, J. W. (1997). Writing about emotional experiences as a therapeutic process. *Psychological Science*, *8*(3), 162–166. https://doi.org/10.1111/j.1467-9280.1997.tb00403.x

Penwarden, S. (2022). Crafting order and beauty from loss: Using found poems as a form of grief therapy. *Journal of Poetry Therapy*, *35*(1), 13–26. https://doi.org/10.1080/08893675.2021.2004370

Perdreau, F., & Cavanagh, P. (2015). Drawing experts have better visual memory while drawing. *Journal of Vision*, *15*(5), 5. https://doi.org/10.1167/15.5.5

Persons, R. W. (2009). Art therapy with serious juvenile offenders: A phenomenological analysis. *International Journal of Offender Therapy and Comparative Criminology*, *53*(4), 433–453. https://doi.org/10.1177/0306624X08320208

Piff, P. K., Dietze, P., Feinberg, M., Stancato, D. M., & Keltner, D. (2015). Awe, the small self, and prosocial behavior. *Journal of Personality and Social Psychology*, *108*(6), 883–899. https://doi.org/10.1037/pspi0000018

Pihko, E., Virtanen, A., Saarinen, V.-M., Pannasch, S., Hirvenkari, L., Tossavainen, T., Haapala, A., & Hari, R. (2011). Experiencing art: The influence of expertise and painting abstraction level. *Frontiers in Human Neuroscience*, *5*, 94. https://doi.org/10.3389/fnhum.2011.00094

Pinho, A. L., Ullén, F., Castelo-Branco, M., Fransson, P., & de Manzano, Ö. (2016). Addressing a paradox: Dual strategies for creative performance in introspective and extrospective networks. *Cerebral Cortex*, *26*(7), 3052–3063. https://doi.org/10.1093/cercor/bhv130

Pizarro, J. J., Basabe, N., Fernández, I., Carrera, P., Apodaca, P., Man Ging, C. I., Cusi, O., & Páez, D. (2021). Self-transcendent emotions and their social effects: Awe, elevation and kama muta promote a human identification and motivations to help others. *Frontiers in Psychology*, *12*, 709859. https://doi.org/10.3389/fpsyg.2021.709859

Pizzolante, M., Pelowski, M., Demmer, T., Bartolotta, S., Sarcinella, E., Gaggioli, A., & Chirico, A. (2024). Aesthetic experiences and their transformative power: A systematic review. *Frontiers in Psychology*, 1328449.

Polzella, D. J., & Forbis, J. S. (2014). Relationships between traditional music audience participation and pro-social behaviors. *Empirical Studies of the Arts*, *32*(1), 109–120. https://doi.org/10.2190/EM.32.1g

Puryear, J. S., Kettler, T., & Rinn, A. N. (2017). Relationships of personality to differential conceptions of creativity: A systematic review. *Psychology of Aesthetics, Creativity, and the Arts*, *11*(1), 59–68. https://doi.org/10.1037/aca0000079

Rabinowitch, T.-C., Cross, I., & Burnard, P. (2013). Long-term musical group interaction has a positive influence on empathy in children. *Psychology of Music*, *41*(4), 484–498. https://doi.org/10.1177/0305735612440609

Ranger, M.-C., Houle, S., Rheault, A., & Thomas, R. (2023). Art-based workshops for women: An opportunity for reflection on identity and transformation following cancer treatment. *Occupational Therapy International*, *2023*, 1828314. https://doi.org/10.1155/2023/1828314

Rathje, S., Hackel, L., & Zaki, J. (2021). Attending live theatre improves empathy, changes attitudes, and leads to pro-social behavior. *Journal of Experimental Social Psychology*, *95*, 104138. https://doi.org/10.1016/j.jesp.2021.104138

Rickard, N. (2012). Music listening and emotional well-being. In N.S. Rickard and K. McFerran (Eds.), *Lifelong engagement with music: Benefits for mental health and well-being* (pp. 209–240). Nova Science Publishers, Inc.

Riggle, N. (2020). Transformative expression. In J. Schwenkler & E. Lambert (Eds.), *Becoming someone new: Essays on transformative experience, choice, and change* (pp. 162–181). Oxford University Press.

Rilke, Rainer Maria (2013). The selected poetry of Rainer Maria Rilke (Ed. and Trans. Stephen Mitchell). Penguin Random House.Ritter, S. M., Damian, R. I., Simonton, D. K., van Baaren, R. B., Strick, M., Derks, J., & Dijksterhuis, A. (2012). Diversifying experiences enhance cognitive flexibility. *Journal of Experimental Social Psychology*, *48*(4), 961–964. https://doi.org/10.1016/j.jesp.2012.02.009

Roberts, J. L. (2013, December). The power of patience. *Harvard Magazine*. www.harvardmagazine.com/2013/10/the-power-of-patience

Roberts, S., Camic, P. M., & Springham, N. (2011). New roles for art galleries: Art-viewing as a community intervention for family carers of people with mental health problems. *Arts & Health*, *3*(2), 146–159. https://doi.org/10.1080/17533015.2011.561360

Rocchi, P. (1998). Il bisogno di chiusura cognitiva e la creativita [The need for cognitive closure and creativity]. *Giornale italiano di psicologia*, *25*, 153–190.

Roche, R., Commins, S., & Farina, F. (2018). *Why science needs art: From historical to modern day perspectives*. Routledge.

Roy, M., Peretz, I., & Rainville, P. (2008). Emotional valence contributes to music-induced analgesia. *Pain, 134*(1–2), 140–147. https://doi.org/10.1016/j.pain.2007.04.003

Saarikallio, S., & Erkkilä, J. (2007). The role of music in adolescents' mood regulation. *Psychology of Music, 35*(1), 88–109. https://doi.org/10.1177/0305735607068889

Sachs, M. E., Damasio, A., & Habibi, A. (2015). The pleasures of sad music: A systematic review. *Frontiers in Human Neuroscience, 9*, 404. https://doi.org/10.3389/fnhum.2015.00404

Saito, Y. (2022). *Aesthetics of care: Practice in everyday life*. Bloomsbury Publishing.

San-Juan-Ferrer, B., & Hípola, P. (2020). Emotional intelligence and dance: A systematic review. *Research in Dance Education, 21*(1), 57–81. https://doi.org/10.1080/14647893.2019.1708890

Sawyer, K. (2025). *Learning to see: Inside the world's leading art and design schools*. The MIT Press.

Schellenberg, E. G. (2005). Music and cognitive abilities. *Current Directions in Psychological Science, 14*(6), 317–320. https://doi.org/10.1111/j.0963-7214.2005.00389.x

Schellenberg, E. G., Corrigall, K. A., Dys, S. P., & Malti, T. (2015). Group music training and children's prosocial skills. *PLOS One, 10*(10), e0141449. https://doi.org/10.1371/journal.pone.0141449

Schellenberg, E. G., & Lima, C. F. (2024). Music training and nonmusical abilities. *Annual Review of Psychology, 75*, 87–128. https://doi.org/10.1146/annurev-psych-032323-051354

Schellenberg, E. G., & Weiss, M. W. (2013). Music and cognitive abilities. In D. Deutsch (Ed.), *The psychology of music* (3rd ed., pp. 499–550). Elsevier Academic Press. https://doi.org/10.1016/B978-0-12-381460-9.00012-2

Scherer, K., & Zentner, M. (2008). Music evoked emotions are different – more often aesthetic than utilitarian. *Behavioral and Brain Sciences, 31*(5), 595–596. https://doi.org/10.1017/S0140525X08005505

Schumann, K., Zaki, J., & Dweck, C. S. (2014). Addressing the empathy deficit: Beliefs about the malleability of empathy predict effortful responses when empathy is challenging. *Journal of Personality and Social Psychology, 107*(3), 475–493. https://doi.org/10.1037/a0036738

Scopelliti, M., & Giuliani, M. V. (2006). Restorative environments in later life: An approach to well-being from the perspective of environmental psychology. *Journal of Housing For the Elderly, 19*(3–4), 203–226. https://doi.org/10.1300/J081v19n03_11

Sen, A. (1999). *Development as freedom*. Oxford University Press.

Shapiro, J., Rucker, L., & Beck, J. (2006). Training the clinical eye and mind: Using the arts to develop medical students' observational and pattern recognition skills. *Medical Education, 40*(3), 263–268. https://doi.org/10.1111/j.1365-2929.2006.02389.x

Sharp, K., & Hewitt, J. (2014). Dance as an intervention for people with Parkinson's disease: A systematic review and meta-analysis. *Neuroscience &*

Biobehavioral Reviews, *47*, 445–456. https://doi.org/10.1016/j.neubiorev.2014.09.009

Shedlosky-Shoemaker, R., Costabile, K. A., & Arkin, R. M. (2014). Self-expansion through fictional characters. *Self and Identity*, *13*(5), 556–578. https://doi.org/10.1080/15298868.2014.882269

Shefik, S. (2018). Reimagining transitional justice through participatory art. *International Journal of Transitional Justice*, *12*(2), 314–333. https://doi.org/10.1093/ijtj/ijy011

Sherman, A., & Anderson, D. (2025). How art contributes to scientific knowledge. *Philosophical Psychology*, 38(4), 1346–1366. https://doi.org/10.1080/09515089.2023.2241499

Sherman, A., & Morrissey, C. (2017). What is art good for? The socio-epistemic value of art. *Frontiers in Human Neuroscience*, *11*, 411. https://doi.org/10.3389/fnhum.2017.00411

Sherman, A., Yamamoto, K., McAlpin, E., Pal, A., AlQatami, A., & Levitan, C. A. (2025). Fostering meaningful engagement and well-being through slow-looking and guided interviews in art galleries. *The Journal of Positive Psychology*, *20*(6), 950–964. https://doi.org/10.1080/17439760.2025.2519304

Sherman, N. (1993). The virtues of common pursuit. *Philosophy and Phenomenological Research*, *53*(2), 277–299. https://doi.org/10.2307/2107769

Shiner, L. (2003). *The invention of art: A cultural history*. University of Chicago Press.

Shiota, M. N., Keltner, D., & Mossman, A. (2007). The nature of awe: Elicitors, appraisals, and effects on self-concept. *Cognition and Emotion*, *21*(5), 944–963. https://doi.org/10.1080/02699930600923668

Silvia, P. J. (2005). Emotional responses to art: From collation and arousal to cognition and emotion. *Review of General Psychology*, *9*(4), 342–357. https://doi.org/10.1037/1089-2680.9.4.342

(2009). Looking past pleasure: Anger, confusion, disgust, pride, surprise, and other unusual aesthetic emotions. *Psychology of Aesthetics, Creativity, and the Arts*, *3*(1), 48–51. https://doi.org/10.1037/a0014632

(2010). Confusion and interest: The role of knowledge emotions in aesthetic experience. *Psychology of Aesthetics, Creativity, and the Arts*, *4*(2), 75–80. https://doi.org/10.1037/a0017081

Silvia, P. J., & Nusbaum, E. C. (2011). On personality and piloerection: Individual differences in aesthetic chills and other unusual aesthetic experiences. *Psychology of Aesthetics, Creativity, and the Arts*, *5*(3), 208–214. https://doi.org/10.1037/a0021914

Silvia, P. J., Nusbaum, E. C., Berg, C., Martin, C., & O'Connor, A. (2009). Openness to experience, plasticity, and creativity: Exploring lower-order, high-order, and interactive effects. *Journal of Research in Personality*, *43*(6), 1087–1090. https://doi.org/10.1016/j.jrp.2009.04.015

Silvia, P. J., & Sanders, C. E. (2010). Why are smart people curious? Fluid intelligence, openness to experience, and interest. *Learning and Individual Differences*, *20*(3), 242–245. https://doi.org/10.1016/j.lindif.2010.01.006

Silvia, P., Winterstein, B., Willse, J., Barona, C., Cram, J., Hess, K., Martinez, J., & Richard, C. (2008). Assessing creativity with divergent thinking tasks: Exploring the reliability and validity of new subjective scoring methods. *Psychology of Aesthetics, Creativity, and the Arts*, *2*, 68–85. https://doi.org/10.1037/1931-3896.2.2.68

Slater, M. D., Johnson, B. K., Cohen, J., Comello, M. L. G., & Ewoldsen, D. R. (2014). Temporarily expanding the boundaries of the self: Motivations for entering the story world and implications for narrative effects. *Journal of Communication*, *64*(3), 439–455. https://doi.org/10.1111/jcom.12100

Smith, A. D. (2015). *Fires in the mirror*. Knopf Doubleday Publishing Group.

Smith, J. K., & Smith, L. F. (2001). Spending time on art. *Empirical Studies of the Arts*, *19*(2), 229–236. https://doi.org/10.2190/5MQM-59JH-X21R-JN5J

Smith, L. F., Smith, J. K., & Tinio, P. P. L. (2017). Time spent viewing art and reading labels. *Psychology of Aesthetics, Creativity, and the Arts*, *11*(1), 77–85. https://doi.org/10.1037/aca0000049

Sonn, C., & Baker, A. (2016). Creating inclusive knowledges: Exploring the transformative potential of arts and cultural practice. *International Journal of Inclusive Education*, *20*(3), 215–228. https://doi.org/10.1080/13603116.2015.1047663

Stamkou, E., Brummelman, E., Dunham, R., Nikolic, M., & Keltner, D. (2023). Awe sparks prosociality in children. *Psychological Science*, *34*(4), 455–467. https://doi.org/10.1177/09567976221150616

Stanley, C. (2010, May 10). Meet the man who sat with Marina Abramović 14 times. *Flavorwire*. www.flavorwire.com/89459/meet-the-man-who-sat-with-marina-abramovic-14-times

Steinbeis, N., Koelsch, S., & Sloboda, J. A. (2005). Emotional processing of harmonic expectancy violations. *Annals of the New York Academy of Sciences*, *1060*(1), 457–461. https://doi.org/10.1196/annals.1360.055

(2006). The role of harmonic expectancy violations in musical emotions: Evidence from subjective, physiological, and neural responses. *Journal of Cognitive Neuroscience*, *18*(8), 1380–1393. https://doi.org/10.1162/jocn.2006.18.8.1380

Stellar, J. E., Bai, Y., Anderson, C. L., Gordon, A., McNeil, G. D., Peng, K., & Keltner, D. (2024). Culture and awe: Understanding awe as a mixed emotion. *Affective Science*, *5*(2), 160–170. https://doi.org/10.1007/s42761-024-00243-3

Sternberg, R. J. (2006). The nature of creativity. *Creativity Research Journal*, *18*(1), 87.

Stoycheva, K. (2025). Tolerance of ambiguity and the creative action: To Engage and endure. *The Journal of Creative Behavior*, *59*(3): e1506. https://doi.org/10.1002/jocb.1506

Stutesman, M. G., & Goldstein, T. R. (2023). Developing emotion abilities through engagement with the arts. In Z. Ivcevic, J. D. Hoffmann, & J. C. Kaufman (Eds.), *The Cambridge handbook of creativity and emotions* (1st ed., pp. 434–458). Cambridge University Press. https://doi.org/10.1017/9781009031240.028

Sumantry, D., & Stewart, K. E. (2021). Meditation, mindfulness, and attention: A Meta-analysis. *Mindfulness, 12*(6), 1332–1349. https://doi.org/10.1007/s12671-021-01593-w

Swami, V., Stieger, S., Pietschnig, J., & Voracek, M. (2010). The disinterested play of thought: Individual differences and preference for surrealist motion pictures. *Personality and Individual Differences, 48*(7), 855–859. https://doi.org/10.1016/j.paid.2010.02.013

Tackett, S., Eller, L., Scharff, S., Balhara, K. S., Stouffer, K. M., Suchanek, M., Clever, S. L., Yenawine, P., Wolffe, S., & Chisolm, M. S. (2023). Transformative experiences at art museums to support flourishing in medicine. *Medical Education Online, 28*(1), 2202914. https://doi.org/10.1080/10872981.2023.2202914

Tangerås, T. M. (2018). *"How literature changed my life": A hermeneutically oriented narrative inquiry into transformative experiences of reading imaginative literature* [Dissertation]. Oslo Metropolitan University.

Tay, L., & Pawelski, J. O. (2022). *The Oxford handbook of the positive humanities.* Oxford University Press.

Tay, L., Pawelski, J. O., & Keith, M. G. (2018). The role of the arts and humanities in human flourishing: A conceptual model. *The Journal of Positive Psychology, 13*(3), 215–225. https://doi.org/10.1080/17439760.2017.1279207

Taylor, G. J., & Bagby, R. M. (2000). An overview of the alexithymia construct. In Reuven Bar-On & James D. A. Parker (Eds.), *The handbook of emotional intelligence: Theory, development, assessment, and application at home, school, and in the workplace* (pp. 40–67). Jossey-Bass/Wiley.

Taylor, Rebecca (2026). Marina Abramović, The artist is present. *Smarthistory, August 9, 2015*. Retrieved January 21, 2026, from https://smarthistory.org/marina-abramovic-the-artist-is-present/Tchalenko, J., & Chris Miall, R. (2009). Eye–hand strategies in copying complex lines. *Cortex, 45*(3), 368–376. https://doi.org/10.1016/j.cortex.2007.12.012

Tegano, D. W. (1990). Relationship of tolerance of ambiguity and playfulness to creativity. *Psychological Reports, 66*(3, Pt. 1), 1047–1056. https://doi.org/10.2466/PR0.66.3.1047-1056

Terracciano, A., McCrae, R. R., & Costa, P. T. (2003). Factorial and construct validity of the Italian Positive and Negative Affect Schedule (PANAS). *European Journal of Psychological Assessment: Official Organ of the European Association of Psychological Assessment, 19*(2), 131–141. https://doi.org/10.1027//1015-5759.19.2.131

The Other Side of Time. (2023). Tanisha Hill-Jarrett. Retrieved October 18, 2024, from www.tanishahilljarrett.com/othersideoftime

The U.S. Arts and Cultural Production Satellite Account (1998–2021). (n.d.). Retrieved October 14, 2024, from www.arts.gov/impact/research/arts-data-profile-series/adp-34

Thoma, M. V., Ryf, S., Mohiyeddini, C., Ehlert, U., & Nater, U. M. (2012). Emotion regulation through listening to music in everyday situations.

Cognition & Emotion, *26*(3), 550–560. https://doi.org/10.1080/02699931.2011.595390

Thompson, W. F., Bullot, N. J., & Margulis, E. H. (2023). The psychological basis of music appreciation: Structure, self, source. *Psychological Review*, *130*(1), 260–284. https://doi.org/10.1037/rev0000364

Tiberius, V. (2006). Well-being: Psychological research for philosophers. *Philosophy Compass*, *1*(5), 493–505. https://doi.org/10.1111/j.1747-9991.2006.00038.x

(2018). *Well-being as value fulfillment: How we can help each other to live well.* Oxford University Press.

Tishman, S. (2018). *Slow looking: The art and practice of learning through observation.* Routledge, Taylor & Francis Group.

Tishman, S., & Palmer, P. (2006). *Artful thinking: Stronger thinking and learning through the power of art.* Traverse City Area Public Schools, Harvard College. https://pz.harvard.edu/projects/artful-thinking

Tolstoy, L. (2021). *What is art?* (A. Maude, Trans., Project Gutenberg E-Book). Funk & Wagnalls Company. www.gutenberg.org/files/64908/64908-h/64908-h.htm

Tommaso, M. de, Sardaro, M., & Livrea, P. (2008). Aesthetic value of paintings affects pain thresholds. *Consciousness and Cognition*, *17*(4), 1152–1162. https://doi.org/10.1016/j.concog.2008.07.002

Trupp, M. D., Bignardi, G., Chana, K., Specker, E., & Pelowski, M. (2022). Can a brief interaction with online, digital art improve wellbeing? A comparative study of the impact of online art and culture presentations on mood, state-anxiety, subjective wellbeing, and loneliness. *Frontiers in Psychology*, *13*. www.frontiersin.org/articles/10.3389/fpsyg.2022.782033

Uc, E. Y., Rizzo, M., Anderson, S. W., Qian, S., Rodnitzky, R. L., & Dawson, J. D. (2005). Visual dysfunction in Parkinson disease without dementia. *Neurology*, *65*(12), 1907–1913. https://doi.org/10.1212/01.wnl.0000191565.11065.11

Ullán, A. M., & Belver, M. H. (2021). Visual arts in children's hospitals: Scoping review. *HERD: Health Environments Research & Design Journal*, *14*(4), 339–367. https://doi.org/10.1177/1937586721 1003494

Ulrich, R. S. (1981). Natural versus urban scenes: Some psychological effects. *Environment and Behavior*, *13*(5), 523–556. https://doi.org/10.1177/0013916581135001

(1984). View through a window may influence recovery from surgery. *Science*, *224*(4647), 420–421. https://doi.org/10.1126/science.6143402

Van de Vyver, J., & Abrams, D. (2018). The arts as a catalyst for human prosociality and cooperation. *Social Psychological and Personality Science*, *9*(6), 664–674. https://doi.org/10.1177/1948550617720275

Vessel, E. A., Starr, G. G., & Rubin, N. (2013). Art reaches within: Aesthetic experience, the self and the default mode network. *Frontiers in Neuroscience*, *7*, 258. https://doi.org/10.3389/fnins.2013.00258

Vezzali, L., Hewstone, M., Capozza, D., Giovannini, D., & Wölfer, R. (2015). Improving intergroup relations with extended and vicarious forms of indirect contact. In Miles Hewstone & Wolfgang Stroebe (Eds.), *European Review of Social Psychology: Volume 25*. Routledge.

Vezzali, L., Stathi, S., & Giovannini, D. (2012). Indirect contact through book reading: Improving adolescents' attitudes and behavioral intentions toward immigrants. *Psychology in the Schools*, *49*(2), 148–162. https://doi.org/10.1002/pits.20621

Vezzali, L., Stathi, S., Giovannini, D., Capozza, D., & Trifiletti, E. (2015). The greatest magic of Harry Potter: Reducing prejudice. *Journal of Applied Social Psychology*, *45*(2), 105–121. https://doi.org/10.1111/jasp.12279

Viding, C. G., Osika, W., Theorell, T., Kowalski, J., Hallqvist, J., & Horwitz, E. B. (2015). 'The culture palette'– A randomized intervention study for women with burnout symptoms in Sweden. *British Journal of Medical Practitioners* *8*(2), a813.

Villanueva, J., Ilari, B., & Habibi, A. (2024). Long-term music instruction is partially associated with the development of socioemotional skills. *PLOS One*, *19*(7). https://doi.org/10.1371/journal.pone.0307373

Visual-Spatial Thinking in Geometry and the Visual Arts | Request PDF. (n.d.). *ResearchGate*. https://doi.org/10.1037/aca0000027

Vogl, E., Pekrun, R., & Loderer, K. (2021). Epistemic emotions and metacognitive feelings. In D. Moraitou & P. Metallidou (Eds.), *Trends and prospects in metacognition research across the life span: A tribute to Anastasia Efklides* (pp. 41–58). Springer International Publishing. https://doi.org/10.1007/978-3-030-51673-4_3

Walden, K. (2015). Art and moral revolution. *The Journal of Aesthetics and Art Criticism*, *73*(3), 283–295. https://doi.org/10.1111/jaac.12173

Walsh, S. M., Chang, C. Y., Schmidt, L. A., & Yoepp, J. H. (2005). Lowering stress while teaching research: A creative arts intervention in the classroom. *The Journal of Nursing Education*, *44*(7), 330–333. https://doi.org/10.3928/01484834-20050701-09

Walton, K. L. (1978). Fearing fictions. *The Journal of Philosophy*, *75*(1), 5–27. https://doi.org/10.2307/2025831

Wang, M., & Wong, M. C. S. (2014). Happiness and leisure across countries: Evidence from international survey data. *Journal of Happiness Studies*, *15*(1), 85–118. https://doi.org/10.1007/s10902-013-9417-z

Wang, X., Ossher, L., & Reuter-Lorenz, P. A. (2015). Examining the relationship between skilled music training and attention. *Consciousness and Cognition*, *36*, 169–179. https://doi.org/10.1016/j.concog.2015.06.014

Ward, T. B. (1994). Structured imagination: The role of category structure in exemplar generation. *Cognitive Psychology*, *27*(1), 1–40. https://doi.org/10.1006/cogp.1994.1010

Webster, D. M., & Kruglanski, A. W. (1994). Individual differences in need for cognitive closure. *Journal of Personality and Social Psychology*, *67*(6), 1049–1062. https://doi.org/10.1037/0022-3514.67.6.1049

Weiskittle, R., & Gramling, S. (2018). The therapeutic effectiveness of using visual art modalities with the bereaved: A systematic review. *Psychology*

Research and Behavior Management, Volume 11, 9–24. https://doi.org/10.2147/PRBM.S131993

Welch, G. F., Himonides, E., Saunders, J., Papageorgi, I., & Sarazin, M. (2014). Singing and social inclusion. *Frontiers in Psychology*, *5*, 803. https://doi.org/10.3389/fpsyg.2014.00803

Westgate, E. C., & Oishi, S. (2022). Art, music, and literature: Do the humanities make our lives richer, happier, and more meaningful? In L. Tay & J. O. Pawelski (Eds.), *The Oxford handbook of the positive humanities* (pp. 85–96). Oxford University Press.

Węziak-Białowolska, D., & Białowolski, P. (2016). Cultural events – Does attendance improve health? Evidence from a Polish longitudinal study. *BMC Public Health*, *16*(1), 730. https://doi.org/10.1186/s12889-016-3433-y

What Is Art Therapy? (2022). *American Art Therapy Association*. Retrieved October 15, 2024, from https://arttherapy.org/what-is-art-therapy/

What Is Parkinson's? | Parkinson's Foundation. (n.d.). Retrieved July 30, 2025, from www.parkinson.org/understanding-parkinsons/what-is-parkinsons

Wheatley, D., & Bickerton, C. (2017). Subjective well-being and engagement in arts, culture and sport. *Journal of Cultural Economics*, *41*(1), 23–45. https://doi.org/10.1007/s10824-016-9270-0

Wiersema, D. V., van der Schalk, J., & van Kleef, G. A. (2012). Who's afraid of red, yellow, and blue? Need for cognitive closure predicts aesthetic preferences. *Psychology of Aesthetics, Creativity, and the Arts*, *6*(2), 168–174. https://doi.org/10.1037/a0025878

Wilt, J. A., Exline, J. J., Sherman, A., Schlegel, R. J., Swartz, S., Blanco, L., Lindquist, M., & Fukada, A. (2025). Behind every artwork is a story: Phenomenological analysis of understandings achieved through engagement with art. Psychology of Aesthetics, Creativity, and the Arts. Advance online publication. https://doi.org/10.1037/aca0000817.

Wiltermuth, S. S., & Heath, C. (2009). Synchrony and cooperation. *Psychological Science*, *20*(1), 1–5.

Wiltsher, N. (2024). Aesthetic selves as objects of interpersonal understanding. *Philosophical Explorations*, *27*(2), 212–224. https://doi.org/10.1080/13869795.2024.2344979

Wimmer, L., Currie, G., Friend, S., & Ferguson, H. J. (2021). Testing correlates of lifetime exposure to print fiction following a multi-method approach: Evidence from young and older readers. *Imagination, Cognition and Personality*. https://doi.org/10.1177/0276236621996244

Winner, E. (2018). *How art works: A psychological exploration*. Oxford University Press.

Winsler, A., Ducenne, L., & Koury, A. (2011). Singing one's way to self-regulation: The role of early music and movement curricula and private speech. *Early Education and Development*, *22*(2), 274–304. https://doi.org/10.1080/10409280903585739

Winterson, J. (1997). *Art objects: Essays on ecstasy and effrontery*. Knopf Doubleday Publishing Group.

Wolf, S. (2010). *Meaning in life and why it matters*. Princeton University Press.

Wollner, G. (2019). Anonymous exploitation: Non-individual, non-agential and structural. *Review of Social Economy*, *77*(2), 143–162. https://doi.org/10.1080/00346764.2018.1525758

Xue, M., Sun, H., Xue, J., Zhou, J., Qu, J., Ji, S., Bu, Y., & Liu, Y. (2023). Narrative medicine as a teaching strategy for nursing students to developing professionalism, empathy and humanistic caring ability: A randomized controlled trial. *BMC Medical Education*, *23*(1), 38. https://doi.org/10.1186/s12909-023-04026-5

Yaden, D. B., Kaufman, S. B., Hyde, E., Chirico, A., Gaggioli, A., Zhang, J. W., & Keltner, D. (2019). The development of the Awe Experience Scale (AWE-S): A multifactorial measure for a complex emotion. *The Journal of Positive Psychology*, *14*(4), 474–488. https://doi.org/10.1080/17439760.2018.1484940

Yassa, N. A. (1999). High school involvement in creative drama. *Research in Drama Education: The Journal of Applied Theatre and Performance*, *4*(1), 37–49. https://doi.org/10.1080/1356978990040104

Yenawine, P. (2013). *Visual thinking strategies: Using art to deepen learning across school disciplines*. Harvard Education Press.

Yu, Y. Z., Ming, C. Y., Yue, M., Li, J. H., & Ling, L. (2016). House–Tree–Person drawing therapy as an intervention for prisoners' prerelease anxiety. *Social Behavior and Personality: An International Journal*, *44*(6), 987–1004. https://doi.org/10.2224/sbp.2016.44.6.987

Zabelina, D. L., & Robinson, M. D. (2010). Creativity as flexible cognitive control. *Psychology of Aesthetics, Creativity, and the Arts*, *4*(3), 136–143. https://doi.org/10.1037/a0017379

Zagzebski, L. (2001). Recovering understanding. In M. Steup (Ed.), *Knowledge, truth, and duty: Essays on epistemic justification, responsibility, and virtue* (pp. 235–251). Oxford University Press, Incorporated. http://ebookcentral.proquest.com/lib/oxy/detail.action?docID=3051905

Zatorre, R. J., Chen, J. L., & Penhune, V. B. (2007). When the brain plays music: Auditory–motor interactions in music perception and production. *Nature Reviews Neuroscience*, *8*(7), 547–558. https://doi.org/10.1038/nrn2152

Zentner, M., Grandjean, D., & Scherer, K. R. (2008). Emotions evoked by the sound of music: Characterization, classification, and measurement. *Emotion*, *8*(4), 494–521. https://doi.org/10.1037/1528-3542.8.4.494

Zhang, M., Li, F., Wang, D., Ba, X., & Liu, Z. (2023). Exercise sustains motor function in Parkinson's disease: Evidence from 109 randomized controlled trials on over 4,600 patients. *Frontiers in Aging Neuroscience*, *15*, 1071803. https://doi.org/10.3389/fnagi.2023.1071803

Zunshine, L. (2006). *Why we read fiction: Theory of mind and the novel*. Ohio State University Press.

Index

For EU product safety concerns, contact us at Calle de José Abascal, 56–1°, 28003 Madrid, Spain or eugpsr@cambridge.org.

www.ingramcontent.com/pod-product-compliance
Ingram Content Group UK Ltd.
Pitfield, Milton Keynes, MK11 3LW, UK
UKHW022148080726
473066UK00010B/843

* 9 7 8 1 0 0 9 3 4 4 3 1 9 *